TRAVELS WITH MY HAT

TRAVELS WITH MY HAT

Christine Osborne

photographs by the author

P.O. Box 33,
Katoomba NSW 2780
Australia

www.travelswithmyhat.com

National Library of Australia Cataloguing-in-Publication entry

Author: Osborne, Christine, author.
Title: Travels with My Hat : a lifetime on the road / Christine Osborne.
ISBN: 9780992324001 (paperback)
Subjects: Osborne, Christine—Travel.
             Voyages and travels.
             Photojournalist—Australia.
             Middle East—Pictorial works.
             Middle East—Description and travel.
             Middle East—Social life and customs.
             Asia—Pictorial works.
             Asia—Description and travel.
             Asia—Social life and customs.
             Africa, North—Pictorial works.
             Africa, North—Description and travel.
             Africa, North—Social life and customs.

956.092

This book has its origins in copious notes and journals from many years ago and certain items stated as facts may no longer be applicable. The names of some persons in this book have been changed to protect their privacy

Page 133: photo by Julian Worker

Design by Margaret Hogan of Red Moon Creative: www.redmooncreative.com.au
Printed by Ligare: 138 Bonds Road, Riverwood, NSW 2210, Australia

Back cover: Migrant worker returning home, Dubai-Sharjah border 1975.

Contents

Chapter 5: No Mocha in Mocha

'… The boy sat in silence with his gun between his knees and studying his lean, sardonic features in the mirror, I decided he made me feel ill at ease. Instead of helping with directions, he had ignored us. Was he leading us into a trap? …'

Chapter 6: May you Never be Tired

'… Boarding at Jamrud, I was swept along in an arsenal of Pathans waving guns and hawkers brandishing cigarettes, sugar-cane and hard-boiled eggs. Chickens, even a cow, were bundled on board as the Mail pulled out of the station …'

Chapter 7: The *Marabout* from Taroudant

'… I've often thought I'd found the middle of nowhere on my travels, only to realise that I was actually on the edge of somewhere, but the Café Lemsid was definitely in the middle of nowhere …'

Chapter 8: Correspondence with Mum

'… I would repair to the nearest café to devour her news. Of how the seeds I'd sent home from the Seychelles had grown into a tree, and of feeding bits of chicken to a blue-tongue lizard living under the house …'

Acknowledgements

Other Books by the Author

Foreword

It was at an American Independence Day party in 1976 that I first met the author and significantly, the word independence, is one of the major clues to the nature of this expatriate Australian.

Fiercely independent and single-minded, she has photographed and written books about countries as diverse as Tahiti and Oman. I occasionally met up with her and witnessed the mix of guts and perseverance, interspersed with the odd tear of frustration, and a hint of the memsahib that seemed to overcome all obstacles. Once, on point of arrest for some minor infringement over photography, with an authoritarian Pakistani army officer, she suggested they have tea first which they both drank, exchanged pleasantries, and Osborne was allowed to go on her way.

Her fondness of small creatures—birds and fish—often manifested itself. A sock was used as a nest to nurture chickens found in a rubbish heap in Beirut. Tiny fish caught in a mountain stream in the Yemen, were carried home in a jam jar to survive for seven years in her fish tank, along with other exotics in her London flat.

A girl's own adventure story, *Travels with My Hat* will put a spring in the step of anyone seeking excitement. It is Christine Osborne's unique life, from scrubbing bedpans as a young nurse in Sydney, to becoming not only a successful travel writer, but a top flight photographer who would accompany Her Majesty the Queen on her riches-laden tour of Arabia.

AILEEN AITKEN

Introduction

I'd noticed her in a waterfront restaurant in Marseilles: an elegant, older woman wearing an exotically patterned kaftan. Seated at a corner table, she was dipping bits of baguette into a steaming bowl of bouillabaisse, the traditional seafood soup in this part of Provence. Where were her friends and family? Was she a traveller, or simply an independent soul enjoying an evening out? Whatever her social situation, I decided she looked like someone who had seen the world. And me. What was I doing in the big French port? I was waiting to board the *Pierre Loti*, a packet steamer on Messageries Maritimes East Africa run. The Kenyan port of Mombasa was my destination at the time.

I got to thinking about the woman again a few years later, in a café-bar in the Canary Islands. Would this be me one day? I drove my fork into a plate of *arroz cubano* (fried eggs and bananas served with sticky rice) and wondered how she might have spent her youth. My thoughts were interrupted when a middle-aged man sat down near my table. Cream flannels dangled at his skinny white ankles and a scarlet handkerchief peeped out of the top pocket of a yachting jacket, rather worn at the elbows. Ordering a drink, he scanned the menu and then called across to me.

'Tell me, what brings a lovely young woman like yourself to the god forsaken island of La Palma?' He spoke with an impeccable English accent.

'I'm just travelling about,' I poured myself a final glass of wine from the earthenware carafe.

'Yes, but why do you travel and what is your aim? Name's Milne.' Christopher Robin Milne—for it was him—looked me in the eye.

'Forgive me if I appear rude,' I said. 'But along with being asked my age (I was twenty-six), I dislike being quizzed about travel. However, if you must know, I'm waiting to catch a banana boat to the Caribbean.'

'Travel,' Milne pronounced it gravely, 'is a form of neurosis.'

'For you perhaps,' I called for my bill. 'But to me, no other experience compares. Especially slow travel and that frisson of setting out to discover something new, only to find that while you were making the trip, the trip was making you.'

Milne looked surprised at this explanation and feeling rather pleased with myself, I stepped out onto the storm-lashed waterfront of Santa Cruz de La Palma, the last port of call for many a boat embarking on a trans-Atlantic voyage.

My thoughts have occasionally returned to this brief encounter. Why do certain individuals refuse to remain hostage to their birthplace and only appear to be happy when on the move? The Scottish writer William Dalrymple suggests that travellers by nature, tend to be rebels and outcasts, and that setting out alone and vulnerable on the road is often a rejection of home. In my own case, it was not a rejection of home, but a 'walkabout' in search of the world, since I knew from childhood that a domestic life anchored at the end of the earth in Australia was not for me.

Apart from a conviction in the human need for adventure, I could not contemplate an existence rendered simple by a deadening routine. Catching the same train each morning with the same announcement—*Mind the step. Doors closing.* Seeing the same pale faces in the office, drinking the same weak coffee from the same clapped-out machine. Sandwich at one. Leave at five. *Mind the step. Doors closing.* Standing room only. Alone travel replaces the monotony of daily grind.

Few activities generate as much excitement as setting off somewhere foreign, where different landscapes, interesting people, and colourful customs await. Every night after saying my prayers, I would fall asleep to dream of destinations in books signed out by Miss Myrtle, the frizzy-haired librarian who never smiled.

I wanted to visit Burma after reading Ethel Mannin's *Land of the Crested Lion*[1] and the Greek islands, immortalised by Charmian Clift in *Mermaid Singing*[2]. I wanted to stand on the spot where Speke discovered the source of the Nile and to follow Freya Stark, to Damascus and Baghdad. I wanted to dance the tango in Buenos Aires and to meet glamorous characters from *The Arabian Nights*: sultans, sheikhs and odalisques in harem trousers serving tiny glasses of mint-flavoured tea. And while I loved mum's roast beef and Yorkshire pudding, I longed to try dishes such as *fesanjan,* a duck and pomegranate dish from Persia, and the aromatic *tajine* stews of Berber kitchens in Morocco.

I grew up in Temora, an old goldmining town in the Riverina area of New South Wales, where my father managed the Bank of New South Wales as it was then known. The main street ended in arid plains with scattered eucalypts and a sprinkling of sheep and wheat stations. Beyond was the great Outback, ending on the west Australian coast, 3,218 kilometres (2,000 miles) away. On weekends I used to cycle down past the newsagent and the Greek café, to where the asphalt ended and the dirt road began. Further on, it dipped into a shallow gully where I would sit by a creek and fish for yabbies[3] as flocks of green-and-yellow budgerigars wheeled overhead. To go yabbying, you only needed a lump of raw meat dangled from the end of a stick by a string. The yabbies would grab it with a claw and you could drag them ashore, often two or three hanging on at a time. But we didn't eat them. In the 1950s, along with rabbits, the small crustaceans were considered vermin, so the pleasure lay in simply catching them and throwing them back.

I remember the day at Temora High School when we discussed what we would do in later life. Janice planned to become a teacher. Pam, the Presbyterian minister's daughter, hoped to train as a hairdresser and the boys all wanted to be rugby league footballers. How they laughed when I announced I was going to see the world. See the world? They found it so hilarious that I never mentioned it again.

On leaving school, I went to Sydney to train as a nurse, only to discover that my calling did not aspire to wearing a starched uniform— the collar used to cut my neck—and to turning my three-piece horsehair

ME (CENTRE) AND RUTH, ROYAL NORTH SHORE HOSPITAL GRADUATES, 1963

mattress daily in Vindin House, the nurses' home. But gritting my teeth, I persevered and after four years study and graduation, I walked out the iron gates of Royal North Shore Hospital with a vow to travel a year for each year I had spent emptying bedpans. The four years became five and by 1968, I had sailed around the world and had flown across it, still unsure of my direction, until one evening, in the south of France, a Spanish gypsy woman took my hand and read my fortune.

'*Usted se convertira en un escritor de viajes,*' she said. And it had dawned: to be a travel writer was my passport to visit foreign lands.

Golden earrings flashing in the candlelight, she stood up in the café and sang a lament to a solitary guitar. I never knew her name, but the craggy faced guitarist was Manitas de Plata—'Silver Fingers'—who rose to fame in the 1960s, even playing at a Royal Variety performance in London, my eventual home.

That night in Les Saintes Maries de la Mer, I dreamt of the white horses and black bulls that still roam the Camargue and of the annual festival when gypsies from all over Europe come to venerate their patron saint, Sarah le Noir whose statue stands in the church. And next morning, ears still ringing with the flamenco, I wrote a story about the festival which was published in the *Sydney Morning Herald*.

It was an auspicious start. The newspaper accepted a second article on Djerba, the Mediterranean island of Ulysses and the lotus-eaters, a third on Djibouti which I'd visited on the *Pierre Loti* and a fourth on Spain, and unwilling to surrender myself to a sedentary life, I kept on travelling, writing and taking photographs. It was not going to make my fortune, but I never looked back, only forward to the next adventure and interesting encounters with people from all walks of life.

Although I have lived in London for thirty-five years, I am still awestruck by the sight of the Tower of London, built by William the Conqueror and Westminster Abbey, constructed five hundred years before Captain Cook discovered Australia. Dirty and overcrowded London may be, but it is an ideal base to travel from one country to another, and my flat near the river Thames is filled with artefacts collected in foreign lands.

In my living room, an African voodoo mask hangs next to a patchwork quilt from Samarkand. A Chinese coffee-table holds a spice box containing fourth century Kushan coins from Gilgit in northern Pakistan, Minaean pottery shards from Baraqish in the Yemen and a speckled egg from Bird Island in the Seychelles. Beside it stand Ashanti fertility dolls from Ghana and a camel skull found in the Wahiba Sands of Oman. A wooden snake, carved by political prisoners in Ethiopia, coils around the staircase; a red rocking horse made in Mumbai has a place in the hall and on the sideboard is a basket from the Banaue rice-terraces in the Philippines containing my collection of 'world seeds'. There are kapok pods from Indonesia, a huge kernel dropped by the *Kigelia africana* 'sausage tree' in Zambia, ylang-ylang flowers picked on Grande Comore in the Indian Ocean, Zanzibar cloves, palm nuts from Malaysia, tamarind from Thailand, pine cones from the Atlas Mountains of Morocco. There is even a coconut from Tetiaroa, the late Marlon Brando's island hideaway off Tahiti.

This basket holds a lifetime of travels. Now friends on both sides of the world have encouraged me to share some of the adventures as a freelance photojournalist. Although the thread may zig-zag a little and double-back to events remembered from one place or another, the tales are basically in chronological order and as the last word is written, I cannot help but wonder what will be the next destination on my ticket.

ABOUT TO BOARD THE *PIERRE LOTI* IN MARSEILLES, AUGUST 1965

Chapter 1

Ticket to Addis Ababa

Mother was a great armchair traveller. Seated on the verandah of our eventual home on Lake Macquarie, she would glance up from reading and say, 'I don't need to see the world: the world comes to me through my letterbox.' A Yorkshire doctor, her grandfather had sailed to Australia in 1841 as Surgeon Superintendent on the 406 tonne barque *Georgiana*. Settling in the Hunter Valley district of New South Wales, he had sired three daughters and six sons; four of the boys he sent back to the 'old country' to study medicine.

A gracious lady more suited to croquet and church fetes, mother should really have been born in the green environment of England, not the sunburnt plains 'down under'. I once found a scrap of paper in her recipe book advising of First Aid treatment in the event of a funnel-web spider bite. It explained her anguish every time she did a spot of gardening.

On sifting through the hundreds of letters I wrote home during more than forty years of travels, I can appreciate why she never wished to go further than the High Street where she shopped at the butcher, Mr Burns, and collected her daily copy of the *Herald* from Cooper's corner store. Some of my letters in envelopes post-marked from places such as Sana'a and Freetown, even frighten me today. Did I really have such adventures? There was never anything gentle, like an appreciation of the Florentine masters in the Uffizi Gallery, or a description of Royal Kew Gardens in spring. Yes, I religiously visited Rome, Paris and Amsterdam, but my real interests lay east of Suez.

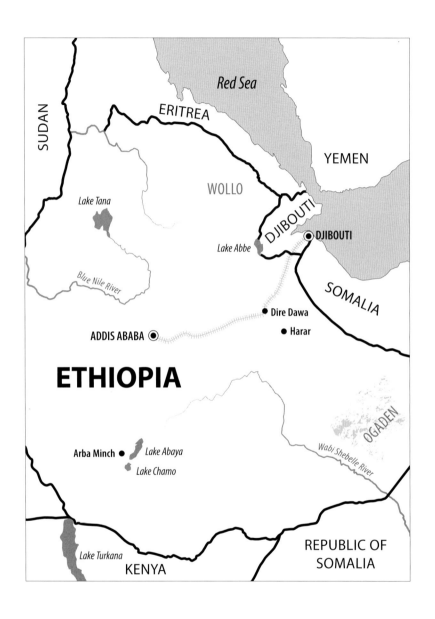

'I wish you would grow a little more cultivated,' she used to say, enrolling me at Wenona Ladies College whose boarders were brought up as though they were daughters of an English country estate, wearing black velvet dresses for dinner and once a week, speaking only in French. But deprived of culture in 1940s Australia, mother yearned for something a little highbrow. When I was nine, she took my younger sister Julia and me to a performance of *Swan Lake* in the Mosman Town Hall. The ballet was a momentous event for Sydney, but when she asked what I thought of it, I'd replied: 'you could see the men's bottoms'.

Poor mum certainly tried while I lived in Australia, but she gave up when I sailed away, only to appear on flying visits ever after. However, she was an excellent correspondent herself. At the poste restante in places such as Rawalpindi or Khartoum, I used to wait patiently for the clerk to sort through correspondence from the pigeon-hole under the letter O. I could spot the thin, blue aerogramme long before he did and snatching it up, I would repair to the nearest café to devour her news. Of how the seeds I'd sent out from the Seychelles had grown into a tree, and of feeding bits of chicken to the blue-tongue lizard living under the house. In Dubai, I once miraculously received an envelope in her neat handwriting, addressed simply: Christine Osborne c/- Hotel InterContinental, Trucial States.

Finding myself short of funds in London in July 1975, I reluctantly put on the dreaded nurse's uniform again and began a day job caring for a bedridden lady living in Chelsea. Mrs Graham's three-storey Victorian terrace was a short walk from my small rented flat off Sloane Square. My brief was to prepare her breakfast and to tidy her bedroom, and when this was finished, I used to sit on a bathroom chair writing articles about my travels.

After five weeks on the case, I returned home to find a letter in my box. Ethiopian Airlines, one of many companies I'd contacted since coming to England, was organising a press trip to Addis Ababa. The invitation was to mark the first anniversary of the overthrow of His Majesty Haile Selassie, Emperor of Ethiopia, whose imperial government had been replaced in 1974 by a Revolutionary Military Council known as the Dergue.

'Addis Ababa,' said Mrs Graham, sharply cracking the top of her egg, 'is where Sylvia Pankhurst is buried.'

The cause of Haile Selassie's death, on 27 August 1975 was given as a cardiac arrest but at that time the whereabouts of his grave remained unknown. Later reports indicated he was likely to have been murdered, and in 1992 witnesses came forward to say his body was buried under a lavatory in the Imperial Palace.[4]

My employer, the Lancaster Gate Nursing Agency, was sympathetic to my request for ten days leave, although accustomed to nurses taking a week off to holiday in Spain, or the Greek islands, they were astonished to learn I was going all the way out to Ethiopia. Just for ten days. A snooty person, Mrs Graham cared not a toss who looked after her, provided her egg was boiled for precisely three-and-a-half minutes. Not a second more. So after writing out instructions for the relief sister, I hung up my uniform behind the bathroom door.

On my first British press trip, I found myself in the company of journalists from distinguished papers such as the *Guardian* and the *Times.* Jonathan Dimbleby, who had covered the Wollo famine of the early seventies for the BBC, was on board with a television crew. In fact, converging on the Ethiopian capital were more than seventy journalists from all over the world.

With time before the Revolution Day parade on 13 September, we were split into sightseeing groups. Mine was to visit Dire Dawa, an important market centre and a stop on the Djibouti-Addis Ababa rail route to the Red Sea. In 1930, a young Evelyn Waugh, sent out to report on the coronation of Haile Selassie, found the entire train had been rented out to the Duke of Gloucester in whose party was Wilfred Thesiger, the first British child born in Ethiopia in 1912, when his father was in charge of the British Legation.

According to Thesiger, the coronation embraced all the pomp and ceremony the emperor could muster. However something happened to the fireworks display, when to everyone's surprise, they all went off at once.[5]

The first serious threat to Haile Selassie's government had arisen not from domestic issues such as the critical need for land reform, but from Mussolini's designs on the Horn of Africa. Abyssinia, as it was then known, was one of the few African countries to escape colonisation and in October

1935, declaring intervention on 'humanitarian' grounds, the fascist dictator had launched a full-scale invasion against the Armed Forces of Ethiopia of whom many were only equipped with muzzle-loaders and spears. In a war remembered for the use of mustard gas, Haile Selassie—225th emperor in a line dating back 3,000 years—Conquering Lion of the Tribe of Judah, Lord of Lords, and God incarnate of Rastafarians—was forced to flee, and in May 1936, Italian troops entering Addis Ababa proclaimed Ethiopia, a part of *Africa Orientale Italiana.*

The male journalists, railway buffs like many Englishmen, watched the night train from Addis Ababa pull into Dire Dawa before retiring to our hotel pool. It was sublime weather for swimming, but I set off to explore with Dorothy, a tall, black reporter from Uganda, in a horse-trap taxi. Spared aerial attack during the conflict, Dire Dawa had become something of an up-country resort for divisions stationed in the capital and as our *garis* clip-clopped along its tree-lined streets, we noticed an Italian influence in several candy-coloured houses and cafés advertising caffé latte.

But here similarity stopped. We'd struck market day and Dire Dawa was thronged with peoples: Oromo and Ahmara farmers from the central highlands, Tigrinya from the Tigray region, Saho from the Red Sea coast and Somali pastoralists all buying, selling and exchanging news in a babble of different languages. There were also Afar tribesmen from the Danakil Desert, a harsh region of intense heat and sulphorous springs abutting on north-east Ethiopia.

Scrutinising one man, I decided his wiry hair was similar to my own and I wondered whether it had ever been washed. His traditional garb, a khaki skirt and shirt affair, was complimented by a *jile*, a vicious looking double-edged dagger, and he wore a bone bracelet on his wrist. Wilfred Thesiger has left a vivid impression of the Afar encountered when he lead an expedition across the depression in 1933.[6] Our driver, speaking *un po'di Italiano* and waving his whip to emphasise the point, indicated that most were camel-owning nomads, coming to sell slabs of salt and to purchase fuel.

The Kefira market, spread out on bags beneath the trees, stocked everything the tribesmen needed for survival in the arid wilderness outside

Dire Dawa: spearheads, knives, tea, sugar, salt, cloth, corn, ropes and camel-halters. Beautiful, but melancholic, Somali women selling baskets of chillies, moved among the traders with the painful, flat-footed gait characteristic of the circumcised female. Swathed in red, white and yellow cotton robes, they pressed around Dorothy, who was wearing a tight T-shirt with Bob Dylan on the front, flared jeans and platform sole sandals. Black, she was obviously one of them, but why did she look so different? No one could explain. Even our press group knew nothing about Dorothy, though rumours said she was the personal emissary of His Excellency, President for Life, Idi Amin Dada, the 'Butcher of Africa'.

Ethiopia's national dish—*wat and injera*—on our dinner menu explained the chillies. Along with other spices, red chillies are a potent ingredient in this palate-scorching casserole made using goat or lamb. *Injera,* a spongy, grey pancake affair, is used to grasp morsels of the meat and to mop up its unctuous juices—slurp, slurp.

Dabbing at tears with a table napkin, Dorothy exclaimed: 'This is even hotter than our own curries.' And soon the entire press group was weeping.

'We also like raw meat in this division of Ethiopia,' said a waiter in a crushed white dinner jacket, smiling broadly as he sliced a steak off a side of beef suspended on a coat-rack behind the buffet table.

I tried it with some *berbere* sauce, another hot local delicacy, but although I love a well-made steak tartare, I found the taste too primitive, even for my by now well-seasoned palate.

'If one must eat meat raw,' said Laurens van der Post, who had tried *berbere* during a visit to Ethiopia, 'it is surely best done in this way, for the sauce gives the impression of being hot enough to cook the meat right on your tongue.'[7]

On our second day, we were to visit Harar, a devoutly Muslim town forbidden to infidels until 1887 when Menelik II incorporated it into 'Greater Ethiopia'.

Travelling by minibus, we left the plains behind for rolling hill country sown under coffee, *teff* (the cereal used to make *injera*) and *qat,* a leaf having mild narcotic properties which is widely chewed throughout the Horn of Africa and in the Yemen. Climbing higher, we passed roadside

AFAR TRIBESMAN LOADING PACK CAMELS IN DIRE DAWA MARKET, 1975

markets selling cheese, eggs, and cow-dung fuel and in contrast to the half-naked tribesmen of Dire Dawa, people here were wrapped in blankets and wore woollen jumpers against the chill. In one place where we stopped, everyone was busily knitting garments, even teenage boys. Eventually we reached Harar, a town perched on the eastern rim of the Great Rift Valley escarpment and surrounded by a medieval wall holding it together like a surgical corset.

Many myths relate to the founding of Harar, but it is usually associated with Sheikh Abadir, a holy man from Southern Arabia who settled there in the tenth century. The town subsequently became the spiritual centre for Ethiopia's Muslims, developing its own language—a mix of Cushite and Semitic—even minting its own coinage. The great wall was built in the sixteenth century by the Emir Ibn Mujahid al-Nur to protect the town from Christian raids. More than 4 metres (13 feet) high, its five gates were bolted at night, locking in the Hararis, and equally keeping out wild animals.

'Jugol, the old walled town, is the sacred heart of Harar,' announced Mr Abdulwasi, our local Harari guide, in the Oxford accent affected by many foreigners when speaking English.

We trailed along behind his dapper figure wearing a green woollen hat and a three button, centre vent tweed suit. Harar is 1,885 metres (6,184 feet) above sea level, and several women who hurried past wore leather leggings against the cold. The cobbled lanes lined with squat stone and clay houses and the shops filled with silversmiths, weavers and leather-makers, bestowed a living museum feel, rather like the medieval town of Fez in Morocco. Everywhere were glimpses of local life, of coffee-sellers, sugarcane grinders and women selling bundles of *qat,* freshly plucked on the misty mountain terraces.

'A carpet draped over the entrance to a house indicates a daughter has reached a marriageable age,' said Mr Abdulwasi as we peeped into the courtyards of buildings likely hundreds of years old.

Mr Abdulwasi said his family had lived in Harar for six generations. One of five children of a wealthy coffee merchant, his paternal grandfather had been a bookbinder who specialised in ornate copies of the Qur'an. A devout Muslim, he used to perform the *hajj* pilgrimage to the holy shrines in Mecca every three years, travelling across the dry plateaus of Christian Ethiopia to Djibouti, where he caught a dhow to Saudi Arabia.

'His boat was lying off Jeddah on the terrible night a pilgrim ship from Karachi caught fire. Pakistani *hajjis* cooking on little stoves were blamed. Leaping overboard to escape, most drowned or were eaten by sharks. Grandfather told us before they jumped, they cried *Allahu Akbar*—God is great'—said Mr Abdulwasi gravely.

Sir Richard Francis Burton, the celebrated British explorer was the first European to visit Harar in 1855, but its most celebrated resident was Arthur Rimbaud, the rebellious child of nineteenth century French poetry. Rimbaud who has been described as both 'a brat and a genius', was certainly one of those individuals in the manner of Henri de Monfreid, Lady Hester Stanhope, or even Dame Freya Stark, who only discover their true focus in life through travel and adventure.

'*Monsieur Rambo,*' said Mr. Abdulwasi, pronouncing his name very carefully, 'spent eight years in Harar, becoming a personal friend of the governor, Ras Makonnen, the father of our future Emperor.'[8] He stopped outside a house, different to others being a double-storey timber affair, with an enclosed upstairs verandah.

'This was *Monsieur Rambo's* house,' he said, moving back for us to admire the building. 'Once owned by the Egyptian conqueror of Harar—hence its name, *House of the Pasha*—it was subsequently rented by the French traders, *Bardey et Cie* in Aden, for their new agent in Africa.'

By the age of nineteen, Rimbaud had ceased to write poetry, but he continued to correspond with his mother in Charleville, a town near the Belgium border. Writing in November 1889, he said: '... The company has founded an agency in Harar, a region that you'll find in south-east of Abyssinia. We'll export coffee, hides, gum and so on ...'[9]

As well as becoming an expert on *bunna,* the Amharic name for coffee, Rimbaud made several excursions into the unexplored hinterland. But while the 'grand house' where he lived with a beautiful Abyssinian woman provided a welcome base, living conditions in Harar were primitive. His letters mentioned a lack of water, lepers, beggars and the constant odour of human excrement. Following an expedition to the Red Sea in 1887, he described the town as a 'cesspit'. With no sanitary arrangements, the good citizens of Harar used to throw their rubbish—the dead included—over the walls to attendant hyenas.

And hyena-feeding was the final bizarre attraction of our own quick visit.

'Ask not what started the custom,' said Mr Abdulwasi staring up at the sky. 'Some say it began during a famine, when people put out *durra* porridge to stop hyenas attacking their livestock. But no one really knows. Lost in the mists of time,' he murmured.

The 'hyena man' was waiting for us outside the Erer Gate where Sir Richard Burton had entered Harar, disguised as an Arab merchant. A farmer by day, at night he transmogrified into the 'hyena man', staging a show for anyone willing to pay for this rustic entertainment.

When we were assembled, the 'hyena man' knelt down, and waving a chunk of meat, he uttered a chilling canine-like call. At first there was no response, but then I discerned four or five animals skulking in the shadows.

'*Batu!'*—come and eat, he called.

Growling the scavengers jostled each other like footballers in a scrum. Then one dashed out and snatching the meat, it loped off with that peculiar canter of the Hyaenidae family. When John Gritten of the *Morning Star* boldly stepped up to repeat this feat, the other men insisted that I follow suit. Barely forty-eight hours had passed since I was preparing Mrs Graham's breakfast: now I was about to feed Africa's second largest predator. Picking up a lump of offal, I stretched out my arm as far as it would go. '*Batu! Batu!*' cried the 'hyena-man' again. But the pack stayed back. What's the matter? I thought. Don't they like the colour of my nail polish? '*Batu,*' he called once more and sniffing the air, a big spotted animal, took a few steps towards me. Head lowered, it edged closer. It was now so near I could smell a putrid, feral odour and its jet-black eyes reminded me of a shark encounter off New Caledonia. Curling back its lips over a fearful set of teeth, it grabbed the meat and made off, leaving me shaking. None of the men said 'well done', but it seemed I had passed a test.

'Are you crazy?' scolded Dorothy on the bus back to Dire Dawa. 'Hyenas can slink into a hut at night and bite the face off a sleeping person.'

The aircraft taking us back to Addis Ababa next morning arrived three hours late, and missing the official press conference highlighting the achievements of the revolution, we were whisked by police escort to the centre of the parade, watched by 100,000 people.

The three strongmen of the eighty member Dergue Revolutionary Council were seated on a platform. In the centre was Chairman Brigadier General Teferi Bente; on his left, the second-in-command, Lieutenant Colonel Atnafu Abate; and on his right, the soon-to-be President of Ethiopia, Major General Mengistu Haile Mariam. Seated beside these atheists and looking very uncomfortable, was white-haired Bishop Abuna Tewofilos, Patriarch of the Ethiopian Orthodox Tewahedo Church who would be executed by the Dergue, in May 1976. Next to him, looking terrified, were three young women waiting to release white doves of peace.

I was standing beside this tense little group as wave after wave of people passed: Wollega blowing long reed pipes; Gambela shaking medieval shields; Arussi tossing lion's mane headdresses; Gurage from the Awash area; dark-skinned Berta and Nilo-Saharan Anuak from the south-west river divisions; Agaw, Irob and scores of other prancing tribesmen who had been trucked in to help celebrate twelve months of dramatic revolutionary change.

However, the parade was not a happy one. Despite the soldiers guarding the route, also marching were unemployed graduate students bravely waving signs reading: 'WE NEED WORK' and 'WE NEED BREAD'. Other people called out for civilian rule and the release of prisoners, among them the twelve Ethiopian princesses[10] detained by the Dergue. When the float from the reviled Ministry of Information drew level with the generals, some 50,000 sat down in protest against the regime we were invited to publicise.

FRONT MEN OF THE DERGUE MENGISTU (L) AND BENTE, 13 SEPTEMBER 1975

Under the late emperor, all fertile land in Ethiopia was owned by a feudal landlord, living in affluence and indifferent to the hardship of the peasant-farmers who were obliged to surrender half their harvest to him. But while the revolution may have been well intentioned, it had turned society upside down, and Mengistu's own ruthless policies were accelerating desertification and starvation.

The situation we found was on the cusp. Studying the grim features of Teferi Bente[11], I decided he wore the look of a doomed man, an expression to become familiar on my later travels in Iraq. As Soviet MiG-23 fighter aircraft swept low overhead, I felt apprehensive and with my colleagues nowhere in sight, I shouldered my camera bag and found my own way back to the Ghion Hotel.

When the crowds had dispersed, I slipped out to explore Addis Ababa, a city of small disconnected neighbourhoods, dotted across the foothills of the Entoto Mountains, 2,400 metres (7,874 feet) above sea level. Most buildings were corrugated iron shacks standing side by side with round, thatched-roof Ethiopian *tukuls* (huts). There were few cars and no traffic lights; in one place, I crossed the road among a herd of goats.

Then suddenly I saw gum trees. Ethiopia's previous capitals had been abandoned when the supply of wood used for cooking and heating, became exhausted. Addis Ababa had faced a similar fate until the introduction of the rapid-growing *Eucalyptus globulus*—Australia's gift to the world. Picking some leaves, I crumbled them between my fingers, releasing a haunting citronella fragrance reminding me of home.

Unlike today's tourists, armed with an abundance of maps, apps and advice from Trip Advisor on where to eat, sleep and locate a cyber café, in 1975 there were no such things. The solution was to find a companion who could speak some English and near the Ghion Hotel, I met Gebre, an eighteen-year-old Christian student. A tall, sad-faced youth, he said he was studying law until the Dergue had closed the university and dispatched its 50,000 students into the countryside to educate the illiterate peasantry.

'We needed change, but no one expected a Phoenix-like Ethiopia to arise without more bloodshed. It's like awakening to a river in the morning that will change its course many times by the afternoon,' said Gebre, fingering a silver cross below a rather pronounced Adam's apple.

Our first stop was the Holy Trinity Cathedral where Sylvia Pankhurst, daughter of the famous suffragette Emmeline Pankhurst, a friend and adviser to Haile Selassie, was buried in 1961. Just as Mrs Graham had said. From here we took a taxi to visit St George's Cathedral built in 1896 to commemorate Ethiopia's celebrated victory over Italian troops at the Battle of Adwa. The Dergue had disestablished the Ethiopian Orthodox religion, and state security forces had slaughtered hundreds of Christians on its steps, but today it was open. To impress the visiting journalists I decided.

'Our leading artist, Afewerk Tekle, designed the stained glass windows,' said Gebre kneeling for a moment of prayer. 'Art in Ethiopia is strongly influenced by faith. You will see this in the *mercato*, but keep your bag closed. It is full of thieves. They're not bad, just hungry.'

I've seen scores of markets in Africa: the 'King Jimmy' market in Freetown while on a commission to photograph Siaka Stevens, then president of Sierra Leone, Kumasi market in the Ashanti region of Ghana, the Sandaga market in Dakar, Senegal (which is certainly full of thieves), Dar-es-Salaam, Lusaka, Harare (during good times in Zimbabwe) and Omdurman filled with bean gourds, ivory and cheetah skin handbags, but the enormous *mercato* in Addis Ababa was the biggest of all. Literally hundreds of stalls and small shops announced by their smells: spices, incense, skins, wood smoke and the rancid odour of the butter market, where Guragué women, wrapped in white robes, squeezed phallic symbols out of greasy, yellow mounds. Asked the significance of this erotic butter sculpture, they said they didn't know, but offered to anoint my head with it for a few *birr* (the unit of currency in Ethiopia).

'It's good for the brains,' they explained, but I declined, disappointing Gebre who said he buttered his own head every morning.

The afternoon slipped by as I sifted through ethnic crafts: baskets for carrying *injera,* charcoal and *qat,* shields, textiles, musical instruments, carvings and carpets. Some traders specialised in equine equipment—saddles, bridles and plumes—a horse being the only means of transport in the rugged highlands.

Elsewhere, merchants seated on three-legged stools were selling icons and religious scrolls. The theme of many paintings—an Ethiopian version of *The Last Supper*—depicted Haile Selassie as Jesus Christ, surrounded by the twelve disciples wearing vivid orange and green robes. Other shops sold religious artefacts cast from the Maria Theresa dollar minted in late eighteenth century Austria and used as unofficial currency in the Horn of Africa where silversmiths found its silver content perfect for making jewellery. In one shop we visited, an elderly jeweller with a prominent nose brought out a cardboard box containing hundreds of silver crosses. 'They are cast by the *cire perdu* lost wax method,' he told me. 'No two are the same.' He held up a delicate filigree Gojjam cross, but I was more struck by his nose. Was he a member of the ancient Beta Israelite community of Ethiopia?

'Yes,' he said, as if reading my mind. 'My name is Rada, and our family comes from Gondar. We are many generations of silversmiths, but times are bad.' He took a quick look at Gebre.

'I'm Christian,' said Gebre. 'You can see my cross.'

'Our people are being murdered by the Dergue,' continued Rada. 'The Beta Jews have lived in Ethiopia since the time of the Book, but they are killing us.' He put a finger to his lips. 'There are only three of us left in the *mercato*.'

Conversation ceased as I sifted through round Solomonic crosses, hinged Lalibela crosses, small hand crosses, the huge processional crosses carried by Orthodox priests at *tingkat*, the Ethiopian epiphany, and finely wrought pectoral crosses such as Gebre wore. Another box held silver jewellery including lion and leopard claws incorporated into pendants, brooches, and other accoutrements to dress. Like the Bedouin in the Middle East, an Ethiopian woman's jewellery, is her personal walking wealth.

Born in October, I suffer the irritating Libran trait of indecision. It may be over something simple, such as whether to paint my nails scarlet or pink, or a complex issue that actually causes personal anguish. Confronted by all Rada's jewellery, after much deliberation I finally bought a silver choker, strung with miniature phalluses whose significance would become apparent a few days later.

Only the political correspondents were invited to the evening banquet in the old Imperial Palace. Back at the hotel, I added my name to the list of journalists interested to visit the famine belt, and next morning, escorted by Ato Shimalis—Ethiopia's Minister for Relief—we took off for Gode in a chartered DC-3.

Gode lies in the Ogaden, a vast swathe of south-east Ethiopia bordered by Kenya and Djibouti, and sharing a historically disputed frontier with

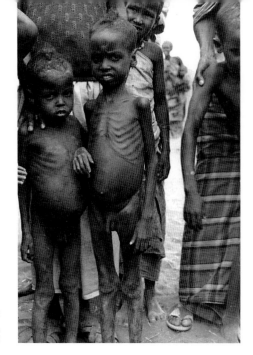

FAMINE VICTIMS
IN THE OGADEN,
SEPTEMBER 1975

Somalia. A semi-desert region, it supports only scraggy shrubs and trees, but the Webi Shebelle River crosses it before flowing into the Indian Ocean, between Mogadishu and Mombasa, more than 1,000 kilometres (621 miles) from its source in the Ethiopian highlands.

'We've had no response to our appeal for medical teams,' Shimalis told us in the Gode refugee camp where one skinny doctor, two tired nurses and three overworked dressers, were attempting to care for 12,000 starving famine victims.

'She will die,' murmured the doctor of a wasted mite whose arms were no thicker than my fingers. 'There have to be mass graves before anyone wants to help, and once you find fresh graves, we have lost our battle against the drought.' He sighed deeply.

Times are never normal, or good in this godforsaken corner of Africa, where Somali nomads roam in a perpetual search for sustenance, for themselves and their herds.

'They are a primitive people who eat food on the hoof, using a special curved knife to slice steaks off the living animal, then packing the wound with mud,' said Shimalis.

Hammered by the sun and buffeted by sand-laden winds, the Ogaden had not received a drop of rain in five years. Wherever I looked, bleached bones punctured the landscape. Even the hardy camel herds were dying. Walking away from my colleagues, I came upon a group moaning softly around a dried-up water hole. One was a mother with twins whose hump had shrunk to a flab of skin. She salivated, rolling her tongue, as they butted her udder in frustration. While I watched, she sank to her knees and rested her chin on the sand. A buzzard took off from a twisted acacia, then another, and looking up, I saw other scavengers circling in the washed-out sky. I had encountered many unpleasant situations on my travels, but conditions in Gode made me weep.

And this was not the first famine in Ethiopia. When the government concealed the Wollo disaster, an estimated 100,000 people perished and it was only when Dimbleby and his team were able to make *The Unknown Famine* in 1973, that the extent of the calamity was revealed. Ian Studdard, the film's director, told us of a sumptuous banquet served by the governor of Wollo, a province in north-east Ethiopia, as people outside the gate were dropping from starvation.

The situation we found in Gode was equally catastrophic. Withered by hunger and racked by disease, the proud nomads had staggered into the relief camp from all over the Ogaden: thousands of refugees, needing thousands of tonnes of high-protein food to survive.

'There's enough for each person to have one bowl of mealy mix a day, but it's a terribly monotonous diet,' said Abdi Nuir, a gaunt-faced worker for World Vision who was clearly in need of a good meal himself. Showing me into a hot, corrugated-iron shed, he pointed out the worst cases lying on palm mats and feebly striking at flies.

'We were expecting blankets with the last aid, but none arrived. As you can see, the children don't have any clothes and at night the desert is freezing.'

Naked, dusty children with Martian-like heads on skeletal frames lolled around as we walked through the camp. Their bellies were distended by kwashiorkor, the result of long-term protein deficiency and gastrointestinal disorders. All had hacking coughs, almost certainly caused by tuberculosis, and their eyes were clogged with mucus feasted on by flies.

Gode's only fortune was the nearby Webi Shebbelle river providing water, but at least one child, or a woman filling her water jar, fell victim to crocodiles each month.

Abdi wiped his face with his sleeve. 'We used to have an American Peace Corps boy helping us, but he went swimming one afternoon, and in two chops he was gone.'

Wherever we went, the refugees—obviously briefed on our visit—burst into applause, making me cringe with embarrassment. Of mainly Muslim persuasion, in normal circumstances they would have refused to let me take their photograph, but dignity had vanished in their new dependence. As our plane took off, the pilot made a low sweep over the tin shed and a few of the stronger children chased after its shadow.

Warder, the second camp, was a wretched settlement of stick-and-bag huts in the bleeding heart of the Ogaden. Its 8,000 inmates were receiving food and sighting the men among us, women made a desperate attempt at modesty, biting a corner of their ragged cotton robes to drag across their emaciated bodies. Their naked children, each clutching a tin, sat in a circle around a pot of high-protein gruel cooking over a fire.

'It takes more than three hours to feed everyone. When they finish, the round starts again, yet the death rate is still five or six a day,' said Shimalis, who had four healthy children of his own.

The Grim Reaper was everywhere in Warder. There was no river, the wells were almost dry and non-Amharic-speaking Somali refugees compounded the situation. Only a dozen inmates of this terrible place spoke both languages. One, a thirteen-year-old boy called Korani, followed me about as I endeavoured to protect my camera equipment from the dust.

As in Gode, the weakest cases lay coughing on bags in a corrugated-iron shed. In a corner, a mournful boy sat alone, his long thin limbs folded under him like stork's legs.

'Is his third time in camp,' Korani told one of the dressers. 'All family dead. He go back to desert, but nothing to eat. Not even ant.'

'Hungry,' said a tiny child tugging at my jacket pockets, which I'd filled with sweets from the plane. My intentions had been kind, but with thousands of watching eyes, I dared not hand out a single one.

'The kids are dizzy,' emphasised the dresser. 'With no clothes and no playthings, all they do is sleep. Sure we need food and medicine, but ask your people to send us some balls to play with before they die from boredom.'

Saving the nomads from death was one thing. It was equally important to re-settle them somewhere sustainable, and at Gen, the last stop on our visit, two hundred families who were fit enough to make a start, welcomed us with beaming smiles.

The government had allocated each family a plot on which to grow maize and 100 hectares (247 acres) were under cultivation. We watched men digging irrigation gutters off the Webi Shebelle, and famine widows who had formed women's cooperatives, were busily weeding the fields. Once peripatetic herdsmen who walked great distances in search of a blade of grass, they were overjoyed by the new green shoots.

'Why doesn't it grow more quickly?' asked one man squatting down and cupping his dusty hands around a tiny bud. Shimalis gently explained that maize needs time to ripen and that providing he never forgot to water it, it would likely yield two harvests a year.

On our way back to the airstrip, the driver lost his way and we spent two hours driving in circles through the sandy wadis. We finally sighted the plane sitting like a giant pigeon on the desert runway. However, fifteen minutes into the flight, the pilot announced we wouldn't make it back to Addis Ababa before nightfall. Bole International Airport had no night-landing facilities so we banked east and headed for the nearest point of human contact. My heart sank—goddamned Gode.

The army quickly assumed responsibility for our unexpected return. They provided us with refreshments and a soldier was sent out to slaughter a goat. Some time after ten, a cook brought out a platter of *wat* and *injera* but in spite of my hunger, I could not eat. It wasn't its toughness, but the thought of the truly hungry, out in the darkness.

We were four women: from the *Boston Globe*, the *Christian Science Monitor*, an irritable Frenchwoman from *Le Nouvel Observateur* and me, the only photographer in the group. We were to sleep on the veranda of one of the late emperor's houses.

'One of the many he never used,' said Shimalis bitterly.

Observing protocol, the soldiers placed our stretchers around a corner, out of sight of the men, but the French woman scornfully decamped and set up her bed between the *Telegraph* and the *Times*. And watching me clean my teeth under a garden tap, she let fly a mocking remark: '*Est-ce que tu portes egalement ta robe de chambre?*'—are you also going to wear a dressing-gown?

I slept fitfully under a cotton blanket and was up at dawn; there was frost on the ground and I learnt that three stiff little bodies had been discovered by dressers on their morning round of the camp.

After thanking the commander of Gode for his hospitality, we boarded our plane and returned to Addis Ababa without further incident. The other press joined connecting flights to various destinations, leaving me with a French reporter, Jean-Emile. Apparently we both had reservations on Tuesday's Ethiopian Airlines flight to Athens, where I planned to spend a few days en route to London. But before then, I had a mission that would take me deep into the steaming heart of equatorial Africa.

In Australia, I'd been travel writer for the women's magazine *Cleo* and on learning of my trip to Ethiopia, its editor Ita Buttrose, had commissioned an article on a child adopted by the magazine through Foster Parents Plan. Conrad Hilton, Julie Andrews and the Boston Symphony Orchestra were some of the famous adoptive parents of the charity, founded in 1937 to provide support for families with needy children in various parts of the world. *Cleo* was fostering Sisay Bonke, a four-year-old boy. My only information was that he lived in Arba Minch, a town in the remote south-west corner of Ethiopia.

At FPP headquarters in Addis Ababa, I learnt that Arba Minch lay on a ridge of the Rift Valley escarpment at a height of 2,000 metres (6,562 feet). Peasant-farmers, the people cultivated coffee and maize, but life had deteriorated under the new Marxist government and as in other parts of Ethiopia, there was increasing dissent.

A message was dispatched to Lloyd Fineberg, the regional director of FPP in Arba Minch, telling him to expect me on the morning flight. So barely twenty-four hours out of the bone-dry Ogaden, I was flying south, to the wettest part of Ethiopia, the only foreigner on a converted military transport aircraft whose passengers included two goats sliding up and down on the metal floor between our uncomfortable webbing seats.

'Do goats ride free?' I asked a man holding a briefcase on his knee who looked like my idea of an Ethiopian civil servant.

'This is nothing.' He fingered his collar. 'I once flew down with a flock of sheep.'

Wearing only a cotton shirt and cargo trousers, I froze as wind whistled through gaps in the perspex windows, but surprisingly for Africa, our plans worked and Fineberg, a fresh-faced, thirty-two year old American, was waiting at the tiny airport.

'It's great of you to come all this way to meet Sisay.' He gave me a warm handshake and a Colgate smile.

'I hope Sisay will like the pens,' I said, pulling out a box of coloured biros from my backpack.

'He'll love them. Most of the people here are illiterate, but with funding from *Cleo*, he'll be able to attend the new primary school,' he grinned.

'Well, this is Arba Minch,' he said as we bumped into a higgledy-piggledy settlement of wooden stalls and corrugated iron shops where flame trees on either side of the road were in flower. Wandering about while Fineberg bought petrol, I saw there was little for sale; corncobs, a few onions and bananas, cotton reels, safety pins and combs and although I was a new white face, no one paid me any attention. People here had the dazed look of the hungry, but not quite starving.

The Bonke family lived in Siskela, a small village outside Arba Minch. Mr Bonke was at work when we arrived, but Beru, the FPP interpreter, introduced me to his wife, Marmite. I wondered about her name. I'd encountered a Rothman and a Culture in Africa, but never anyone named after the dark-brown vegetarian spread.

Marmite was thrilled with the beaded bag I'd brought as a gift and, gripping my hands, she bowed almost to the ground. Sisay was hiding behind her skirts but called by Beru, he emerged shyly, eyes focused on his toes, and extended a grubby hand. He was a serious little fellow missing two front teeth. His head was shaved, except for a woollen topknot, and his belly, distended by worms, strained against a pair of grey shorts held up

SISAY BONKE, THE CHILD SPONSORED BY *CLEO* MAGAZINE 1975

by string braces. Despite the heat, he was wearing a green woollen jumper bought out of sponsorship money received from *Cleo*.

'He won't take it off,' said Marmite introducing her other children, eight-year-old Shyate and her runny-nosed younger brothers, Tamene and Berahun. In the family *tukul*, she pointed to another child who lay crying on a burlap mat.

'I had him here.' Picking him up, she offered a breast. 'There is an old village woman who helps, but five is enough. I don't want any more.'

'Has she heard of birth control?' I asked Beru.

'My neighbours speak of something, but we don't know what it is, or where to find it,' she told him.

A cane partition in the *tukul* divided the cooking, living and sleeping areas. Marmite's utensils were arranged neatly along a log: a large enamel bowl, a small enamel plate, three glasses, a wooden spoon and a chipped cup and saucer. Bean gourds, corncobs and a bag for carrying *injera* hung from the beams and two earthenware jars stood against the wall—fetching water was also a woman's chore.

Asked what they ate, Marmite whispered that they'd never eaten *wat*.

'They've never eaten meat,' explained Beru, who was wearing a navy suit and tie for the occasion. 'And they've never drunk tea or coffee. Even milk is a luxury they can't afford.'

Before coming to Ethiopia, I'd planned on taking the Bonke family out to dinner, but while well-meant, the idea was preposterous. There was nowhere to eat in Arba Minch and instead, the Bonkes invited me to share their supper, and while concerned as to whether I would enjoy the experience, Fineberg finally left me with Beru.

Helped by Sisay and Shyate, at sunset Marmite rounded up their animals and lit a rusty hurricane lamp. At seven o'clock, Mr Bonke returned from a day building roads in Gemu Gofu province of which Arba Minch was the regional town.

'Ten hours a day, six days a week for thirty dollars a month,' he said wearily. 'Without help from this *Cleo* person, I don't know how we'd manage.'

We were now fifteen squeezed inside the *tukul* since Bonke's seven goats—including a rank-smelling, billygoat standing beside me—had staked out places for the night. And tonight, just as they did yesterday and would do so again tomorrow, the Bonke family was eating corn.

Marmite uncovered a bowl of eight uncooked patties she had mashed with water and squeezed into lumps, with *haleko* leaves—a sort of spinach—draped across them. The thought that mother would be horrified to learn I was eating uncooked food mixed with river-water crossed my mind. Fiddling with my portion, I managed to swallow a mouthful, or two. Its taste was negligible and the texture was like plasticine, but I was glad to have eaten a little so as not to offend this poor Ethiopian family.

'Is there something they might like to drink?' I asked Beru, who was seated next to Mr Bonke on the only bed.

'People here drink *tella,* a fermented corn beer,' he replied. 'I know Bonke loves it, but they've only had it twice in their lives.'

'Tonight's the night,' I said, giving Sisay some coins to run and fetch some *tella* from a neighbour.

Bonke's eyes lit up when he returned with a ketchup bottle filled with amber fluid. A glass was poured for me, but now obsessed with thoughts of guinea worm and dysentery, I declined as politely as was possible in the circumstances.

'With one dollar I could start a small *tella* business and make a profit of two dollars a week,' said Marmite, staring dreamily into the fire.

As contented snorts came from the animals, I stood up, a good head taller than both Beru and Bonke, and pressing the equivalent of a dollar in Marmite's hand, I wished her luck with her enterprise.

'She asks may she keep the plastic bags you've brought their presents in. They will be great for carrying her corn,' said Beru courteously.

Back at Arba Minch's timeworn hotel, I pictured Mrs Bonke walking about Siskela with Sainsburys[12] carry bags. But I could not sleep. Stomach cramps sent me scurrying to the lavatory where I remained racked by diarrhoea and attacked by mosquitoes as big as bumblebees zooming in through a broken window. Back to bed for a bit. Then up again. Up. Down. All night long, but though utterly drained, next morning I accompanied Fineberg back to thank Marmite for her hospitality. She was at the river fetching water and having loaded her heavy jars into the Land Rover, we drove her back to the *tukul*.

'Thank you,' she smiled. 'It has saved my back and I've never ridden in one of these things before.'

'Goodbye Sisay,' I told the little boy. 'I hope you'll do well at school.'

'I'm not excited,' he whispered hoarsely. 'But I think I would like to go.' And he ran off surrounded by leaping, skipping children.

I had given the Bonke family powdered milk, rice and biscuits, but as in the Ogaden, I was troubled at not having enough for their neighbours. And everything considered, I even questioned the wisdom of raising one family's living standards in the unstable political climate of Ethiopia.

Sure enough, between 1975 and 1991, the general situation deteriorated under the violent leadership of Mengistu who mounted a 'Red Terror' campaign against all opponents of his wretched regime.

'Death to the counter-revolutionaries,' he cried in 1976, and standing in the centre of Addis Ababa, he'd smashed bottles filled with pig blood to demonstrate the fate awaiting them. Students refusing to obey government orders were arrested, given a gun and sent to the front-line battle zone with Eritrea. State security forces tortured anyone suspected of belonging to opposition movements and thousands of 'dissident' peasants were killed, at which point *Cleo* lost contact with Master Sisay Bonke.

After leaving Siskela, Fineberg invited me for drinks with Father John Gannon, an Irish priest who'd spent twenty-five years in Africa and whose parish was now in Arba Minch. A great raconteur, the father was quick to tell me about a local tribe, the Gujis (pronounced just like the iconic Italian fashion label).

'I recently took an Irish engineer out to survey possible dam sites,' he said as we sat watching the sunset on his back verandah. 'We were deep inside Guji Oromo territory when I mentioned their custom of presentin' a severed penis to the bride on their wedding night. He got quite upset, so he did, but don't worry Paddy, I told him. If the Gujis attack us, I'll offer me own, seeing I sort of don't need it like.' Slapping his knee and roaring with laughter, he got up and poured us another belt of whisky as the significance of the necklace from Rada's jewellery shop dawned on me.

'But it seems so peaceful here Father, and your garden is lovely.' I inhaled the intoxicating scent of night jasmine.

'Ai. During the dry season, we sit out here playing the *Messiah* and watching bushfires. Now don't you be taking them Gujis lightly.' He looked sternly at Lloyd.

'You're takin' our friend here to the Neche Reserve. Well, that's where we saw them. You ask Sister Shelagh now. She'll be after tellin' you. She and another of the good sisters went to a Guji village to inspect a clinic. Suspended on six trees were four legs, two torsos and three heads. Work that out. And only last week we found a young lad in the parish who had bled to death in the garden. Turnin' him over we found he was missin' his member. The Norwegian doctor here has treated several men who have had their penises amputated by the Gujis. Christine's all right, Lloyd, but you'd better watch out. Ho! Ho!'

There are moments in travel to far-away places when the mind cannot keep pace with the physical flight—it may find itself in a body seated somewhere foreign, and while not exactly an out-of-body experience, the two are somehow separate. This was how I felt on hearing Father Gannon's stories, but I'd seen so much since leaving London it was no surprise.

After a second night fighting Arba Minch mosquitoes, I was ready to leave long before Fineberg and a companion came to collect me. The plan was to do some crocodile-spotting on Lake Chamo and to visit the adjacent Nechisar Plains set on a plateau overlooking the Rift Valley.

'You're not driving through Guji territory are you?'asked Fineberg's friend, a tall, lean Swedish pilot, known as Captain Karlsson.

'There shouldn't be any Gujis this far north,' said Fineberg, strapping a canvas water-bag onto the bumper bar of the Land Rover.

Karlsson belonged to a church relief team making food drops to starving nomads in this remote corner of Ethiopia, abutting on the Kenyan border.

'Around here it's not so difficult,' he told us on the way to the lake. 'But elsewhere rivers and villages on our old maps can be as much as 15 kilometres (9 miles) off course and when this happens, without radio contact, we fly entirely by the seat of our pants.'

'When we're searching for a settlement, our routine is to pick a land-mark, go left, drift for thirty minutes, then go north. Sometimes we land near a settlement only to find everyone has left because of the tsetse fly. It also happens, like your own experience in the Ogaden, that we reach a place just on dusk. These bush strips are so short that in this event, we just cross our fingers and go down as fast as possible.' He ran a hand through his blond crew cut.

'Occasionally we also find ourselves carrying a patient or two. One man had been hit in the brain with an axe. Another, working for the Swedish mission, had his genitals hacked off, but survived a week lying out in the bush. We later heard he'd married and got his brother to fertilise his wife who had three children by him.'

The smaller of two Rift Valley lakes in South Omo, Lake Chamo is fed by a jungle-lined channel pouring into it from the higher elevation of Lake Abaya. Fineberg had organised a boat, but with room only for two, Karlsson agreed to wait with the Land Rover.

As I was about to step on board, a man popped out of the bush and unfurled a python skin twice as long as the jetty.

'Souvenir, gimme twenty dollars,' he said and I noticed tribal scars, like crossed bananas, on his chest.

Powered by an old outboard, we set off, travelling some way along the lakeshore before veering into a reed-lined channel where the propeller churned up clouds of insects. Wearing only a T-shirt and swimming costume, I wished I'd brought a jacket, but the thought had not occurred to me in the oppressive heat.

As we chugged further along the narrow waterway, the boatman pointed to the carcass of an enormous Nile perch washing among the reeds. 'Dem grow much bigger dan dat. Bigger dan dis boat,' he grinned. 'Fishing easy here.'

To demonstrate, he swatted a dragonfly with his shoe, threaded it on a hook, and immediately pulled up a struggling tilapia. Then he put a finger to his lips, although it was him doing all the talking. Ahead a huge crocodile lay asleep on the bank. The world's largest freshwater crocodiles are said to inhabit Lake Chamo: this one was no exception.

'Easily four metres (fifteen feet),' whispered Fineberg crouching in the bow.

As we drifted closer, terrified it would wake up and jump into our boat, I begged the boy to start the motor, but my request had the opposite effect. He picked up a paddle and slapped it on the mud.

'Hey, wake up crocodile. Mister and Missus want to see you,' he yelled.

Startled, the crocodile rose up and dived in, drenching us with water. Other crocodiles, disturbed by the noise, did similar bellyflops, setting the boat rocking and our boatman shrieking as only an African can. Lake Chamo was crocodile heaven. We counted ten more monsters, but by noon, all were cooling off with just their eyes showing above the surface. I longed to swim, but crocodiles apart, like most freshwater in Africa, the lake was teeming with the parasitic worm, bilharzia. I had to be content with Karlsson tipping the waterbag over me when we were back at the Land Rover.

The appeal of Nechisar is its proximity to Lake Chamo, but the track winding up was very rough. We stopped on several occasions for Karlsson to roll away rocks, but once on top we found ourselves in a stunning landscape of waving yellow grassland backed by blue-green mountain ranges.

'Wow. It's just like Nebraska,' whooped Fineberg enjoying his day off.

Startled by the noise of our vehicle, a herd of zebra took to its heels while a nervous wart-hog, tail stuck straight up like a flag, made a dash for safety. Farther away, thick black side-stripes identified Thompson's gazelle. Dik-diks and hartebeest grazed peacefully out on the savannah where a large eland raised its head in curiosity.

However it was the birdlife that fascinated us. Fineberg pointed out a lilac-breasted roller and a colony of weaverbirds, both inhabitants of high-altitude grasslands. We saw golden-breasted starlings, red-beaked hornbills, paradise flycatchers, shining sunbirds and others with equally brilliant plumage. I spotted a black-chested snake eagle and Karlsson saw a Kori bustard with a group of bee-eaters, riding on its back. Quails whirred out of the undergrowth and we disturbed a helmeted guinea fowl, which scuttled across the road, trailed by nine cheeping young.

Suddenly my attention was caught by a circle of bare-chested men, standing 300 metres (328 yards) away under a thorn tree. Focusing my binoculars on them, I saw they were clutching bloodstained spears and staring intently at something on the ground.

'Guji!' hissed Karlsson.

Gamewatching stopped as Fineberg drove on in silence. We needed to make our way back to the lake road without showing sign of alarm. From being one of joy at the wildlife, the atmosphere was tense and as we proceeded in a wide arc around the Gujis, no one mentioned a pair of giraffes that seemed to float across the horizon.

'Want a smoke?' asked Karlsson.

He passed a joint across to Fineberg, filling the vehicle with the sickly scent of hashish and convinced we'd all be hacked to death, I dictated a final message into my pocket tape-recorder.

Now we were passing the place where I saw the Gujis, but strangely there was only the thorn tree, pricked out against the blue sky. Where could they have gone?

'Can we quickly go and see what they've killed?' I asked.

'They might be lying in the grass,' said Karlsson. 'Where else can they be? The place is flat as a pancake.'

Reaching the track again, Fineberg slipped into low gear and skidding and sliding on the muddy road, we began the descent.

Halfway down, a man clutching a spear, stepped up in front of us.

'Shall I stop?' asked Fineberg.

'Keep going,' yelled Karlsson.

'He might want a lift,' said Fineberg naively.

'Let him walk,' I shouted and pressing down on the accelerator, Fineberg shot past the man, showering him with stones.

Even back at Lake Chamo, we remained uneasy. Where could the Gujis have gone? No one was talking when a bushbuck bounded across the road and swerving to avoid it, we spun off into mud.

'De-plane!' ordered Captain Karlsson, clearly under stress.

Jumping out, I disturbed thousands of yellow butterflies that fluttered around us like confetti as the men began breaking off branches and packing them in front of the wheels. A family of olive baboons, attracted by the noise, climbed onto a rock and blinked curiously at the unfamiliar commotion. After some minutes scrutiny, a large dog-faced male dropped down and walked purposely towards us.

'Get in Christine. He can rip your face open,' yelled Karlsson.

I didn't need to be told again and seated in the Land Rover, I realised with beating heart, that it would soon be dusk when animals come down to drink. Bugger the Gujis—my new concern was being surrounded by a herd of trumpeting elephant.

'Okay. Start her up,' called Fineberg, and as he and Karlsson leant against the vehicle, up popped the man with the python skin.

'Gimme twenty dollars,' he said once again.

'Put your foot down,' yelled Fineberg and as I struggled to control the spinning wheel, rocking and squelching, the vehicle roared free.

I reflected that the racket must have been audible to Gujis all over the Nechisar and perhaps also to Father Gannon seated on his verandah back in Arba Minch.

'Gimme fifteen dollars,' said the man and passed half that amount by Karlsson, he rolled up the note, stuck it behind his ear, and disappeared into the undergrowth.

Every six weeks, Fineberg visited Addis Ababa for supplies and on this occasion, he'd waited so I might join him on an uneventful trip when compared to our experience in the Nechisar. We passed farmers working their fields with wooden wish-bone ploughs and groups of peasants carrying loads to market. Near Sodo, an ancient town on the Omo River, we stopped for an old woman carrying a bag of charcoal. Getting out she pressed a roasted corncob into my hand that may have been her lunch.

It took us seven hours to complete the journey, and to my surprise, the first person I saw back at the Ghion was Jean-Emile, a dapper figure with a burgundy silk cravat knotted precisely at the neck of his bush jacket.

' 'ave you found this child?' he asked with a wry smile.

'Yes, and I've changed my plans to stop in Athens. I have exclusive photos of the Ogaden and want to get back to London.'

To Jean-Emile's regret, I changed my ticket, but we enjoyed dinner in the hotel and afterwards took an evening stroll. With Addis Ababa under curfew, few pedestrians were about, but outside the gate, several youths beckoned to us.

'Shouldn't we listen to what they may have to say?' I was astonished by the French journalist's apparent lack of interest.

He frowned. '*Non.* They bother me all the time you are gone.'

'Please listen. Something will happen,' one boy pleaded.

'It's always going to happen in Ethiopia. *Faites-les, alors,*' Jean-Emile retorted.

My flight left on schedule and touching down at Heathrow, I went straight to News Limited at Wapping and deposited my film of the drought with the picture desk.

On my way to Mrs Graham next morning, I stopped to buy the *Times* at the kiosk outside Sloane Square Station. My picture of the famine widows weeding maize fields in Gen was on the front page! Dodging traffic, I flicked through to an item of news: police had opened fire on students distributing anti-government literature at Bole International Airport. Several Ethiopian

Airlines employees had been killed and passengers were among the injured. It was the Athens flight I had been due to take with Jean-Emile.

'Well, Sister. Did you enjoy your holiday?' inquired Mrs Graham when I took in her breakfast tray. 'Oh! The egg is too soft. I told you how I like it cooked.'

In the following weeks, I sold several articles and photographs of Ethiopia and while none-too-rich, I felt confident enough to hang up my nurse's uniform for good.

It was a start. But only a beginning. I made the rounds of London newspapers and magazines. Some took my work, most rejected it. Then Elizabeth de Stroumillo[13], the travel editor of the *Daily Telegraph* made a suggestion that would change my life.

'You might be known as a travel writer in Australia, but no one here gives a hoot. If you want to make a name in London, you will have to write a book,' she told me.

MY PHOTO OF THE FAMINE WIDOWS WEEDING A FIELD AT GEN,
ON THE FRONT PAGE OF THE TIMES, 29 SEPTEMBER 1975

Chapter 2

Red Sea Adventure

I was seated in the Colony Room in Soho with Haile Selassie's grandson who was passing a dummy cover of my book around the drinkers, a mix of actors, artists, publishers and PRs. Muriel Belcher, the butch bar-owner was pouring us whiskys. At two in the afternoon. Somewhere between then and midnight I made it home. I have no recollection of how I came to be out with Ethiopian royalty and Muriel was too acerbic to call to inquire if anyone had handed in the cover which I'd lost. She'd referred to me as 'Missy' but she could just as easily have called me 'c...y', her favourite name for drinkers of either sex in her London watering-hole that managed to be louche, yet fashionable at the same time.

The Gulf States and Oman that took me two years to write was published in 1977 by the fledgling team of Croom Helm. Filled with facts for business visitors, the book examined the remarkable changes linked to the discovery of huge oil and gas fields in the eastern states of the Arabian peninsula. Travelling up and down the Gulf, at a time when there were no tourist offices and few hotels, I had been humiliated, propositioned, frightened and led up the garden path on so many occasions, that it was a miracle I'd finished the book at all, but illustrated with my pictures, it attracted good reviews in the Australian media as well as the *Gulf News*, the daily paper in Bahrain. Elizabeth de Stroumillo called it a 'riveting read'. A further review said '... her text is good...clear and brisk...but depth is given by her truly remarkable photographs showing a traditional people on the brink of an unimaginable future ...'

The book lent clout in the competitive world of freelance travel writing in London. I received commissions for articles on the Middle East, and the prestigious photo-agency Camera Press agreed to market my pictures. Tom Blau, the Hungarian photographer who founded Camera Press in 1947, called me into his rabbit warren office in Russell Square. It was stacked from floor to ceiling with photographs of every conceivable news-making event, those of popular film stars, rock bands and royal persons. Cecil Beaton and Lords Snowdon and Litchfield, were just two of its celebrated photographers.

Courageously, bridging the Gulf

By P. T. PLOWMAN

The Gulf States and Oman, by Christine Osborne. Published by Croom Helm (London).

CHRISTINE Osborne, Sydney-born journalist and photographer, has made several trips to the oil-rich States along the Arabian Gulf. Her travels were attended by certain risks because, from her account, she frequently aroused the inflammable passions of Arabs.

The perils of taxis in Kuwait forced her to rely for transport on the Hilton Hotel bus. "Some of these Bedouin drivers get ideas about Western women," a businessman explained. "Many have never even seen their wives naked — the women keep their robes on in bed."

When not warding off lascivious locals, the observant Osborne collected material for her book. It mixes dry statistics with bizarre information. Bahrain has a population of 250,000, and a spring called "the Virgin's Pool" which is used as a car-wash. In the emirate of Ras-al-Khaima there are five cement factories, and censors ink in bras on bare-topped girls in *The News of the World.*

This grab-bag of facts conveys well the mixed-up character of the region. Building laborers at work on new high-rise blocks in Kuwait let bricks fall on the roofs of passing cars. Dame Violet Dickson, an Englishwoman of 83 described as "the grand old lady of Kuwait," remembers when "the mad used to shuffle about in shackles."

The Kuwait Hilton nominally

Sheik Zayed: falcon fancier

observes the Islamic prohibition of alcoholic drinks. It supplies whisky and calls it "lobster" on the bill. The de luxe Tri-Stars operated by Gulf Air provide air-to-ground telephones for the use of passengers. Some of the latter carry falcons on their wrists.

Osborne carefully records the improvements that wealth has brought. Kuwait, where the infant death rate used to be 90 percent, has hospitals. Children go to schools. A few women, especially in sophisticated Bahrain, have escaped from their traditional oppression by Arab men.

Yet the general scene is not exhilarating. Ornate old buildings are pulled down to make way for lumps of concrete. The well-off, as Osborne puts it, behave like people who have just won the pools and don't know what to do with the money. One of the telling pictures in her book shows a damaged car beside a road. In Kuwait when a driver hits something he leaves the car there and buys another.

'See these pictures,' Mr Blau pushed a sheet of contacts across his desk. 'We've made this American photographer £500. Your pictures might do even better.' He gave an encouraging smile.

With the *Gulf States* on sale, I returned to travel journalism and in the autumn of 1977, I was invited to Egypt with a party of scribes from the London dailies. Among them were Shauna Crawford-Poole, the travel editor of the *Times*, Reg Grizell from the *Daily Express* and the historian and former war correspondent, Tom Pocock. Our program included sightseeing in Cairo, Luxor and Aswan, where staying at the Old Cataract Hotel, Agatha Christie penned her murder mystery *Death on the Nile*. I would not accompany the others on the return flight to London. I was to visit Hurghada on the Red Sea coast, a small fishing village, that was being groomed for package tourism and the diving facilities to be offered by a new Sheraton Hotel were of special interest to me.

The underwater world has been a lifelong passion. On holidays at my aunt's house on Lake Macquarie, I would be up at dawn, netting baby squid, prawns, miniature jellyfish, and other fascinating creatures from the weeds (to everyone's horror, I once innocently caught a small, but deadly blue-ringed octopus in my hand).

Encouraging this early interest in ichthyology, my parents gave me T.C. Roughley's *Fish and Fisheries* featuring colour plates of every species of fish in Australia. On my thirteenth birthday, I received *The Silent World* by Jacques Cousteau, the famous French diver who pioneered the aqualung. *Under the Red Sea,* written by the Austrian diving team of Hans and Lottie Hass, was a prize received for coming first in biology at Temora High School and holidays away from the wretched hospital were spent diving on the Grande Recife off the island of New Caledonia, a two-hour flight from Sydney.

I was already familiar with Hurghada. Arriving in Europe in 1964, I had embarked on a marathon journey with Ruth Bicknell, a nursing colleague from Royal North Shore, when we'd hitchhiked from London, down through France and Spain to Morocco, and across North Africa to Cairo. Wearing sunfrocks! Ruth, a slightly built brunette, wore the same pink frock, washing it every evening, all the way from Morocco. Naïve young Australians, we'd shared many adventures on the way, but nothing untoward had occurred until we reached the Red Sea coast of Egypt.

Some people aspire to attending the Vienna Opera Ball, or Carnival in Rio de Janeiro, but it had been my dream to dive in the Mare Rostrum, as the Red Sea was known in antiquity. Informed that Hurghada lay only 500 kilometres (310 miles) south of Port Suez, I begged Ruth to come. Although we'd had several spats, as most travellers do, Ruth was an easy-going companion and seeking similar company in later life, I was to find that people like her are hard to find.

An alert to two young females hitchhiking brought the Suez police speeding down the road with their siren wailing and their blue light flashing.

'*La!*—no hitchhiking,' admonished a sweating officer ticking off the reasons why, on lecherous fingers: bandits, a breakdown in the desert, and above all, the Red Sea coast was a military zone. He flagged down a bus, two passengers were ordered to surrender their seats, and we were bundled on board.

But the bus proved serendipitous. Among the veiled women and men—Ruth and I thought they were wearing pyjamas—we discovered four Anglo-Egyptian students from the University of Alexandria. They were going on a diving holiday in Hurghada and we could join them.

'You'll be safe with us,' assured Morris, a lean, green-eyed medical student.

Hurghada had none of the historical attractions of other towns in Egypt. A small coastal village, it was never more than a meeting point for Saudi fishermen selling dried fish to camel caravans from Upper Egypt. A score of coral stone houses were built around a tiny mosque and surrounding them were palm frond shacks likely to become airborne in a strong *khamsin,* the hot, sand-laden wind blowing off the Sahara.

'Al Ghardaqah has one tree and no water,' announced a passenger using Hurghada's Arabic name. 'Most of us work in the fish factory owned by a businessman from Cairo who drives around like God, in a grey Jaguar. That is where tourists stay.' He pointed to a white circular building on the seafront.

The Red Sea Tours Hotel was a luxury that Ruth and I could not afford. On our journey across North Africa, we'd never spent more than five

MY PICTURE IN THE EGYPTIAN
MAGAZINE *HURGHADA*, 1964

shillings a night on accommodation and on several occasions, because we
were the first Australian visitors, we were not charged anything. For us it
was the Hurghada Youth Camp where canvas stretchers in an army tent
cost only five piastres (about one shilling) each.

As we were settling in, a middle-aged Egyptian bearing an old Eastman
bellows camera waddled up and introduced himself. A magazine in Cairo
was doing a destination feature on Hurghada. He would like to take our
photographs. 'I've got a German girl here on a diving holiday for the cover.
But I need more pictures to show that tourists are trickling back since the
Suez crisis,' he explained politely.

We were photographed beside the skeleton of a dugong and a large
leatherback turtle in the Hurghada Museum, a small wooden shed. I also
posed in my bikini, with a lacquered red lobster on the beach. With a cheap
camera bought especially for our trip, I had no inkling that one day I would
become a professional photographer. And the event was to be of major
significance for the German cover girl.

With the photo session over, Ruth and I set off to buy supper only to find
Hurghada's three stores all sold the same thing: onions, over-ripe tomatoes,

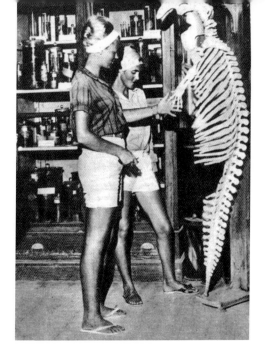

WITH RUTH IN
HURGHADA MUSEUM, 1964

khoubz (Arabic bread), and tins of Chinese corned beef. Dug out with our penknives, the latter made a meal of sorts as we sat on the wharf watching fishermen preparing their nets. On hearing us chatting, a whiskery old chap announced he used to work for the Suez Canal Company, nationalised by President Nasser in 1956.

'Things were better under the British,' he said. He looked up from baiting lines. How long were we staying? Had we seen the museum? 'Dugong weigh 300 kilograms (660 pounds). Our boat catch,' he said proudly.

We wandered back to the youth camp for an early night, but I'd barely closed my eyes when I heard someone fiddling with the tent flap. A turbaned man slipped inside and crossing to my stretcher, he ran rough hands over my breasts.

'Hey!' I yelled, but jumping up, I was tripped by the regulation youth hostel sheet that is sewn across the bottom and the intruder, running across the sand, leaping here and there over odd bits of detritus, made his escape.

Curiously for a former night nurse, Ruth slept through the fracas, but I explained what had happened next morning when a row of Arabs was seated cheekily outside our tent. Clearly one was the culprit and he'd brought his friends to laugh at my expense. For the first time on our travels, we felt unsafe, and after a brief discussion, we decided to return to Cairo. This news dismayed the boys.

'We know of another great diving place where there is no one to bother you,' said Sharif, a muscular engineering student with a mop of chestnut brown hair.

'It's a great bay called Dishdaba. The Germans were there a few days ago making underwater movies,' Morris chimed in.

'But how do we get there?' asked Raouf a small youth who was studying law.

'Hitchhike,' Ruth and I chorused.

The Red Sea coast being only sparsely populated meant there was little traffic between Hurghada and Dishdaba, but finally a truck slowed down and pulled up. It was delivering bags of concrete to Safaga, a port under construction farther south.

'*Y'alla.* Let's go,' called Morris scrambling up beside the driver. The rest of us climbed on the back with Sharif and the fourth boy, Muhammad, taking care not to spill our precious tin of water.

The journey south was thankfully cooler than our wait by the boiling tarmac. I estimated we had driven about 25 kilometres (15 miles) when the driver suddenly turned left onto a track in the dunes, but after travelling only a short distance, the truck shuddered to a stop and standing on the cabin roof, I saw we were marooned in seas of sand.

As night dropped its skirts over the Sahara, we jumped down and the men began digging us out. An hour passed, then two hours, until with the six of us pushing, the truck jumped free, but without even a wave, the driver reversed and we watched its tail-lights disappear back up the road to Hurghada. Morris quickly assured us he had paid the man to return with water, but at this point, we had no alternative but to walk, and helping each other on with our haversacks, we began trudging east, the direction of the coast.

Bored by the delay, at first we made steady progress, but our feet soon ached from walking in the soft sand. Stopping a moment, Ruth and I threw away our sleeping bags to lighten our loads. Ahead the boys strode on manfully under the stars, but finally, they too called a halt. Putting down the tin of water, Morris and Muhammad discarded their flippers for some puzzled Bedouin to find. And despite his protests, Raouf agreed to abandon his tent. Checking my watch in the moonlight, I saw it was 3am. We'd been walking for six hours and especially tired after last night's episode, I sank down for a few minutes sleep only to be jolted awake by Morris shaking my shoulder.

'Get up. We'll fry if we don't reach the sea before sunrise,' he told me.

By 5am, we were crawling on hands and knees when the boys let out a shout.

'We've made it! I can see the sea,' Morris called back over his shoulder and after staggering up a final dune, there was the Red Sea, spread out before us like a dark-blue satin bedspread.

'Yippee,' we cried, running down and plunging into the water just as the hot eye of the sun popped onto the horizon.

We'd emerged from the desert at one end of a vast bay, desolate except for a concrete house, once a weekend retreat for expatriates working in the Egyptian capital. Now it was just a shell, its walls covered in swirling Arabic graffiti. The rooms had lost their doors—probably used as firewood by Bedouin, but they would afford Ruth and me a degree of privacy. The roof would also shield us from the sun, if not the heat. Carrying in the water tin, the boys placed it reverently in a corner, but on opening the lid, I found it was only a quarter-full of very rusty water.

'It's the youth camp garbage-bin,' said Muhammad, a serious third-year veterinary science student.

This was awful news. Ruth and I had only a bottle of water each to last until the driver returned. To be thirsty was one thing, but to get a stomach upset was unthinkable. We'd been laid up with dysentery in the Mahdia Youth Hostel in Tunisia; our lavatory in Dishdaba was a shit-pit in the dunes.

But we'd made it. Pulling on my mask and snorkel, I followed Morris out into the bay where I looked down on an underwater Eden. Corals covered every inch of the reefs. Some were soft pink and yellow 'flower' corals, feathery tentacles waving in the current as they sifted in plankton from water around their colony. Others were hard, limestone corals—mosaic, organ-pipe, brain and grass coral interspersed with lacy sea fans. Still others like the light brown stag-horn coral, tipped in blue, were the size of small cars. Moreover, the abundance of fish was extraordinary. Now I appreciated why Cousteau was so enthusiastic about the Red Sea where marine biologists have recorded more than 1,200 species of fish and invertebrates.

In the first minutes, I spotted a school of black-white-and-yellow butterfly fish, red banner fish, rainbow-coloured wrasse, yellow striped goatfish and a cheeky blue-and-black mottled triggerfish. As I was admiring this colourful galaxy, a giant silver trevally rose up from the deep. A member of the *Caranx* genus of fighting fish beloved of anglers, it swam slowly towards us as Morris placed the butt of his speargun in his belly and drew back the rubbers.

Unwilling to see such a regal fish killed, I gave him the diver's 'palm down' signal not to shoot.

'There'll be others,' I said as we both surfaced for air, then dived again.

Visibility was good. A wall of soft corals dropped 5 metres (16 feet) to a plateau bristling with coral like the antlers of a highland stag. I spotted a red hawkfish resting in the branches of an orange sea fan, a graceful angelfish hovering above a cluster of lemon-coloured anemones and green-and-mauve parrotfish grinding coral polyps with pharyngeal teeth. A school of eight squid, my favourite marine creature, jetted through the water like a team of Red Arrows. When I swam after them, they flushed brown, then yellow and green, and the last animal squirted a defensive puff of sepia-coloured ink. Surfacing again, I was brushed by a soft, brown and turquoise-trimmed nudibranch (gastropod mollusc) known as a *badia* in Egypt for its undulating movements resembling those made by a belly dancer.

Swimming farther out over the trench, I observed a brown mass hovering in the distance. Surely it couldn't be a whale shark? As the mass moved closer, it resembled a swarm of bees. It was a quivering bait ball of millions of immature anchovy, which sprayed out in all directions as they were attacked by jack and bonito. Sensing my presence, the ball moved away, forming, re-forming and exploding like a catherine-wheel each time a predator zoomed in. Then suddenly it vanished, leaving a few silver scales drifting slowly down to the bottom.

Morris and the other boys speared several fish, but there was no wood to build a fire to cook them. More than a thousand years ago, the Baghdadi scholar Ali al-Mas'udi had described the Red Sea coast as barren, so unlike the Pacific Ocean there was no driftwood on the tidemark. Ruth and I had brought a tin of Chinese corned beef, and a packet of biscuits from Hurghada, but they would not stretch far when shared between six of us. The boys had brought nothing at all.

'How can you go camping without even a little primus stove?' I asked with astonishment.

'Mother gave me one for our holiday, but it was thrown away on our walk,' said Raouf wistfully.

Muhammad and I decided to check if the Germans had left anything at their camp-site. We returned with leaves of rock-hard *khoubz*, a lump of dried-out salami, some rotting grapes and a sandy, but unopened plastic bottle of mineral water. We shared this for supper, and later I lead the smokers in a treasure hunt for cigarette butts. That evening saw us happy, if slightly peckish. As the sky darkened we scooped out holes in the sand for our hips and shoulders and lay down to sleep among the ghost crabs.

Next morning found us thirsty enough to start sipping water from the garbage-bin, but diving acted as a remedy of sorts. I ventured out again with Morris and Ruth accompanied Sharif and Muhammad, leaving an increasingly miserable Raouf by the house.

This time we swam further out to where the coral was anchored around 20 metres (65 feet) deep. Morris, who said he dived in the mouth of the Nile, easily reached this depth on a single breath, stalked and shot a fish. At one stage a bronze shark, accompanied by an escort of remora suckerfish, glided out of the green, but when we swam towards it, it vanished with a flick of its tail. I watched a spotted eagle ray wing past, and to my delight, a big blue-green Napoleon fish swam up to goggle at me.

After an hour or so, we were snorkelling back to shore when I spotted a solitary barracuda zooming in behind Morris. Its jerking sideways movements indicated a possible attack. *Turn around*, screamed a voice inside my head, but before I could signal, a wave washed me onto the reef and I was bowled over and over in stinging fire coral.

As I stood there spluttering, Morris scrambled up behind me.

'Sharks don't bother me, but I don't fool with old man barra.' He grinned, but his smile faded at the sight of scarlet wheals across my back.

With nothing to relieve the pain, suddenly Dishdaba had become quite threatening. We rationed the last water and at Sharif's suggestion, we began chewing raw fish whose salty taste exacerbated our increasing thirst. When midday passed without sign of the driver, we reluctantly accepted he wasn't coming back, and little Raouf, the youngest among us in his red, white and blue striped bathing trunks, began to cry.

Habitually uncomplaining, Ruth seemed unaware of our plight, but I was now seriously concerned. How would we explain that we had gone off with strange men in the desert and without food or water? Trifling things assumed importance. An anemone swallowing a shrimp, or a crab missing a claw brought us running to look. Muhammad complained of a headache, that Ruth and I agreed was due to salt loss: we were all sweating profusely in a temperature of more than 40° Celsius (104°F).

That evening, Sharif did not join us on the beach. Instead, he headed off in hope of encountering the camel corps that patrols the Red Sea coast for smugglers. He returned at dawn, his brown curls were full of sand grains, and his eyes were bloodshot with fatigue.

'*Mahfeesh*,'—nothing, he said and flopped down beside us.

On the third day we were seriously hungry. Clearly someone had to walk back along the coast to Hurghada. But could he make it under cover of night? Morris snapped some matches and the boys drew lots. Morris picked the shortest one and would set out at dusk. We agreed he must have the last sip of water, but going to the tin, I found only a dry orange crust.

All that morning we lay in the tepid sea. Around 3pm, a dhow passed 800 metres offshore, but its crew gave no indication of seeing our frantic waving.

Exhausted by the heat, Ruth and the boys stretched out on the concrete floors of the house, but I pottered along the water's edge. Stooping to pick up a spider shell, I was startled by the sight of a camel in the distance and after making sure it was not a mirage, I let out a cooee. The rider had discovered Sharif's footprints, and believing him a smuggler had come to investigate. Dropping down from the saddle, he listened to Morris' explanation of our improbable situation. Then eyeing Ruth and me in our bikinis, he loped off to radio Hurghada from his lonely camp-site.

We had changed into our sunfrocks long before two officers bounced up in an army truck and accused us all of being spies. But following a vigorous exchange with the boys, they were finally convinced we were tourists of sorts, and we were driven back to Hurghada.

Our first bite to eat was a *khoubz* wrap of onion, over-ripe tomato and Chinese corned beef, but washed down with tins of Indian mango-juice, it was little short of a feast. There was no chance to rejoice, however, as the police put us all on the night bus to Cairo. Our travels from London to Dishdaba had taken four months: a rich experience, though possibly not to have been undertaken without adequate preparation, or at the height of a North African summer.

Back in London during the winter months, I earned a living working as a waitress at The Contented Sole, a trendy fish-and-chip restaurant in South Kensington. Gerry, its Irish chef, smoked like a chimney and the batter around many a sole contained a liberal sprinkling of his cigarette ash. We waitresses wore straw boaters, frilly white blouses, and tight black skirts, and sang along to a honky-tonk piano. It was hard work singing and running up and down the stairs, but within six months, I'd saved enough to spend the summer in Spain.

In Malaga one day, I was leafing through an old copy of *Hola!* the Spanish news and celebrity magazine when, among articles on film stars and bullfighters, I chanced on a story of some German tourists who had perished while on holiday in Egypt. The four men, a woman and her poodle had been attempting to visit a remote archaeological site in the Western Desert, but travelling by minibus, they had run out of petrol and water and had succumbed to the August heat. Eventually located, their bodies were found to be withered like prunes, the last to die being the woman who'd kept a diary of their agonies. At this point, my eyes flew to a small

picture obtained to illustrate the feature: it was the cover photograph from
the Egyptian magazine of the German girl at Hurghada.

***

Thirty years had passed since my Red Sea adventure and I imagined
Hurghada would now be a mass of hotels, shopping malls, and seaside
restaurants. The British writers had just departed and I was waiting for
a friend, a former stewardess with BOAC[14], who had taken a few days off
to visit Hurghada with me. We'd packed evening wear for cocktails and
I'd thrown in a mask in hope of a dive. Our hosts, the Cairo Sheraton, had
advised that their hotel was still under construction, so our accommodation
was to be a bungalow. Everything seemed to have been well-organised and
I was looking forward to Aileen's plane that was due in behind a Royal
Jordanian Airlines flight from Amman.

As our departure to Hurghada was not until the following afternoon,
I left her asleep, and took a taxi to the City of the Dead, the huge cemetery
in northern Cairo where I needed to shoot some photographs for a book
on Islamic art. The Mamluk sultans, rather like latter-day pharoahs, had
selected this area just outside the city walls as a suitable burial ground to
erect magnificent monuments to their dead. The dusty heritage included the
funerary complex of Sultan Sayf ad-Din Barquq, who founded the dynasty
in 1382, the mausoleum of Sultan Qaitbey, and the Qaitbey Mosque that
features on the Egyptian one pound note.

Over the years, due to Cairo's chronic housing shortage, many poor
families had taken up residence in the necropolis. A spooky place, at the same
time it resembled a village community, though lacking the amenities enjoyed
by the city's more affluent citizens. I passed women hanging out washing on
lines strung between headstones, children drawing pictures using the tombs
as desks, and youths kicking a football among *madrassas* (religious colleges)
more than five hundred years old. A dead black cat lying outside the funerary
complex of Sultan al-Ashraf Barsbey was an ominous sign.

Over lunch in the Cairo Sheraton, we heard British guests earnestly
discussing an incident of the previous evening, but unable to establish the
cause of their concern, we left for the airport.

DEAD CAT LYING
IN THE CITY OF
THE DEAD WAS AN
OMINOUS SIGN

'There seem to be lots of police about,' said Aileen, an attractive woman in her early forties who had flown as Cabin Crew Superintendent with various members of the Royal family on their worldwide jaunts.

The flight to Hurghada took an hour and as we approached the coast, I was surprised by the lack of high-rise. Had we come in further south over Dishdaba? Our mood had been upbeat until we disembarked onto a windswept runway where three young men from the Sheraton Hurghada greeted us wearing jeans, gym-boots and zipped puffer jackets. When I remarked on the cold, one boy who identified himself as the Sheraton-to-be-sports-monitor, told us the inclement weather had been around for weeks.

The short drive into Hurghada took us through a bleak landscape punctured by abandoned motor vehicles and one or two tanks, casualties of the 1967 war with Israel. As we neared signs of urbanisation, I was appalled by the sight of feral dogs worrying a dead companion. A large husky-like animal was tearing at the dog's head while another animal dragged on its haunches. It was macabre start to our visit and I suggested that Aileen, a rather prudish Scot, should look the other way.

'Hurghada,' announced one of the boys.

'Are you sure?' asked Aileen. 'I can't even see a Kentucky Fried Chicken.'

The grafting of a Sheraton onto the old Red Sea Tours Hotel had acted like a beacon. Bedouin from as far away as Sinai had pitched their tents and around them lay the trappings of civilisation: discarded generators, broken television sets, polystyrene packing cases, plastic bags and mountains of soft drink cans. Hurghada was a slum. Only the old white-washed mosque showed any sign of care.

'There's the Sheraton,' said one of the lads pointing to a large construction site.

'We can see it tomorrow. I think we would like to change for dinner,' I replied politely.

We ascended a stony plateau devoid of vegetation, a monotony relieved only by a row of shabby wooden shacks on stilts. When the driver stopped outside one of these splintery structures, I realised with dismay it was our accommodation. Far from obtaining the keys to a seaside bungalow, we were staying here; but the future sports monitor had remade our beds and stacked his gym-boots in a corner of our room.

'When is the next flight back to Cairo?' asked Aileen, plonking down on her suitcase.

'I'm sure there is a daily service,' I said, less than enthusiastically.

Presently there was a knock on our door. A pimply faced youth wearing a Second World War cowhide flying helmet, a helmet he was to wear day and night for the next three days, informed us dinner was served. It was only 6pm, but joined by the boys, we sat down to a meal of boiled eggs, *foule* (fava beans) and a limp salad. A bottle of *Cleopatra* wine thoughtfully provided by the Cairo Sheraton was consumed in ten minutes flat.

When efforts at conversation petered out we retired, but growling dogs beneath the floorboards made sleep impossible. Getting up to close a shutter, I pulled off the entire window frame, which clattered onto the ground outside.

'Who's attacking?' cried Aileen, sitting up in bed so violently she knocked a photograph of Manchester United football team off the wall.

'No one. Lie down and pull the rug over your head,' I told her.

At dawn, a wind was blowing in the window and peering out I saw it had begun to rain. We were dressed by seven—neither of us had attempted a shower (the bathroom was ghastly)—when members of the Town Council arrived to welcome us to Hurghada. By the time they left, our breakfast of boiled eggs and *foule* was cold and going into a tiny kitchen in hope of heating it up, I found the youth in the flying helmet peeling potatoes into an overflowing bin, and a fish on the sink was crawling with little black flies.

Backing out, I suggested to Aileen that we might go to see the Sheraton—the purpose of my visit—but we arrived to find the hotel at that stage when it was impossible to make a complimentary remark. Wires protruded from the plaster, workmen were laying tiles, and there were holes in the corridors through which one could fall and end up in Melbourne. Ankle-deep in building rubble and cigarette ends, I tried my best to imagine it filled with sun-tanned guests enjoying candle-lit seafood dinners, gentle music, and the pat of tennis balls, as notebook poised, I tramped about, trying hard to appear awestruck.

When the weather lifted a little, the boys suggested the swim for which I was hoping. Aileen who did not so much as put a toe in water (she claimed to have nearly drowned during a stopover in Sri Lanka), would find a sheltered spot to sit on the beach, however, excrement dotted the sand wherever we looked. Deciding one of the bunkers might be a good spot out of the wind, she disappeared inside only to emerge foul-mouthed and ashen-faced: it seemed the entire Egyptian Army had been stationed in Hurghada during the Six-Day War.

With sunbathing out, we were taken to the Hurghada Museum where I found the same specimens looking older and dustier. A few bones had detached from the dugong skeleton and the coiled womb of a stingray and young floated in a jar of milky-coloured fluid. Opening the comments book with a flourish, the caretaker asked us to sign our names and flicking back a page, I saw R. Bicknell and C. Osborne 25.8.64, with precisely twenty signatures between then and now.

Dogs and the banging shutter disturbed our sleep on night two and with no prospect of a flight out of Hurghada for another day, we discussed possible escape routes.

'There's a new road link to Luxor, but it's 500 kilometres (310 miles), so a taxi will cost a fortune,' I said. Leaving early would also offend our Sheraton hosts, so how could I most effectively spend my time? One day Hurghada might be a fantastic resort, but right now it was a dump.

'What about a feature on how the locals feel about impending tourism?' suggested Aileen. Would it corrupt their Muslim moral values? Would Hurghada become another Limassol or Torrelmolinos?

'Good idea,' I replied, endeavouring to ratchet up our mood.

Next morning, we drove into town where I pounced on a man selling shells on an up-turned oil-drum. What would he likely be doing when Hurghada was crawling with tourists? Might he open a crafts shop or shrewdly switch to Dunkin' Donuts? Raising my camera to take his picture, I was stopped by one of the men from the Hurghada Town Council.

'No pickchiz. Hurghada military zone.' He slapped a hand across the lens.

Since there was no point in arguing with such a mentality, I suggested a fishing expedition. Provided we caught some fish, Aileen could pose as a photographic model, as I had in Hurghada all those years ago.

We set sail in a small launch, Aileen, the future sports monitor of the Sheraton and our two minders. At first choppy, the sea soon grew rough, and the smaller minder leant over the rail and vomited. Seated downwind Aileen turned pale again, but the boatman, averted a potentially ugly situation by landing a large Spanish mackerel.

'Hold it up while I take your picture,' I said.

'No pickchiz,' said the security man who had not succumbed to mal-de-mer.

Frustrated and depressed, we decided to wait for our afternoon flight in a café below the plateau. With torn parasols flapping against a slate coloured sky and shabby cane chairs stacked around us, the setting was grim and hardly surprised that it did not sell alcohol, we managed to convey the message that we wanted two Sprites.

THE BOATMAN, AILEEN AND OUR MINDER, HURGHADA, 1977

'*T'nin Sprite,*' I held up two fingers, emphasising the Arabic word.

A child aged about ten, eventually brought out two lukewarm bottles with straws. Wiping our table with his sleeve, he set them down and stood back looking at us. Were we the first Western women he had ever seen? Overhead the sun disappeared and from being simply melancholy, Hurghada assumed a sinister air, but happily our flight arrived on time, and I left the Red Sea again, my cocktail dress unpacked, without a tan, and without the slightest regret.

Landing in Cairo for a final night in Egypt, we noticed that police were still milling around the airport and a uniformed official carefully recorded the licence plate of our taxi. But what bliss to be back in civilisation. Checking into the Sheraton, we poured ourselves huge gin and tonics from the mini-bar and ran a bath. While Aileen soaked off Hurghada, I went downstairs to buy an airmail copy of the *Daily Telegraph* whose main article highlighted the continuing investigations into the death of David Holden, the chief foreign correspondent of the *Sunday Times*.

Reading down, I learnt he was a passenger on RJ503, that had landed ahead of Aileen's flight on 6 December. He'd had his passport stamped at immigration, collected his Samsonite off the carousel, cashed $200 in traveller's cheques and strode out of the airport to catch a taxi. Eight hours later, his body was discovered by the road near al-Azhar university, not far from the City of the Dead—the labels had been cut off his jacket, and a single bullet had entered his back.

Who killed David Holden? Referring to the murder in his book *My Paper Chase,* Harold Evans—then editor of the *Sunday Times*—advances several theories. That Holden, whose own book *Farewell to Arabia* I'd read, was a case of mistaken identity. Had he been confused with David Hirst, the *Guardian* correspondent whose articles about the extravagant lifestyles of the Sadats had infuriated the Egyptian president? Was the fifty-three year old journalist who had known Kim Philby, the homosexual KGB agent in the blurred world of spy and counterspy in Beirut, an undercover agent? Like other curious assassinations, notably that of Lee Harvey Oswald in Dallas, on 24 November 1963, it is unlikely we shall ever know.

***

In December 2008, seeking an escape from Arctic winds sweeping England, I surfed the web for a winter sunshine break. Turkey wouldn't be warm enough, Zanzibar was too far away, and while Aswan was ideal, getting there involved several changes of aircraft. Suddenly my eyes hit upon Hurghada. Dare I return? Due to the credit crunch, the fare was half the normal price and I was suddenly curious as to what may have happened to Dishdaba.

By extraordinary coincidence, it was exactly thirty years to the day when the captain switched on the seatbelt sign for landing. Peering out of the window, I saw winking turquoise swimming pools and a string of lights stretching all the way down the coast. Was this the same Hurghada where I slept in a shack all those years ago?

On this occasion, I was to stay at the exclusive Oberoi, which had been voted The World's Best All Suite Hotel. Its VIP list included Arab sheikhs, prime ministers, and fashion designers, but indecision was kicking in. Suite 119 which I was allocated, didn't feel quite right. Even I couldn't believe it.

'Which direction is sunrise?' I asked Ibrahim, the gangly front office porter anxious to please, but thrown into a state of confusion by the question. He revolved, rather like a slowly whirling dervish.

'Out there,' he said, pointing vaguely into the night.

I attempted to explain feng shui: how I prefer to sleep in an end room and with my head aligned to the rising sun. And please, not next to any Saudis, or Kuwaiti families (I remembered an Arab who had beaten his wife, in the room next to mine in Dubai). Or indeed any children, of any nationality.

We eyed each other across the beautiful tiled suite with its Arabic-style arches, Egyptian wall-hangings, private courtyard, two televisions and elegant furniture imported from Mumbai, the headquarters of the Oberoi chain. Then retrieving my suitcase, Ibrahim replaced it on the golf buggy and we motored back to reception, a domed edifice with a huge display of *Strelitzia reginae*—Bird of Paradise—flowers by the fountain.

Bounding up the steps, he returned with keys for suites 110 and 222, and an assurance that all 102 hotel suites were identical.

'Except the twelve Grand Suites each of which has a private swimming pool. But all face the same direction,' he assured me.

We were now standing outside suite 110, an end suite as I had requested. Ibrahim inserted the key in the lock and flung open the door. Televisions were switched on, minibar doors were opened and the procedures for locking my valuables in the safe were explained in detail.

'The swimming pool, gym and restaurants are just across there,' he said, swinging an arm like a weather-vane. 'Or if madam prefers suite 222, she can then simply walk down to the beach.' He wrung his hands in desperation.

It was now 8pm. We had been motoring around the Oberoi site for nearly an hour and pulling up outside suite 222, I observed that Ibrahim had developed a rictus smile.

'This will be fine,' I said, feeling a burden lift from my shoulders. And I should think so, I told myself. The bed was heavenly and after a swig of Scotch, I was sound asleep, ready to renew my acquaintance with Hurghada next day.

I had steeled myself for change, but the humongous hotels ranged along the road into town left me speechless. The Mamoluk (sic) Palace, the Aladdin Beach, Jasmine Village, Pick Albatross and the Aqua Blue Resort—apparently modelled on the sixteenth century Mughal fort of Fatehpur Sikri—were an architectural soup of Pharaonic, Indian and Islamic-style elements in gut-wrenching colours: turmeric yellow, ox-blood, biscuit, vanilla and Sea Island sauce pink. But there was no sign of the Sheraton Hurghada.

'I want to find the *Funduq Sheraton*,' I told my taxi-driver, a young man wearing designer stubble and a red number 7 David Beckham football shirt.

'Road closed.' His brow knitted in the rear vision mirror.

'*Izmi Hurghada thirty years ago*,' I tapped my chest with a certain pride since I had clearly graced Hurghada before he was born. But he was right. The old road was blocked by a rusty, corrugated-iron fence plastered with posters advertising an 'Eid Concert' at the Ministry of Sound, and other extravaganzas for *Eid el-Fitr,* the imminent Muslim feast of sacrifice.

'*Funduq Sheraton,*' he suddenly exclaimed as we pulled up beside a crumbling circular building surrounded by leaning lamp posts and dusty trees. Grey, shabby and clearly unloved, I recognised it as the old Red Sea Tours Hotel, a large Marriott that had risen beside it being one of 160 new hotels.

Hurghada's long main street was still known as Sharia Sheraton, even though a new Sheraton had re-located to Soma Bay, far away from bungee jumping, kite-surfing, glass-bottom boat rides, submarine tours and other entertainments for holidaymakers flocking to the Red Sea resort. Wherever

I looked there were hotels, cafés and shops selling tourist tat, but a sign, 'Harrads Hurghada', captured my attention.

On the pavement outside, glass water pipes, brass trays, wooden animals, leather pouffes, and camel-shaped backpacks were displayed beside baskets of *karkady*, the dried red hibiscus flowers that Egyptians make into tea. As I raised my camera to take a photo, an intense-looking man who clearly hadn't shaved for days, got up from a dirty plastic chair.

'Everything inside 1 GBP,' he said, holding up a finger.

Going into his shop, I picked up a fish from a display of onyx marine life.

'Fish 4 GBP,' he corrected himself.

Removing the stopper, I sniffed one of the pee-coloured flagons of perfume.

'Perfume 10 GBP for 100 grams.' He cleared his throat. Then all of a sudden he flew into a rage.

'Tourist just lookin'. No buy anythin'. Flecks of spit appeared in the corners of his mouth as he shouted. 'Every tourist fuggin' Russhin'. Old woman wantin' sex. Fuggin' rubbish. Only lookin'. Pay nothin'. Russhin' fuggin'! Fuggin'! Fuggin'! Oh Allah. What we do?' He clasped his hands together and concerned my presence might bring on a seizure, I left him shouting to continue my walk along the Sharia Sheraton.

Every second shop was stuffed with souvenirs. In the window of a leathergoods store, a lizard skin handbag, including the head, half-chewed away by insects, was marked 145 Egyptian pounds. I wanted to buy a plain white T-shirt, but everything had either a shark or a pyramid on it. There were hotels that looked like mosques and mosques that looked like hotels. Hundreds of vacant tables and chairs stood on the forecourt of a pink edifice called La Pacha. Cafés were also empty; the only tourists in sight were two old babushkas dragging cheap orange suitcases across the road.

Halfway along, I came to a tiny public garden where faux-Pharaonic statues, including a replica of Ramses II's broken feet from Luxor, lay among the weeds. Sitting down on a concrete bench, I took out my plastic bottle for a drink of water; it was at least 20° Celsius (68°F) warmer than the temperature in London.

'The last time it rained in Hurghada was 1966,' said a man seated on the bench opposite me.

Abdul Rashid was a former diving instructor who had injured his back and could no longer wear a heavy SCUBA tank. 'But the fish have gone,' he said. 'Too many divers and the Russians break off coral. They are stupid people. I go to collect them at seven o'clock and they are drinking vodka. Good for diving. They tell me.'

'Is the old fishing wharf still here?' I asked hesitantly.

'Now we have new Hurghada Marina. Come. I show.'

Turning off Sharia Sheraton, we followed a lane covered with flattened soft drink cans, fish backbones and used phone cards, where mournful sheep awaiting slaughter, stood tied up outside the shops. Before leaving London, I'd asked Aileen whether she would like to return to Hurghada. I was thankful she had decided not to come.

But Hurghada did have a new marina, crammed with yachts registered in ports such as Guernsey and Bermuda, and designer shops and restaurants, where the cost of a grilled sea bass would feed a local family for several days. We passed Timberland, Inter Moda, Jackie B. and a dive shop where Abdul Rashid stopped to stare at the window display.

'We never had such things in old days,' he said, refusing my offer of a coffee as he obviously felt uncomfortable in such surroundings.

Back at the Oberoi, I decided that Dishdaba must be further down the coast in the area now known as Sahl Hasheesh. *Hasheesh* is rather confusing. It's Arabic for grass, rare green grass, beloved of a wee grey-and-white bird known as *Abu Fasad,* which scurried about the hotel lawns like a winged mouse.

With no transport this far from Hurghada I had started walking when a small silver sedan, driven by a bespectacled man wearing a suit and tie, pulled out of the hotel gates.

'Where are you going?' I called across.

'Sahl Hasheesh Resort,' he replied, and without being asked, I ran over and jumped in beside him.

Forty-four years on and I was hitchhiking to Dishdaba again, but this time we were driving along a tarmac road lined with street lights and date palms.

'Do you mind if I smoke?' the driver asked.

'No of course not,' I said, noticing his top lip had beads of perspiration.

'This is a small community and I have a very jealous wife,' he said, nervously ashing his Marlboro out the window.

'You must promise not to tell anyone I have given you a lift.'

'I won't breathe a word,' I said, aghast at causing such anxiety.

There was a tense moment as a security guard checked his ID card at the entrance to Sahl Hasheesh, but waved in, we pulled up in the parking lot of the Pyramisa Hotel, 28 kilometres (17 miles) south of Hurghada.

'I work in the hotel bank,' said the nervous man. 'Do you mind if we don't go in together?'

'Not at all, thank you so much for the lift.' I moved to shake his hand, but he hurried up the steps.

If Hurghada's hotels were frogs, the Pyramisa Sahl Hasheesh was a cane toad. Its 815 rooms overlooked swimming pools, water slides, children's pools and poolside bars, all interconnected by tiled walkways and hump-backed bridges. Taking one or two pictures, I tiptoed down to the beach where hundreds of obese Russian tourists lay stretched out on sun-beds. Some were sleeping, others were stuffing their mouths with pizza and ice-cream, and all, including those asleep, were swatting flies.

Instantly I recognised Dishdaba. The behemoth was built at the end of the vast bay where we had slept on the beach, and the desert hinterland where we'd walked for our lives that summer, was now covered in hollow-eyed construction sites. As I stood there reminiscing, a water-skier streaked across the water where we dived all those years ago and suddenly I missed my old companions: Morris was probably a wealthy doctor practising in Alexandria, and Raouf could well be on the Supreme Court bench in Cairo. I was lost in thought, when four women emerged from a swim, and snapping out of it, I asked could I take their photograph.

'Where are you from?' I addressed them in a friendly fashion.

'Russe,' replied the largest woman while drying herself with a yellow beach towel.

'What you doing here?' she asked, since clutching my spiral notebook, I was clearly not on holiday.

RUSSIAN HOLIDAYMAKERS AT THE PYRAMISA HOTEL DISHDABA, 2010

'I came here forty-four years ago,' I said, feeling rather strange.

'You from where?' she asked.

'Sydney,' I replied.

'Australia is nice?' She shook her wet hair like a dog after a bath.

'Yes, you should go there.' I smiled.

'Are many Russe in Australia?' She was becoming interested.

'No, but they seem to be everywhere else,' I muttered, though uncertain if she appreciated the joke.

Dear old Dishdaba. The Pyramisa Hotel was even larger than Cheops pyramid, and I learnt that the Sahl Hasheesh Resort would eventually have ten hotels, with banks and boutiques along the 12.5 kilometres (7.5 miles) corniche planted with hibiscus shrubs and baby date-palms. Counting an 'old town' médina, a marina, four golf courses and villa-type housing for a projected population of 200,000, it was billed as the biggest, splashiest resort in the Middle East, but I wouldn't be buying there: the Dishdaba from our young, free-spirited days had been laid to rest.

Chapter 3

A Member of the Royal Press Corps

The third of February 1954 was a very exciting day in Sydney. Her Majesty Queen Elizabeth II accompanied by the Duke of Edinburgh was making her first visit to Australia. For the great occasion, I had chosen to wear patriotic colours—blue-and-white check frock and red shoes—and with mum and Julia, I stood in Macquarie Street amid thousands of people cheering and waving flags. As the royal car flashed past, I had a brief glimpse: never in my wildest dreams imagining that twenty-five years later, I would travel with the queen myself.

'You're either a journalist or a photographer. You can't be both,' declared Terry Fincher, spokesman for the 'royals', the motley bunch of photographers who earn a living by pursuing royalty around the globe.

It was February 1979 and we were flying over the eastern Mediterranean to Kuwait, the first stop on the British royal tour of Saudi Arabia and the Gulf States. Ita Buttrose, now editor-in-chief of the Australian *Women's Weekly,* had commissioned me to cover the three-week visit and underlining its importance, she had paid £2,000 for my seat on a Dan-Air Comet, the official carrier of the Buckingham Palace press corps. Her Majesty's party would travel on a British Airways Concorde, a controversial decision until Westminster decided the oil-rich Arabs should be impressed.

I had attended a briefing in Buckingham Palace conducted by Her Majesty's press secretary, Michael Shea[15], a distinguished former diplomat who would play a key role in the proceedings. The other photographers

and journalists were familiar with royal protocol, but although experienced in Arab etiquette, I was hesitant to ask about the myriad formalities surrounding the British monarch. There had even been gentle badinage between Shea and Court Reporter Grania Forbes, whose circular of royal engagements appeared daily in the *Times*.

Though ignored by the press, I was clapped by members of the public as I walked out the palace gates on The Mall. This had raised my spirits, but just four hours out of Gatwick Airport, I was upset by the aggressive attitude of the 'royals'. After four years working in the Middle East, freelancing as a writer and photographer, I wore both hats with ease, but sensing conflict on this occasion, I opted to be a photographer.

'Then you'd better not miss any of the pool shots,' remarked Tim Graham, a ginger-haired, young snapper known as 'Squirrel'.

The only woman photographer on the tour, I was to find myself caught between the two groups that had little contact. I had more in common with

*The Master of the Household
is commanded by Her Majesty to invite*

Miss Christine Osborne

*to a Reception to be given by
The Queen and The Duke of Edinburgh
on board H.M. Yacht "Britannia" at Shuwaikh Harbour
on Monday, the 12th February, 1979, at 9.30 p.m.*

R.S.V.P.
British Embassy
Telephone: Kuwait 432047
*Guests are asked to arrive
between 9.10 and 9.30 p.m.*

*Dress: National Dress
Lounge Suit*

the six journalists, but I found myself stuck with the photographers who were to reveal themselves almost as uncivil towards each other as they were to me. A good snapper earns big money tracking royalty and guards the privilege as a divine right. Tim Graham who went on to become the photographer of choice for special royal family occasions is likely now a millionaire.

Gazing down on the gas flares of northern Iraq, I compared our visit to the journey alledgedly made by the Queen of Sheba to Jerusalem in the second century BCE.[16] Accompanied by courtiers bearing gifts of frankincense and myrrh, the Sabaean queen had undertaken a similar tour to seal trade links with the Holy Land. Evidently her caravan of some eight hundred camels was also followed by faithful scribes who left a colourful record of her meeting with King Solomon.

Accounts describe how Sheba arrived, bejewelled and wearing dazzling gold-embroidered robes. Of how Solomon had made available a luxurious palace apartment adjacent to his own, sending gifts of fruits, rose-trees, silks, linens, tapestries and eleven bewitching garments. Daily he sent her and her 350 attendants, 45 sacks of flour, 10 oxen, 5 bulls, 50 sheep (in addition to goats, deer, cows, three gazelles, and chickens) wine, honey, fried locusts, rich sweetmeats and 25 singing men and women.[17]

The Queen of England's whirlwind tour of the Arab States was seen in the context of a colossal public relations exercise to promote British technical expertise in a region hungry for everything under the sun. British companies had laid a sound infrastructure in the desert sheikhdoms, building ports, airports, and dry docks; Sir William Halcrow, Sir Alfred McAlpine and George Wimpey were household names. Kuwait was to be Her Majesty's first impression of the Arab world. Indeed, never before had a reigning British monarch set foot in *Arabia Deserta*.

A flat desert state bathed by the tepid waters of the Gulf, Kuwait was one of the seven countries on our itinerary. The others were Bahrain, Saudi Arabia, Qatar, Abu Dhabi and Dubai, the biggest and most developed of the seven members of the United Arab Emirates, and Oman, ruled by one of the world's only two sultans, Sultan Qaboos bin Said al-Sa'id (the other is Sultan Hassanal Bolkiah Mu'izzidin Waddaulah of Brunei Darussalam).

Kuwait, a diminutive of the word *kut* (fortress), was founded in the early eighteenth century when a prolonged drought in the Nejd drove the ancestors of the ruling al-Sabah family out of Saudi Arabia, a search for water rather than oil that instigated similar Bedouin migrations in the other Gulf States.

Kuwait's fortune comes from oil and shrewd foreign investments made by the Kuwaiti Investment Fund. Until oil was discovered in 1938, the highest point in the desert state was the peak of a sheikh's tent which eventually gave way to the top of an oil derrick, and this to Kuwait's iconic water towers covered with 50,000 gleaming steel plates, and sensitive of its humble background, Kuwait subsequently destroyed every link with its past: traditional coral and limestone houses, city walls and even some of the mosques.

Having left London in a blizzard, the gleaming white Concorde glided down in Kuwait like a migrating snowbird. Waiting to receive Her Majesty was the Emir, Sheikh Jabar al-Ahmad as-Sabah, a slightly built man with a sharp black beard. He wore the white ankle-length *dishdasha* (gown) covered by a *bisht* (black cloak) and Arab headdress worn to great effect by Peter O'Toole in the film *Lawrence of Arabia.*

Until this moment the *Daily Telegraph* reporter Ann Morrow had not acknowledged my presence, but as the queen descended the aircraft steps dressed in an elegant apricot silk ensemble, Ann nudged me.

'What's that gear the Arabs are wearing?' she said.

I explained about the *d-i-s-h-d-a-s-h-a,* carefully spelling out the word. Then, with no knowledge of millinery, I asked how to describe Her Majesty's hat.

'Who are you and who do you work for?' she retorted before stalking off in pursuit of the other journalists.

A strict Muslim country, Kuwait prohibits the consumption of alcohol and with nothing to steady my nerves, I'd fretted about the press reception on the royal yacht *Britannia* at 9.30pm. The sleek, 125 metre (410 feet) long vessel had conveyed the queen and other members of the royalty on 696 foreign visits, voyages of more than a million nautical miles. In Arabia, the ship would act as the queen's personal living quarters so Her Majesty could return the lavish hospitality expected in her own home, as it were.

At the palace briefing, Shea had informed us there was no requirement for formal dress, but since Her Majesty would receive us following the state banquet, I felt it necessary to show some sartorial respect. Scouring London boutiques, I'd settled on a long, blue Grecian-style gown which was glamorous, but sufficiently covered up so as not to offend our conservative Kuwaiti hosts. None of the seasoned women journalists had bothered to dress. Having met the queen on numerous royal tours, most were blasé about the occasion, and waiting in line on the deck of *Britannia,* I stood out like a sore thumb.

Wearing a silver gown, a diamond-and-emerald tiara with matching earrings the size of quail's eggs, Her Majesty looked every inch Queen of Great Britain and the Commonwealth. When she extended her hand, her twinkling blue eyes indicated I had done the right thing by my wardrobe— a small acknowledgement of her status, perhaps.

ROYAL VISIT TO AHMADI IN KUWAIT WHERE OIL WAS DISCOVERED IN 1946

'You're Australian? And you've written a book about the Gulf, so you must know all about it,' she addressed me.

'Yes Ma'am. How did you enjoy the Arab food?' I inquired politely of the state dinner.

'Oh, it was lovely, but I had barely started to eat when everyone got up to leave,' she smiled.

'You're bound to get sick of all the coffee Ma'am,' I wittered on. '*Qahwa* is not like Turkish coffee. It's made with tea leaves and cardamom husks and is rather bitter to taste. One is expected to drink at least two or three cups at every meeting.'

'Oh, we had some this evening. It was rather strange,' said Her Majesty, and reputed for an excellent memory, she would recall this brief conversation in Saudi Arabia.

Next morning the royal party was to visit the Kuwait Oil Company Gathering Centre at Ahmadi, some way from Kuwait City. It was a unique opportunity to photograph Her Majesty against a rags-to-riches backdrop, but we were too many for the bus and bundled into a car with former war office photographer John Shelley, I reached Ahmadi to find no sign of the 'royals'. The press bus had lost the way and we were the only ones to obtain pictures of the queen in this setting, but as punishment, we were made personae non grata. From that moment, not a single photographer would address me.

At noon the Duke of Edinburgh left to visit al-Jahra, a small village where a few dhows, the classic lateen-rig ship of the Gulf, were still being made with traditional tools such as an adze and bow drill. This time I was on the bus whose driver, a terrified Pakistani of the Ahmadi fiasco, lost his way again and travelling in the opposite direction, the duke gave us a cheeky wave. In the melee of our eventual arrival, a photographer's boot ground my foot into the sand, an incident observed by the duke, who subsequently became my ally on the mission ahead.

That evening, Her Majesty had returned Kuwaiti hospitality when she invited the emir, together with local dignitaries and a select number of British expatriates, to dine on *Britannia*. Among some fifty Bedouin sheikhs who arrived without their wives, were three women guests. One was eighty-five year old Dame Violet Dickson, widow of the former political agent Colonel H. R. Dickson, and a witness to the metamorphosis of Kuwait from its desert origins to modern state.

I had called on Dame Violet when researching *The Gulf States and Oman*. Well-built and taller than me (I am 1.72m) she was a serious, dominating character. Standing beside a brass-studded Zanzibar chest, she tossed down three, then a fourth cup of *qahwa* without inquiring whether I might care for a refreshment—an unthinkable discourtesy in Arab society.

'How can you expect to write about Kuwait on such a brief visit?' she demanded. 'We've lived here forty years and I still don't know everything. In the old days, we used to see camel caravans hobbled outside the city walls. There was no hospital. The mad used to shuffle about in shackles. Life was hard. The Bedu only ate meat when they shot a gazelle. There were no hotels like you're staying at. If we went outside the city, we slept under the stars.' She had left me feeling utterly demoralised.

Britannia docked in Manama, our second port of call, in brilliant sunshine. As usual, Her Majesty was exquisitely dressed, but on this occasion she was outdone by Sheikh Isa bin Salman al-Khalifah, the Emir of Bahrain, swathed in a cream *bisht* edged with gold and with a solid gold *khanjar* dagger stuck in his belt. A tubby little man, 'Happy Jack' as he was known among expatriates, was the nattiest dresser in the Gulf.

The islands of the Bahrain archipelago were now poor by comparison with their oil-and-gas-rich neighbours, but in ancient times, Dilmun as it was known, was one of the most prosperous places in the Middle East. Babylonian records refer to it as '... an earthly Paradise and rendezvous of Gods...' Evidence of its past wealth was a vast necropolis of some 10,000 tumuli since only an affluent society could have afforded such large, individual tombs.

The royal couple were to visit the cemetery, a series of dun-coloured mounds, extending to the horizon. They arrived in a gold Mercedes, but evidently our driver had instructions not to damage any of the historic graves, and stopping on the perimeter of the necropolis, he told us to walk.

Hopping off our bus, the 'royals' floundered in pursuit of the queen, but struggling to keep up, I had only got halfway through the mounds of the dead when I saw the limousine on its way back and drawing level, both Her Majesty and the Duke of Edinburgh gave me encouraging waves. It was the start of a warm, though largely unspoken bond and as the tour progressed, I felt genuine affection for the handsome duke with his slicked back, golden-wheat hair and flirtatious grin.

The Bahraini hosts shared the British monarch's passion for horse racing and the next event was a race meeting of Arab thoroughbreds.

Seated on a concrete bench, thoughtfully covered with a prayer rug, the queen trained gold binoculars on the twenty-seven horses, all owned by 'Happy Jack,' as they belted around the sandy circuit. I concentrated on trying to take photographs, a dangerous business since without a press stand, I had to lean out to snap the horses flashing past the rails. When Her Majesty and Sheikh Isa stood to leave, the 'royals' hurdled the barrier, but endeavouring to emulate this feat, I tripped and fell on my face. The incident, which brought an audible gasp from the crowd, was to be repeated at an even more inopportune moment at the state banquet in Saudi Arabia.

VISIT TO BAHRAIN HOSTED BY THE EMIR SHEIKH ISA BIN SALMAN AL-KHALIFAH

The queen looked very happy in Bahrain. Perhaps the initial stress had worn off, but then jolly Sheikh Isa would put anyone at ease. I'd attended an exclusive luncheon hosted by Bahrain at the London Dorchester Hotel when he'd taken my hand between his own and, smiling sweetly, had thanked me for inviting him.

At the Budaiya Agricultural Gardens, both Sheikh Isa and Her Majesty were beaming. Wearing a floral-patterned dress, imminently suited to the botanical backdrop, the queen smiled directly into my camera, making up for her knitted brow in Kuwait. To the sound of bagpipes, I photographed her pretending to eat a date as she watched a man shin up a palm, a sight she had doubtlessly witnessed on numerous visits to Commonwealth countries.

Date farming and pearling were traditional activities in Bahrain in former times. At the start of the diving season, hundreds of pearl-lugger crews, beating drums and singing shanties set sail for the pearl beds as the entire population lined the bays to bid farewell. The boats could remain at sea for weeks as their water supply was topped up by divers filling goatskin bags from sweet water springs bubbling in the seabed.

On a previous visit to Manama, the capital of Bahrain, I'd come upon some fishermen opening oysters in the souq. As I watched, one man, feeling between the yellow lips of an oyster shell, had discovered a shiny orange pearl.

'Ten dinar,' he announced as the pearl was passed from palm to palm for everyone to admire.

'Twelve dinar, fifteen dinar,' he popped it into his mouth, spitting it into his hand for any newcomers to the auction.

Noticing my own interest, an Arab had reached into his robes producing a massive pearl, which he held out for me to see. The fisherman looked disappointed, but he needn't have worried. I wasn't bidding, and while certainly big, it was not perfectly contoured like the small orange pearl.

That afternoon the queen and the duke were shown a priceless pearl collection owned by a leading merchant who allowed Her Majesty to hold a *dannah*, a perfect pearl, the size of an olive. 'Provided you keep it away from scent, a pearl should last for five hundred years,' he informed her.

Handicapped by our slow-flying Comet, we missed this advice. While the royal couple completed engagements, we were flying across the Empty Quarter in Saudi Arabia, 403,000 square kilometres (155,610 square miles) of burning sands, where dunes are taller than the Sydney harbour bridge.

At one point during preparations, it was thought that female members of the press corps would be forbidden to cover the Saudi section of the tour, but the Saudis managed to circumvent the gender issue by receiving the monarch in the capacity of an 'honorary gentleman'. The badges issued to Her Majesty's companions, Fortune Fitzroy the Duchess of Grafton, (Mistress of the Robes) and Lady Susan Hussey, (Woman of the Bedchamber) also referred to them as 'him'. As did my own: 'His name has been registered with the responsible Arab authorities ... and he should be allowed to the appropriate functions', was printed on the press pass I wore on a chain round my neck. But all of us—Her Majesty included— had to wear neck to ankle dress. A long blue *galabia* (a casual garment worn by Egyptian men) was my own choice, although I worried how I would manage three hectic days of photography without tripping over.

The atmosphere was tense as we awaited the Concorde at Riyadh International Airport. The queen's choice of outfit for her meeting with King Khalid had caused much speculation. Royal milliners Simone Merman and Freddie Fox had a problem designing hats to match Her Majesty's full-length dresses with one fashion writer wondering whether the queen might appear like Salome, in seven veils.

The scribes stood wilting in the afternoon sun. Among them, I saw Ann Morrow, wearing a frilly white high-neck blouse and a long Laura Ashley-type skirt. Notebook ready, she stood beside ebullient Cathy Cousins from the *Daily Star*. My mates, the photographers, were jostling each other for the best position along the red velvet carpet. Just as everything seemed ready, the Saudi royal bodyguard elected to pray and placed their chrome-plated guns on the tarmac. They were still prostrate when Concorde appeared in the eastern sky.

Called to attention, members of the Saudi Royal Air Force could not control their curiosity. First one man turned his head, and finally the entire platoon twisted round to look, a final note of disorder being an irritating wind which set the carpet flapping. Indian lackeys were still laying bricks along it as King Khalid, walking up to the aircraft steps, smashed through centuries of protocol to welcome the British queen onto Saudi sand.

Her Majesty's full-length sapphire blue dress and matching turban seemed to please the crowd. A murmur of approval greeted the two monarchs as they walked side by side, flouting all rules in Saudi Arabia, where a woman traditionally trails a man. As they approached where I stood, the anxious snappers knocked down the crush barrier. This was quickly corrected by security men, but disregarding anything but their pictures, they knocked it down again, and raising their guns, the guards glared in my direction.

'Stop it,' I shouted, furious at taking the blame for this behavioural lapse.

My photo of the moment captured the queen with an amused expression, and unlikely ever to have heard a woman address men in such a manner, King Khalid and his interpreter are grinning from ear to ear.

Suddenly there was pandemonium. Everyone was running this way and that and after years of working alone, I forgot our strict orders not to leave the press group and dashing outside the airport, I hailed a passing taxi.

'Quick, the Nasirya Palace,' I told the driver.

The queen and the duke were to spend their only two nights on land at the palace while *Britannia* sailed to Dhahran, in the Eastern Province of Saudi Arabia. A photo-call there was not on our itinerary, but I hoped to sail in on a bit of bluff. Especially since I was a man.

The old Indian taxidriver entered into the spirit of the moment as though his country was still under the British Raj. Speeding along Riyadh's sandy highways, he screeched to a stop in front of a mammoth building flying the Union Jack, and above it Her Majesty's personal standard.

'The Nasirya Palace, memsahib,' he said, reversing the dented red Datsun in between a line of black limousines.

Racing up the palace steps I nodded at the Bedouin guards. Did they think I was an advance on the ladies-in-waiting? Without inquiring, they waved me inside a vast foyer lit with chandeliers the size of flying saucers.

It took all my courage to stand there surrounded by many princes of the estimated 7,000 members of the House of Āl Saūd: tall, erect men all wearing the *bisht* edged with gold, the mark of nobility. My eyes roamed over onyx tables and huge vases of flowers, but my flashgun sparked a buzz of conversation and feeling vulnerable, I wound my long black scarf around my face like one of their own women.

When a Rolls Royce drew up at the palace steps, attention shifted from me to the queen. Trained not to flinch, Her Majesty passed with only a brief look of surprise. Had I gone completely native? Trailing behind her, the duchess and Lady Susan looked perturbed. Could Buckingham Palace have erred? Should they also be veiled? Long dresses brushing the marble floor, they swept towards the audience room and before anyone inquired why I didn't join them, I scampered back to the taxi.

'It's the most exciting day of my life,' said the old driver, who was saving up to put his daughter through university in Bangalore.

Back at the Riyadh Inter-Continental, my luck was in when I met a helpful Middle East Airlines pilot who offered to take my films to

London. Ita had been insistent that we beat rival *Woman's Day* to press and leaving Riyadh at midnight, the films were collected next morning from the Kensington Hilton and put on a Sydney-bound plane.

A week later, my first report—*CARRY ON DOWN THE GULF MA'AM—THE SHEIKHS LOVE YOU*—captured readers' attention 'down under'.

'Well done,' cabled Ita from Sydney.

On Sunday in Riyadh there was no church for the queen. With his last breath on 8 June 632, the Prophet Muhammad had outlawed Christianity from Saudi Arabia and while today even conservative Qatar has built a church, if a Christian dies in Saudi Arabia he must be flown home, or interred in the Christian cemetery in Bahrain.

Over breakfast of fried eggs and beef rashers (pork is *haram*— forbidden—to Muslims) I studied the programme for the 18 February, the equivalent of 20 Rabi' ul-awal 1399 on the Arabic Hijri calendar. Departing from the Nasirya Palace at 10am the British royal party was to inspect Bedouin crafts at the National Museum, to listen to an announcement of the new Five Year Plan at the Ministry of Planning, to visit the Armed Forces Hospital, and to lunch with members of Riyadh's expatriate community. At 8.10pm their Royal Highnesses would attend a banquet hosted by King Khalid, who had succeeded the Saudi throne in 1975 when his half-brother, King Faisal, was shot by a nephew.

For me it was to be the most stressful day of the tour. It started badly when I stepped on the toe of Michael Trestrail the queen's detective, outside the National Museum. I was profusely apologetic, but he threw back his head and caused himself further injury by striking his rather prominent nose on the branch of a tree and horrified at causing such a rumpus, I retreated to the gate.

'Having fun?' called a blond youth in jeans and green check shirt.

'Hi, yes, who are you?' I replied.

'I work for Saudi Pritchard. They've got a $10 million contract to keep this filthy city clean. Name's Ian McGhee.' He extended a dirty hand.

'I'm not supposed to leave the tour, but have you got a minute to show me a bit of Riyadh?' I asked boldly.

IAN AND HIS DREAM CAR BUILT OUT OF EXPENSIVE WRECKS IN RIYADH

'If you don't mind riding in a refuse truck,' he grinned and when the press moved inside the museum, I jumped into the big blue waste-disposal truck parked nearby and we roared off with empty bins clanking in the back.

Riyadh struck me as a curious city. Mammoth palaces were the only sign of its massive oil wealth and never entirely out of sight, the desert lapped at shops and ramshackle houses on the city limits.

'Riyadh is the world's biggest rubbish-tip. We shift over a million kilos (2.2 million pounds) of garbage a day.' said Ian. He pointed a tanned arm at overflowing bins, broken packing cases, and a stained mattress hanging from the window of a block of flats.

'This is execution square. Yesterday they chopped off an Iraqi's hand for stealing a car. I once saw an execution. It's family entertainment in this godforsaken place. When the head flew off, the kids began kicking it about like a football. For Christ's sake don't take a picture here. You'll get us arrested. Would you like lunch? Nothing special. It's in the mess.'

Lunch with Riyadh's refuse collectors was a good story. I accepted without hesitation, only to grow uneasy as we drove to the outskirts of town. 'Where are we going?' I asked McGhee, who was twenty-six and from Staffordshire.

'We're going for a ride.' He smiled. 'You say you're not supposed to leave the group. Aren't you afraid of being raped?'

An incident involving a local was always on the cards, but an assault by a British garbage man had never dawned. 'What? A member of the Buckingham Palace press corps?' My reply was angry, but also nervous.

At the Saudi Pritchard compound, Ian parked outside the mess, a simply furnished, but blissfully airconditioned shed. Two men finishing lunch did not even bother to look up. Was it finders keepers, I wondered?

'You think you're smart doing this sort of work,' said Ian pulling up a chair. 'All these places you've visited and nothing's happened. Sex with an Arab doesn't last long you know. In and out and it's all over.'

Attempting a diversion, I inquired about his girlfriend, but he wasn't interested. After working three months straight, the man was fed up. Would I like to see his room?

'Sure. But we mustn't let me miss the camel races.' I flicked my press credentials.

Suddenly the rape fantasy vanished and youthful immaturity replaced the macho image he was trying to project.

'I want to show you my pet,' he said, almost humbly.

Opening the wardrobe, he removed a biscuit tin in which an eight-inch long jet-black scorpion was rattling its tail.

'Found it under a garbage bin. It eats live cockroaches and an occasional mouse.' He replaced the tin between rows of dusty cowboy boots.

'Charming,' I muttered, impatient to be off.

'There is something else,' he said, leading me to behind his cabin to where a metallic blue limousine sat parked on a concrete slab.

'It's all mine.' He stroked a mudguard. 'The chassis is a Cadillac Fleetwood, the wheels are off a Mustang, and the horn is out of a Ferrari. All wrecked by the Arabs. Rolled through excessive speed, or just left by the roadside due to a minor fault they couldn't be bothered to fix. They have no notion of death or injury. Swerving around a camel at 160 kph (100 mph), they say *Inshallah* the Arabic for 'if God wills'. Anyway, the showrooms are full of imported cars so it's easier to buy a new one. When I finish building this, it will be the world's most expensive car.'

'How will you get it back to England?' I asked the garbage man who kept a pet scorpion, built dream cars from desert debris, and invented rape fantasies to prevent himself from going mad.

'Drive it. All the way.' He grinned boyishly.

It would have been great style to arrive at Riyadh racetrack in such a vehicle. Instead, we rumbled up in the garbage truck just as the scribes drew up in their minibus. They hurried into the stadium, leaving me with the 'royals', glaring across another red carpet. I could read their thoughts. Where had I been? Had I seen something important? The look from sullen Tanzanian born photographer Anwar Hussein could have melted an iceberg.

I decided that Prince Abdullah bin Abdul Aziz Āl Saūd, the tall head of the National Guard, was a suitable person to stand beside. Even then, one of them called out cheekily, 'Roll your sleeves down. We can see your arms.'

The usual buzz of anticipation heralded the arrival of the queen. Obviously excited by her first camel race, she stepped out of the black Rolls Royce wearing a smart red and white polka-dot outfit and matching pillbox hat.

Pursued by the 'royals', Her Majesty's party moved inside, but I hung back to observe the silent crowd of Indians, Yemenis, Baluch and other migrant workers who had lined the streets for an official occasion to admire a woman, but at a word from Prince Abdullah, Saudi mounted police suddenly unfurled long bullwhips and charged the bystanders. At first transfixed, I too took flight. I was there to record the pleasant aspects of the visit, and keeping quiet about the incident, I pushed my way through to the racetrack.

The highlight of the program was the 3,000 metre (3,280 yard) Taif Cup in which six of Saudi Arabia's finest racing camels would twice circumambulate the sandy course. At a word from the starter, a handler gave them a brisk tap on the backside and they were off. The riders, tiny Pakistani and Bangladeshi boys, sat back on the haunches, knees clinging to the base of the hump. Far from being a romantic event, the camel race was a testy affair, accompanied by groaning and teeth-gnashing, the winner being a jockey only seven-years-old. Thinking this information would interest Her Majesty and her entourage, I approached the ladies-in-waiting as they left the grandstand.

'Only seven?' responded the Duchess of Grafton, a woman even keener on racing than the queen. 'Do you think it was rigged?'

I did not reveal that only one camel was facing the start when its handler had shoved a stick up its bottom. Why spoil a lovely story for Royal Ascot? Our program read: *8.10pm. Dinner on carpets and cushions in a tent on the road to al-Khurais.* The road to Mandalay? The road to Damascus? I had travelled on both, but where the hell was al-Khurais?

With ten minutes to spare, I raced into the Inter-Continental to change. The task of working in evening dress lay ahead. The desert is freezing at night but I longed to look attractive after my dowdy *galabia*. Rummaging in my suitcase, I selected a black-and-silver striped jumper and a long black skirt. Black, the colour of mourning, was the most suitable choice in Saudi Arabia, I decided. It was too cold to go barefoot and as trainers would look stupid with this outfit, instead of being sensible, I trooped out to the bus in black patent leather sandals.

The journey from the warm hotel took us into the chilly night to an enormous tent adorned with fairy lights. An oriental carpet the size of a football pitch covered the sand, and Bedouin sheikhs, who looked as though they would prefer their traditional places on the ground, occupied hundreds of chairs arranged around the walls.

The scribes were dispatched to the rear of the tent and photographers were told to stand near the entrance.

'You will have a photo-call when Her Majesty is seated with King Khalid,' Michael Shea told a few protestors.

I did not join them. I had to cope with the onset of menstrual pain. One of the men, indeed. Perhaps sensing I was unwell, a kindly Saudi suggested I sit by a roaring fire in the centre of the tent. But just at that moment, King Khalid arrived, leaning heavily on an ebony stick. Although he had a gentle face, in 1977 he'd agreed to the execution of the tragic Saudi Princess Masha'il for adultery. Now he, King Khalid bin Abdul Aziz Āl Saūd was himself about to entertain a woman (it may have aggravated an ailing heart, for he died soon afterwards).

More desert patriarchs shuffled into the tent, took their seats and stared straight ahead as if awaiting their own execution. A bearer, swinging a smoking censer, did the rounds, followed by a statuesque Nubian pouring *qahwa*. Were it not for the photographers in their ill-fitting dinner jackets, it could have been a scene from *One Thousand and One Nights.*

Suddenly they charged towards King Khalid who, unnoticed by me, had been joined by the queen and her party, which now included British foreign secretary David Owen.

'Stop it!' said Her Majesty addressing the scrum. But out for blood, the 'royals' ignored her and continued pushing, shoving, and firing their flashguns.

Barred by this manic barrier, I dropped to my knees and groped my way through their legs to the front. I even managed to take several pictures before the inevitable happened: catching my hem with the heel of my sandal, I pitched forward at King Khalid's feet. Panic-stricken, he made a gesture of sorts to help, but quick as a flash the duke saved me further embarrassment.

'Come on, have another bash,' he called out to me.

Hearing him laugh, the Saudi monarch looked relieved: he wasn't going to be assassinated after all. My fall had brought comic relief. Even the queen managed one of her grim smiles, but standing up to straighten my skirt, I found the photographers had withdrawn and I was alone in front of the dignitaries.

'Please come forward and take your pictures madam,' called Prince Salman bin Abdul Abdul Aziz Āl Saūd, the gracious governor of Riyadh.

For a second I considered this opportunity. However, with half the tour to go, such a privilege would be viewed as favouritism.

'No thank you, sir, I've had enough.' I replied with equal courtesy, unaware that my flash cord had torn loose and that none of my photos would turn out.

Prince Salman and the king now rose to escort the queen and her entourage into the dining tent. And to the amazement of the experienced reporters, we were also invited: Bedouin hospitality was even extended to the press. Just as I could never have imagined lunching with a garbageman, the queen could never have thought that she might one day sit down with the hacks. A concerned Michael Shea told us to leave our cameras outside the tent.

'No pictures. Absolutely no pictures of Her Majesty eating,' he called.

From my own position at the end of a long trestle table, the royal party was obscured by mountains of mutton, pyramids of rice, and stacks of glace fruit. Fifty lambs had been roasted for the banquet; lobster had been flown in from Jeddah, turkey from Britain, cheeses from France, and orange juice from the citrus orchards of Lebanon.

Ignored by all, Detective Trestrail sat near me. Feeling guilty about the toe incident, I passed him a date tart, an offering he gratefully accepted. Then just as the queen had experienced in Kuwait, dinner was over and she was being escorted out.

Caught off guard, the photographers were still eating as I dashed outside to witness an amazing scene. King Khalid accompanied Her Majesty to her car, and stood back for a tall Nubian bearer to pour her a cup of *qahwa* from a gold coffeepot. It was a stunning photograph of the queen, in full evening dress, flanked by black servants, moonlight flashing on their scimitars, but suddenly I sensed her unease. Where were other members of her party? A gloved hand accepted the *qahwa,* but I saw it shaking slightly and lowering my camera, I gave what I hoped was an encouraging smile.

It was not the last time I was to find myself alone with Her Majesty. For the most part nothing was said. On this occasion, she murmured, 'This is my sixty-fifth cup of coffee since arriving in Arabia.'

And the tour moved on. Leaving Saudi Arabia ahead of *Britannia* meant that we had a day's wait in Doha, capital of Qatar, a thumb-shaped country the size of Kent, that projects into the Gulf from the Arabian landmass.

My arrival in Qatar as a member of the Buckingham Palace press corps was in stark contrast to a previous visit. In December 1976, stopping to check the manuscript of *The Gulf States and Oman,* I got no further than the airport where an official had scrutinised my Australian passport and announced bluntly: 'You can't come in. You've written bad things about us.'

'But my book isn't published,' I wailed.

VISIT TO THE QATAR NATIONAL MUSEUM ACCOMPANIED BY (THEN)
CROWN PRINCE, SHEIKH HAMAD BIN KHALIFAH AL-THANI (CENTRE)

'We have it on authority that you've written wicked stories about Qatar.' He squinted through wire-rimmed spectacles.

Suddenly I understood. They were confusing me with Linda Blandford, author of the recently published book *Oil Sheikhs* whose scathing comments about Arab society were causing shock waves across the peninsula.

'You will return to Abu Dhabi,' he announced it like a prison sentence.

'But I've just come from Abu Dhabi,' I said.

'Well, then you must go on to Bahrain.' And although I could see my old friends from the Ministry of Information waving from the Arrivals Hall, I was marched onto the first flight to Manama.

Britannia received a colourful aquatic welcome in Qatar. Scores of cruisers and dhows escorted her into Doha, but while officials had years to prepare for the royal visit, teams of Indians were still washing trees, hanging up flags and sweeping away sand as the royal couple began a hectic round of visits.

At one o'clock, the Emir Sheikh Khalifa bin Hamad al-Thani was hosting a traditional Bedouin lunch at a picnic spot about 16 kilometres (10 miles) outside Doha, where we found two army tents pitched on the limestone conglomerate that covers most of the country. As the press was admiring a herd of captive Arabian oryx, I wandered around behind the dining tent where a perspiring Egyptian chef was supervising lunch: Danish turkey, rice and smashed baby marrows whose smell had attracted swarms of flies, hysterical at finding something to eat other than rotting corpses on the desert highways.

'Where is Her Majesty to sit?' I inquired of one of the Pakistani helpers.

'There,' he replied, pointing to a place in the centre of the tent.

Each setting had a moisturised tissue in a packet on the side plate. However, this one at the head of the table was without.

'Where is Her Majesty's tissue?' I asked.

'Queen will wash hands outside,' he replied.

'Where?' I asked him.

He indicated a wooden hat stand plunged in the sand. A neatly folded orange towel hung from a hook, and a pristine cake of pink Lux toilet soap sat on a wooden side table.

'Bearer will pour water for queen to wash.' Picking up a kettle, he rehearsed the procedure.

Now thoroughly concerned, I explained that Her Majesty would probably prefer to use a tissue. 'The queen does not normally wash in public,' I told him gently.

Entering the picnic tent, I scrutinised the royal place setting. Instead of a dessert fork, Her Majesty's place had two large dinner forks. Astonished that no one from the British Embassy was supervising arrangements, I quickly swapped the queen's cutlery with the next setting. Another moisturised packet of tissues was found, and all was complete.

A cloud of dust on the horizon indicated it was just in time and I quickly joined the ranks. The day was still and hot, but just as in Riyadh, a puff of desert wind stirred as Her Majesty was shaking hands with Sheikh Khalifa. It lifted her dress, sending it swirling about her waist, a moment I was not quick enough to catch, but it would win the *Daily Express* photographer, 1979 Picture of the Year.

Back in Doha again, I visited the nearby Sailing Club to search for someone to take my films up to London. A British Airways steward agreed to help and that evening, I wandered across to his hotel and left them in his pigeon-hole. I was almost back at our hotel when two youths on a motorcycle roared past and leaning out, the pillion rider punched me in the stomach. As they swung around—although winded—I stepped back and cuffed his ear but luckily disturbed by people in the car park, they sped off into the night.

Inside the foyer, I encountered a woman from the picnic. An Egyptian broadcaster with Radio Doha, she introduced herself as Layla al-Moghy.

'I wanted to interview one of the journalists, but they've all gone to their rooms. Can you help me out?' she asked wistfully.

'Okay, but I'm too tired now,' I told her.

'Lovely. What time do you get up?' She clapped her hands.

'Seven,' I muttered reluctantly.

'I'll be right there,' said Ms al-Moghy bidding me good night.

I was still asleep when she knocked at 6.45am and after first ordering tea, I sat up in bed watching her set up a large tape recorder.

'Right now, you're on *Desert Island Discs* in Doha,' she announced.

'What? I've had no preparation. Besides, I'm still in my pyjamas,' I crowed.

'Never mind. Ad-lib is more natural,' said Ms al-Moghy fiddling with the dials.

'Good morning listeners: we have a special guest today. She is Christine Osborne, an Australian writer and the only woman photographer on the British royal visit which began yesterday in Doha.'

'Now Christine, you were born in Sydney where you trained as a nurse. Right? And this is your third visit to lovely Qatar. Yes? What is your first choice of record?'

'*Dancing Queen*, by Abba,' I mumbled the title of the Swedish song currently topping the hit parade. There followed the most banal choice of music ever heard on *Desert Island Discs* as barely awake, I floundered under Ms al-Moghy's questions.

'*Espana Cani* the music of the bullring,' I said, recalling summer holidays in Spain.

'Chopin's piano concerto,' I tried to upgrade my taste.

'And which concerto is your favourite Christine?'

'Any one. They're all wonderful.' I said, but disregarding my discomfort, Ms al-Moghy pressed on.

'Christine, being so well-travelled, I'm sure you must be equally well-read. Can you tell us what book you would take to your desert island?'

I glanced anxiously at my reading material: *Bad Blood: My Years in an Indian Prison,* the story of the drugs killer, Charles Sobraj would never do.

'An English-Arabic phrase book,' I replied lamely.

'Now listeners, isn't that thoughtful. When Christine returns to Qatar she'll be able to talk to you. Finally, Christine. One item only. What item would you choose on your desert isle?'

I struggled to respond. Like being cast in wax at Madame Tussaud's, or starring on *This is Your Life,* an appearance on *Desert Island Discs* is a sign of status. Though unfortunately not in my own case. Tea? Too simple. Whisky? Can't say that in a Muslim country. Fish hooks? Boring.

'*Monoi,*' I shouted.

'*Monoi?*' queried Ms al-Moghy.

'Yes. *Monoi* is a Polynesian love potion made from jasmine and coconut oil. You rub it on your body and pray someone will come along,' I said triumphantly.

'We can't air this!' she cried and cutting off the tape and lifting the huge recorder like a feather pillow, she had charged out the door.

In fact, the program was aired. Two years later, I ran into Ms al-Moghy in Trafalgar Square when she told me what a problem she'd had locating *Espana Cani* out in Doha.

When Britain announced its withdrawal from the Trucial States, Qatar had joined the federation of Arab emirates but following disputes, in 1971 it had declared its independence. In 1979 it was still a sleepy coastal state exhibiting no signs of the development transforming its neighbour, Abu Dhabi. A major problem was the inability to agree on who owned the prime real estate along West Bay although away from the waterfront, a national stadium, a national theatre and a national library had been built.

On a previous occasion, visiting the library to do some research, I had asked a Qatari manning the Information Desk where I could find the toilet.

'Ladies can only use WC on Thursday,' he replied.

'But it's only Tuesday,' I exclaimed before running back to my hotel as fast as my legs would carry me.

On this trip, a pleasant twenty-five year old man from the Ministry of Information, black—indicating slave blood in his not so distant past—had acted as my guide.

'Would I like a drive after work?' he asked and, being alone on a balmy evening, I'd accepted.

As we set off, he'd opened the glove box and produced a bottle of Tanqueray gin, tonic and two glasses.

'Never mind the cost,' he said. 'We can go and drink it in the park.'

Before I could say *inshallah*, I found myself sipping a gin and tonic in Qatar's first ever public garden. Groups of masked women, out for a stroll, stared as if I was a she-devil, however, we were merely chatting about life in Qatar, and he drove me back to my hotel for dinner.

As I debated whether to have grilled *hamour* (reef cod) or lobster thermidor, the young man had leant across the table.

'I need a new wife,' he announced, 'and I'm so happy with you. You like reading and fishing, same as I do. And you don't like camel meat, same as me. Perfect. I really want to marry you. We will be very happy. I am building a house with a big garden in al-Ruwais. What colour do you want me to paint it? $8,000 worth of furniture from Jashanmal department store. Very good bed. German I think. I have three cars. A Peugeot, an Oldsmobile and a Mercedes. You can have the Mercedes. And a boat. And we'll go to Europe whenever you like. I'm serious. I will tell my father tonight. I don't care what he says. He has seven wives. Christian? That doesn't matter. You see I am not a real Muslim, as I drink. He picked my first wife. I never spoke to her before we married. You must marry an English, American, or Australian so you can to talk to them first. My wife looked all right, but she wasn't kind, so I divorce her. Puff! Three times. Just saying once no good. Three times and you're free. I'm tired of living at home with my family. How much you pay your flat? Only £300 a month? We'll keep it on. You live here and it will be there when we go to London. In fact let's get married before we go fishing on Thursday. This is good.

You go to Abu Dhabi, Australia, come back to Qatar to live. I trust you. And we can both work and earn $1,200 a month. Think about it not too long.' He was out of breath when he finished.

'I'll let you know after we go fishing,' I said quietly.

In the desert, Bedouin will offer you their last drop of water, a natural generosity that continues in oil-rich urban Arabia. A pearl choker, whispered to be worth more than £500,000 was Sheikh Khalifa's gift to Her Majesty, who had already received the Mubarak pearl necklace from the Emir of Kuwait. Other gifts from the State of Qatar included a ruby-studded brooch in the shape of a dhow and a lapis lazuli fruit stand with prancing stallions, encrusted with diamonds. Neither was the duke forgotten. He received a solid gold sword in a scabbard encrusted in rubies and other precious gems. Her Majesty returned the compliment in presenting her Qatari host with a silver salver engraved with *H.M.Britannia*, and the royal yacht departed for Abu Dhabi, capital of the United Arab Emirates.

As I stood with the photographers watching *Britannia* berth, a Bedouin security guard kept telling me to move. It was all I could do not to push him into the harbour, but deciding this was inappropriate behaviour for a member of the Buckingham Palace press corps, I gritted my teeth and ignored him.

Sheikh Zayed bin Sultan al-Nahyan, the ruler of Abu Dhabi, was on hand to welcome the queen at the bottom of the gangplank. Together they walked to a podium, and stood side by side. The Royal Marine Band struck up God Save the Queen as the 'royals' bounded about like kangaroos, but I remained at attention, also for the national anthem of the UAE. Thus rooted to the ground, I missed the best pictures, but someone in the crowd had noted my decorum—we'll meet him in the chapter on Iraq.

Vast oil and gas deposits were changing Abu Dhabi from a simple fishing village into a major player on the world stage. Zayed's generosity with his spectacular oil income was legendary and his forestation programs had won international awards. Abu Dhabi municipality counted some 150 million trees planted since he became ruler in 1966. Acacias, orange trees, Indian almonds, and native *ghaf,* were flourishing in public gardens and rhododendrons from Zayed's own farms enlivened its roundabouts. On one

SHEIKH ZAYED INTRODUCING HER MAJESTY IN ABU DHABI

visit, I passed a row of cauliflowers planted along the seaside corniche—clearly a horticultural error by one of the 20,000 Indian gardeners.

New tree cover had brought wildlife back to the former sand island. Jerboas and sand rats scuttled about and birds that used to overfly the inhospitable Trucial States to winter in Africa, now alighted in their thousands. The Duke of Edinburgh, a keen bird-watcher and author of *Birds from Britannia,* was delighted to hear of this progress which was not limited to birds. Sheikh Zayed's private fish farm at *al-Ajban,* started with 700 tilapia imported from Egypt four years before, now counted 20 million fish living in a network of canals carved out of the desert. The lucky tilapia even had bridges under which to shelter from the sun and consuming 50 kilograms (110 pounds) of food a day, they were in no danger of being eaten as Zayed prohibited anyone fishing them.

Abu Dhabi was the only occasion when women scribes would have an advantage as Her Majesty's meeting with Sheikha Fatima bint Mubarak, favourite wife of Sheikh Zayed, was to be strictly women only. Men are not permitted in the harem, the section reserved for female members of an Arab household. As well as wives, it invariably counts an assortment of relatives, friends and retainers, as I had experienced on previous efforts to meet the elusive desert queen.

The Ministry of Information in Abu Dhabi had advised it would be considered discourteous in Bedouin society were I not to call on the ruler's wife. Nevertheless, each time I'd attempted to see her, with appointments arranged for anything between eleven in the morning to nine at night, Her Highness had cancelled the meeting. The most startling excuse on one occasion was that the ceiling had collapsed on the harem dining table, but construction errors in the early days of development gave most buildings only a three-year life span—I was walking past the National Bank of Abu Dhabi in 1977 when three concrete blocks fell off the top.

Late one afternoon, as I was about to leave for Oman, I received a call from the sheikha's Egyptian secretary.

'Sheikha Fatima will see you at 8pm.' she told me.

Delighted at this luck, I bought some roses at great cost and wearing a full-length black evening gown, I took a taxi to the Manhal Palace. A final obstacle was a sentry who raised his gun and refused to let me in the gate. Older guards were seated around a large platter eating mutton and rice, but one got up slowly, and called the harem on a walkie-talkie.

'*Y'alla,*'—go in, he said, and I started walking down a gravel path towards the harem quarter.

Slipping off my shoes, I entered a salon through glass doors flanked by two stuffed lions where a dozen masked women, seated on divans, watched a large television screening an American western starring the man who would become the fortieth president of the United States of America. Passing around the room, I shook all their hands and found a seat in a corner with my flowers. A servant brought me a mango juice. More masked women arrived, among whom was a pretty, unveiled girl who sat down beside me.

Speaking good English, she said she was Abu Dhabi's first woman graduate from Baghdad University and she was now 'head master' as there was no one else. Suddenly all the ladies rose and she invited me to accompany them in to dinner.

'*La,*—no,' the sheikha's personal retainer swept up. 'I am very sorry but Her Highness has a sore throat and she isn't seeing anyone.'

Retrieving my shoes, I walked back to the gate, gave the roses to the sentry and returned to my hotel only to receive a new call next morning fixing an appointment for eleven that day.

Passing the African wildlife again, I entered the inner sanctum where a long table was generously spread. But not with the Arabic sweetmeats I had anticipated. It was entirely covered with digestive biscuits, shortbread, ginger snaps, Kit-Kats and glass bowls of Quality Street chocolates. Servants placed a Sprite on a marble side table. Secretary Hayat entered and wearing a cream diamante-sewn robe and the shiny black beaked mask of the Gulf States, finally Sheikha Fatima herself.

Tall and voluptuous, she extended a hand, its henna-stained fingers charged with tiger-eye rings. 'Ahlan wa asalan,'—welcome. Her eyes crinkled behind the *burqa* as she summed me up, motioned me to sit, and popped the first question.

'Her Highness wishes to know what changes you notice in Abu Dhabi?' said Hayat.

I replied how the trees had grown taller and the sheikha's raisin coloured eyes crinkled again. Like her husband, Zayed, the greening of the desert was dear to her heart and translated, my comment caused a ripple of satisfaction among members of the harem who had filed quietly in.

Generous with her time on this occasion, the sheikha and I chatted for nearly an hour. Born near the inland oasis of Buraimi, she had taken the biggest step of any woman of her generation in founding a women's association and publishing a magazine. But oh, my goodness, no. She would never have her picture in it.

'I have never had my photograph taken and I never will. It's work that counts,' she replied, sliding a memento of our meeting across the table. It was a box containing a watch, but not just any old watch; it was a winking, diamond-studded, Favre Leuba.

Already aware of the sheikha's views on photography, I joined the female members of the royal party in the *majlis* (audience-room) of the Qasr al-Mashrif, an older style blue-tiled palace near Abu Dhabi's racecourse. The queen, her lady companions and two young embassy wives arrived precisely on time. But time passed without sign of Sheikha Fatima.

Seated bolt upright on a faux-Louis XV beechwood sofa, Her Majesty looked straight ahead. On either side of her, the duchess and Lady Susan looked concerned by the delay and across the room, the embassy wives were clearly terrified. Scattered around the *majlis* even the scribes seemed uncomfortable, but to me it was typical that the harem could not keep an appointment and sensing that I should take the initiative, I slipped outside to inquire of the problem.

'Someone give wrong message. Her Highness Sheikha Fatima is late. Queen must wait,' said a woman flashing past. 'Perhaps she go bathroom.'

'The Queen of England is not going anywhere,' I told her crossly. 'What's more, no one keeps Her Majesty waiting.' And glancing into the *majlis,* I observed the queen was drumming white-gloved fingers on the back of the sofa.

Fifteen minutes late, Sheikha Fatima and her entourage drew up in a fleet of black Cadillacs and when they were seated, servants carried in censers of smoking frankincense which we waved under our armpits. All except for Her Majesty who swatted at it like a wasp as seated on her right, Hayat began interpreting the conversation.

'Yes, Anne no longer lives at home, she is grown up and married now,' I heard the queen say. Then casually and with a deadpan expression, she inquired of the sheikha: 'Do you go to London often?'

'Yes,' replied Hayat on her behalf. 'We have a house in Bolton Gardens and a Scottish estate.'

It was now time to exchange gifts, a sensitive matter since the munificence of the Arabs was overwhelming. 'I'm afraid this is rather small,' muttered Her Majesty handing over a signed photograph of herself.

Suddenly a large unveiled woman wearing a shocking pink gown appeared brandishing a Polaroid camera.

'You don't mind?' inquired Hayat of the queen, who looking mildly surprised, said she understood the sheikha did not allow her picture to be taken.

'It's for the family album,' she was told.

Angry at this favouritism, I motioned to Lady Susan that I too should be allowed to take a photograph and Her Majesty, clearly aware of the situation, gave me an almost-imperceptible nod of royal assent.

I felt like Virginia Wade winning Wimbledon. What a scoop. Dashing out to retrieve my cameras, I had raised my arms to take a picture when two uniformed female security guards pounced.

'*La sura!*' said one grabbing the camera and the other my wrists.

Disappointed, but hardly surprised, I returned to my seat just as the woman pulled the picture out of the Polaroid. It was completely black. Something was wrong with her camera.

'How very strange,' said the queen, looking at the picture and standing to leave.

Next morning found us speeding down the road to al-Ain, the burgeoning city in the dead heart of Abu Dhabi. Having attended a meeting of the Supreme Council of Rulers of the UAE, watched Morris dancing at the British school and made a walkabout in the British Embassy, Her Majesty and the Duke of Edinburgh were flying to al-Ain to visit the United Arab Emirates University—and we had to arrive before them.

On an earlier visit to al-Ain, a Bedouin, driving a silver Pontiac provided by the Ministry of Information, had suddenly pulled over and got out in the desert. Seated in the back, I'd imagined he was about to kill me, but he simply walked away to relieve himself on the only clump of grass in a hundred kilometres. Now, with five of us packed into the car, it was a race to reach the inland town. There was no chance to photograph Zayed's roadside forests. I arrived hot and crushed and we rushed to the university just as Sheikh Zayed and the dean were receiving the royal party.

Before federation, the Trucial States counted only two schools, so locals were justifiably proud of the university, that opened in 1976. Tribal elders and Bedouin girls swinging long black hair were dancing with Zayed in their midst. A whirling figure in brown-and-gold robes, he beckoned to the queen to join in, but Her Majesty shook her head while laughing at such an idea.

The visit was proceeding well until the royal party, escorted by scores of male students, reached the lecture rooms where a tutor, declaring they were blocking the corridor, locked the Duke of Edinburgh and sixty boys in the science laboratory. And it was at al-Ain where the 'royals' committed the cardinal sin of racing into the university mosque with their shoes on and anguish clouded the former smiling face of the UAE president.

'Get out!' he thundered in Arabic.

With the queen scheduled to arrive in Dubai at 5pm, it was another race across the desert to Abu Dhabi's neighbour.

I set off with journalist Norman Luck of the *Daily Mail,* and a man I knew only as 'Ed of the *Express.*' On our dash through the dunes, we made three stops: the first where a Land Rover had collided with a camel, the second for me to photograph the men pretending they were dying of thirst, and a third occasion for our driver to say the mid-afternoon prayer. Arriving seconds before the royal party coming in from the airport, I raced up to the Dubai Municipality building to find I was the only photographer.

'Go away. You're not allowed to take pictures,' said a policeman pushing me roughly.

'Leave her alone. She is a member of the Buckingham Palace Press Corps,' called Michael Shea leaping out of the leading car like a knight in shining armour.

Her Majesty was welcomed by Sheikh Hamdan, Chairman of the Municipality who presented her with an 18-carat gold key to the City of Dubai, watched by Mahdi al-Tajir, the shrewd UAE ambassador, a former customs officer who owned among many assets, a Cayman Islands bank and Highland Spring, the second biggest supplier of bottled water in the United Kingdom.

Dubai which means 'locust' in Arabic, occupies a special place in my life. It was here, during a stopover between London and Sydney, that I found the subject for my book. Standing on top of the Mazda building—the tallest structure at the time—I'd looked down on the big teak *booms*— massive two-masted dhows used for smuggling gold to Bombay (now Mumbai)—and smaller dhows from Lamu and Zanzibar. It was a scene from the *Arabian Nights* and as I watched lean Somali crews unloading motorcycles and televisions, I knew I had my theme: the discovery of oil and its sweeping effect on traditional Bedouin society.

Oil was struck in the offshore al-Fateh field in 1966, but Dubai has a long history of maritime trade due to the safe mooring in its saltwater creek. Development began in the 1970s under Sheikh Rashid bin Saeed al-Maktoum of the highly regarded al-Falasi section of the Bani Yas, the dominant tribe in what became the United Arab Emirates. A craggy old Arab known as the 'Fox of the Gulf', Rashid who ruled Dubai with a council of merchants, considered that any sort of trade that was good, was good for Dubai. At six one morning, I watched him point out where to start digging a road tunnel under the creek: an idea expatriates had described as madness.

If Rashid had plans for Dubai, his third son, the present ruler Sheikh Mohammed bin Rashid al-Maktoum, envisaged turning Dubai into an Arab city like Córdoba, the most sophisticated city in medieval Europe when there were more than a thousand mosques and six hundred *hammams* (public baths). Among his ventures are mega shopping malls, indoor ski runs and Burj Dubai, the tallest building in the world, but the queen and duke were to see 'Old Gulf Coast' Dubai before it disappeared.

Five years before, I had stayed in a flat on the creek, with a sixty-year-old British Airways ground engineer, whom I'd met by chance at Singapore's Changi Airport, on the night of 21 September 1971. Our BOAC VC10 had just taken off when there was a loud explosion—boom, boom—right side, rear when the plane had become unbalanced and we were all gripped by fear.

Following earlier visits to Singapore, I knew that taking off from the island, an aircraft heads straight out to sea, but as our pilots struggled to gain height, we circled the city at an altitude so low, I could see people eating dinner in upstairs tenements. After what seemed an age, but was likely to have been about ten or twelve minutes, we made it back although the weight of fuel and baggage burst our tyres. As one of the first passengers to hurtle down an emergency slide, and racing through fire engines to the bar, I'd bumped into Frank in his oily overalls.

'Are you off that plane? he asked. 'Consider yourself lucky. It was coming in with a sheet of fire underneath it.'

Frank and I had kept in touch and we caught up again in Dubai when I'd stopped there, en route home for a family Christmas dinner in Australia in 1974.

Although Arabs are partial to goat, it was not on the menu when the queen invited the seven UAE rulers to dinner on *Britannia* among whom

BOOMS ON DUBAI CREEK USED FOR RUNNING GOLD TO BOMBAY, 1974

was Sheikh Hamad bin Mohammed al-Sharqi, the thirty-year-old ruler of the mountainous emirate of Fujairah, on the Arabian Sea coast. I had met Sheikh Hamad at the inauguration of the Fujairah Hilton in 1978, when tribesmen had danced in the palace courtyard, hands clasped behind each other's backs as they shuffled backwards and forwards among plastic bags blowing about the gravel.

'Why did you write in your book that Fujairah looks like a garbage tip?' The sheikh called me out of my bed to his palace at ten that evening.

'I'm sorry Your Highness, but I'm afraid it is,' I told him.

With dinner over, the Royal Marines beat the retreat and *Britannia* cast off into the dark waters of the Lower Gulf. On board two solid gold camels flanked by gold palm trees with bunches of ruby dates had joined other of Her Majesty's gifts: a pinafore of gold chain mail set with pink amethysts, a gold incense burner, gold goblets and a coffee jug in the shape of a falcon, several gold brooches and dhows, and a necklace studded with sapphires, surrounded by 300 diamonds, with matching earrings and a ring—a present from Sheikh Rashid.

BEDOUIN CELEBRATE THE OPENING OF THE FUJAIRAH HILTON, 1978

Carrying this fabulous cargo, the royal yacht sailed along the former 'Pirate Coast' of Ras al-Khaimah, through the Straits of Hormuz—the strategic entrance to the Gulf—and around the Musandam peninsula, to set a course for Muscat, capital of the Sultanate of Oman.

'Muscat and Oman' as it used to be known, occupies a 2,092 kilometre (1,300 mile) coastline on the underbelly of Arabia. As early as 200 BCE, its dhows were trading copper mined in the Hajar Mountains and frankincense from the southern province of Dhofar, with Mesopotamia. An Omani, Abu Ubayda bin al-Qasim, had sailed to Canton eight hundred years before Colombus discovered North America, but latter-day development was obstructed by the ruler, Sultan Said bin Taimur, who considered the West a harbinger of evil. Anything foreign was forbidden, even sunglasses and cigarettes, at dusk a cannon was fired and the Bab al-Kebir (big gate) closed off Muscat from the outside.

The transformation of Oman began in 1970 with the accession of his son Sandhurst-educated Sultan Qaboos. Schools, roads and hospitals were built and electricity was brought to remote villages, but with much to accomplish on a limited budget, development had bypassed Oman's two great souqs: Muttrah on Muscat Bay and Nizwa, planted in an inland date oasis, and when *Britannia* dropped anchor, neither had changed in more than a hundred years.

Nizwa was high on the royal itinerary. The historic capital of the Imamate of Oman, its dark, labyrinthine souq was the last authentic bazaar in Arabia. Turbaned silversmiths squatting in box-like shops fashioned jewellery and *jambias,* the curved dagger worn by Omani men. Other shops stocked textiles, swords, sharkskin shields and the British Martini-Henry rifles still carried by many tribesmen. The whack of meat choppers, the thump of women pounding grain, and a sticky-sweet smell of *halwa*[18] made visiting the souq a memorable experience. And for everyone, including the queen, it was to be the experience of the tour.

At noon, Her Majesty and the Duke of Edinburgh, accompanied by Sultan Qaboos, were scheduled to visit Nizwa by air. The Buckingham Palace press corps was travelling by bus along with hundreds of cars and buses carrying villagers in to see their beloved ruler who distributed a bag of rice to every family on his wedding day in 1975.

It is hard to say when things began to go wrong in Nizwa, but it became the stuff of nightmares for Michael Shea. In my own case, knowing the royal party was a jump ahead, I leapt off the press bus, which had become locked in a traffic jam.

'You must stay with the group,' bellowed a security man, but knowing where to find the souq tucked in the shadow of the great fort of Nizwa, I ignored him.

Thousands of tribesmen lined the alleys and women, who wear colourful African robes in this part of Oman, were gathered in doorways like butterflies emerging from cocoons. Finding a good vantage point, I perched on a ledge outside a spice shop. There was no sign of either the journalists or photographers, but at the far end of an alley, I saw a small group marching towards me at military pace.

It was the royal party, led by the Duchess of Grafton, in a flowery frock and floppy hat more suited to a palace garden party than an Arab market. I was tempted to salute them as shoes slipping on the stones, they drew level.

'Good morning,' said Sir Philip Moore, Her Majesty's Private Secretary as they marched on into the souq.

Hurtling out of another alley came a distressed Michael Shea, grey hair ruffled and spectacles steaming in the heat.

'I've lost the queen,' he cried in an anguished voice.

Alarmed I jumped down and pointed into the souq. 'I haven't seen Her Majesty but the others have gone that way,' I advised him.

At this moment, a chilling cry erupted inside the souq as sighting their sultan, traders and tribesmen gave a feudal roar. Stopping in his tracks, Shea loosened his old school tie, and belted back into the bazaar. By then, even I was concerned. Was the queen in danger?

Suddenly the queen and the sultan, followed by scores of chanting tribesmen, emerged into the sunlight. Her Majesty looked quite white as indeed she might. 'I was looking for your blue hat,' she said, sailing past me.

Accustomed to only seeing their sultan on television, his subjects rushed forward to shake his hand. I was forced back in the crush and looking alarmed, Sultan Qaboos instructed police to form a barrier so the queen, clutching a white handbag, could reach her limousine. Stopping to chat, the duke had been left behind, and the duchess and others had clearly taken a wrong turn.

My own worry was to locate the press bus so as not to be left in Nizwa, but turning abruptly, I ran straight into a tall, fair man in rolled-up shirtsleeves: it was the duke!

'How do you do, sir?' I asked in a stricken voice.

'I'm all right, are you?' he replied. Then looking anxious, he said, 'The queen. Where's the queen? Is she all right?'

'Yes sir,' I replied. 'She just left in a silver Cadillac.'

'That's my bloody car,' exclaimed the duke of a second Cadillac in the motorcade.

'Stop,' I banged on its windscreen. 'Stop you fool, this is the Duke of Edinburgh.'

To the driver however, the duke was just another *ferengi* (foreigner) and reaching back, he locked the door which left the duke and me blocking the road and a police car switched on its siren.

Unable to believe the situation, the duke clapped his hands over his ears and when this had no effect, he thumped on the bonnet and yelled, quite reasonably in my view: 'Switch that bloody thing off!' That evening, I was obliged to repeat his words to the scribes, who had been watching from a nearby hill. *DUKE LOSES HIS COOL* were next morning's headlines in the British newspapers.

And having disgraced myself in Riyadh and now in Nizwa, even worse was to follow on our final evening in Muscat.

Weary after three weeks on the go, I decided to miss the press party for the Dan-Air stewardesses for an early night. We were staying at al-Ghubra Guest House, one of the Sultan's palaces reserved for special guests with the royal crest, crossed swords and a *jambia* featuring on the stationery. After writing to mum on such elaborate paper, I washed my hair of the Nizwa dust and went downstairs.

The only person about was Malcolm Brown, a young freelance photographer from Bahrain who hated the 'royals' as much as I did.

'I'm going down to the harbour to watch the fireworks,' he said. 'Why not come?'

The last event was a private occasion with the queen and her party invited to attend a state banquet in the sultan's palace in Muscat: *9.50pm. Fireworks display over Muscat Bay. Dress: Mess Kit/D.J. (Decs) T.* read the code.

'I've got wet hair and look at this beach robe. It has SWEATSHIRT written on it,' I said.

'You can stay and watch from the jeep,' he assured me.

Winding a towel around my head and pausing neither to put on underwear, nor to pick up my cameras, I set off down to Muscat where the sultan's blue-and-gold palace, flanked by ancient Portuguese forts, stands on the waterfront where a huge crowd was assembled outside.

When Malcolm left to take pictures, I got out of the jeep and perched on the bonnet of for a better view.

'You must go inside the palace,' said an Omani policeman stepping up.

'No, I'm just here to watch the fireworks,' I told him.

'Press,' he indicated the credentials around my neck. 'Press.'

Then more firmly: 'Press must go inside.' And he escorted me around the front of the palace where a row of blue-and-gold velvet-backed chairs was arranged on the lawn.

'Press to sit here,' he said and instructed to sit down, I found myself alone under the stars.

Suddenly a rocket launched behind the palace drew a roar of approval from the crowds and as their clapping ricocheted off the cliffs, I looked up to see Her Majesty and the sultan appear on a balcony above me. Hearing an echo of the applause, the queen automatically raised her hand to wave, but there was only me, and standing there in my lime-green beach robe, I put my hands together, wishing the ground would swallow me.

I sat down again only to stand up when the royal party arrived in the garden. Weighed down with jewels and decorations, the Duchess of Grafton seemed as though she could hardly believe her eyes. SWEATSHIRT. Even the fatherly Sir Philip Moore looked as if to say, this is a wee bit overdone, and leaning over to Bill Heseltine, the Deputy Private Secretary to Her Majesty, and a fellow Australian, I whispered earnestly.

'It's a mistake Bill, the police made me come and sit here.'

'It's nice to have you with us Christine,' he replied in the manner of a born diplomat.

For the next thirty minutes, Muscat was lit up by fireworks ending with silver catherine-wheels forming a giant EIIR on the walls of Fort Jelali which until recently had been Muscat's jail. The royal party then moved to join the queen and the duke who appeared to board the Royal Barge waiting to take them out to *Britannia.*

Several hours had passed since their arrival at the palace and the tide now covered the red carpet under a metre of water. Golden handrails leading down the steps seemed to beckon to a nautical kingdom and attracted by the lights, schools of small sharks were swimming across it. Holding onto her tiara and lifting her gown, Her Majesty jumped on board, and the royal tour of Arabia was over.

Chapter 4
Middle East Nightmare

When I set sail for Europe in 1963, Australia remained a close-knit Anglo-Saxon society, a situation due as much to the 'White Australia policy' restricting immigration, as to its location—a long way from anywhere. Growing up in this closeted environment saw many Australians develop an irrational fear of anything foreign. Especially anything relating to the 'Yellow Peril', the term used to describe the threat of invasion from Asia, most notably from China.

My great-grandfather, Dr Richard Ryther Steer Bowker[19] had made the ninety day voyage from Liverpool to Melbourne in 1841, but travelling overseas, or 'going abroad' as it is known Down Under, was a huge step in the reverse direction. People were cautious, almost frightened of venturing into the great unknown. One could even obtain an official letter from Canberra, personally signed by the Australian prime minister, to present in event of need in a foreign land.

This charming introduction—To Whom It May Concern—is still in my possession:

The Bearer of this document, Miss Christine Osborne
of Sydney, New South Wales, is proceeding on a visit overseas.
Any facilities, or courtesies, which may be accorded the Bearer
whilst absent from the Commonwealth will be appreciated.

Signed Robert Gordon Menzies
Prime Minister

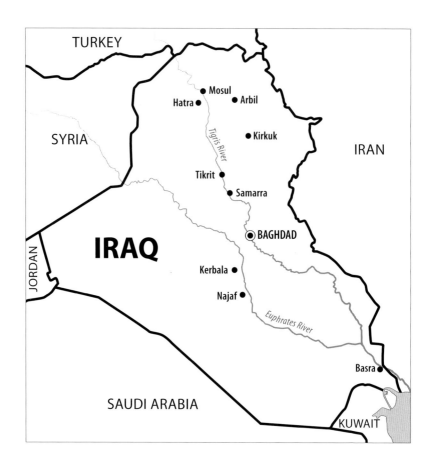

13 February 1980 found me standing at a bus stop in Putney, in south-west London. I was about to leave the 'Commonwealth' to fly to Iraq and to facilitate my trip to Heathrow Airport, I had sent my luggage ahead with my friend Aileen who worked at Terminal 3. Half-an-hour later, shivering in a wind off the Thames, I was still there.

'Number 33 is never on time,' moaned a woman behind me in the queue.

'If it doesn't come soon, I'll miss my flight to Baghdad,' I muttered into my upturned collar.

'Baghdad,' she guffawed. 'Where's your flying carpet?'

I had never been to Baghdad. Capital of the Abbasid dynasty, the second great Muslim caliphate, it reached its apex in the eighth and ninth centuries, when merchants and travellers spoke in awe of a great city—a rival to Constantinople—with magnificent mosques, palaces and caravanserais, built along the banks of the Tigris River.

The Abbasids were not only builders, they were learned scholars with the caliphs themselves taking a personal interest in science and the arts. The Bait al-Hikmah—'House of Wisdom'—developed by the fifth Caliph, Hārūn al-Rashīd (786-809) had attracted the cream of Muslim intellect and extended by the Caliph Abū Jafar Abdullāh al-Mā'mūn[20], it became a centre of learning and research without equal in the ancient world.

Scrolls acquired from libraries throughout the Middle East and the eastern Mediterranean were brought to the Abbasid Court. Muslim scholars translated classic Persian, Greek, Latin, even Sanskrit texts. Abū Yūsuf Yaqūb ibn Isāq al-Kindi[21]—known as the 'Philosopher of the Arabs'— translated the works of Aristotle. He also wrote several hundred treatises on mathematics, astronomy, meteorology and medicine. *De Materia Medica,* one of the most influential discourses ever written on herbal medicine, was translated from the Syriac—an offshoot of Aramaic, the language spoken at the time of Christ. Observatories were established—the world's oldest surviving astrolabe was made in Baghdad—and the Persian mathematician Muhammad ibn Mūsā al-Khwārizmī,[22] introduced the decimal system. Students attending more than three hundred institutes for higher learning were able to draw on this remarkable collection of knowledge to create new discoveries that included the distillation of rosewater and experiments in determining the early use of chemical pesticides.

But the Abbasid caliphs did not always study. Possessed of a great capacity for enjoyment, they were fond of organising hunting trips and hosting lavish banquets. Ancient cookery manuals refer to *bazmaward*— meat-stuffed dough, '... sprayed with a little rose water and leaves of mint, vinegar, salted lemons and walnuts [was] a favourite dish among men of elegance in Baghdad[23]...' Dates, together with cow, sheep, goat and camel milk, formed a staple part of diet with the Caliph Hārūn al-Rashīd reported to have been especially fond of gazelle milk.

Chickens were popular, especially the plump Kaskar chickens from this village in the fertile strip between the Tigris and the Euphrates rivers. Castrated cocks were considered to be the tastiest fowl, and fish was widely eaten—Tigris river carp as well as lobster from the Persian Gulf. On festival days, people employed cooks who specialised in the preparation of rich desserts and sweetmeats. *Muhallabia* a ground rice pudding and *ma'mounia*—a concoction of semolina, butter and pine nuts (two recipes from my book *Middle East Cooking*[24]) were almost certainly enjoyed more than a thousand years ago.

Abbasid society further displayed a keen sartorial sense. Tailors designed elaborate costumes for the haute bourgeoisie. *Washi*, a fine silken fabric woven from gold thread that reached Baghdad via the Silk Route was especially desirable, and it seems the illustrious Hārūn al-Rashīd may have even been something of a dandy. On his death, the following garments were found in his wardrobe: 4,000 cloaks of variegated silk, 10,000 shirts, 10,000 kaftans,10,000 pairs of trousers of different materials, 4,000 turbans and 5,000 silk handkerchiefs.

This knowledge inspired me to take more care than usual when packing for Iraq. I was wearing an Australian red fox fur jacket with fine wool slacks for the flight, and I had even squashed a pair of 'wellies' into my suitcase. It is my habit to pack something for every occasion—usually far too much—but I thought waterproof boots might be useful should we visit the Tigris-Euphrates marshlands near the southern city of Basra.

Just thinking of Baghdad made my imagination take flight. Although stripped by Mongol raids in the thirteenth century, to me it conjured up Scheherazade, the storyteller of *One Thousand and One Nights* and the exotic society of *Aladdin and His Magic Lamp*. Iraq normally banned journalists from the United Kingdom, and as I understood it, no photographer had set foot there in years.

My invitation had come via the roundabout route of the Arab Information Office in Melbourne. Its director Rudolph Abu Kater, a Palestinian-born naturalised Australian, was organising a small press trip to promote Iraq in the local media. Apparently the Iraqis were smarting over adverse publicity following allegations of their association with

Sydney menswear retailer Reuben F. Scarf and several Labor politicians. They evidently hoped a good press coverage would dispel doubts about their courting influential friends.

Abu Kater was an observer of the British royal visit to the Gulf States and my demeanour had evidently impressed him. My own participation was to write an article about Iraqi women, contrasting their freedoms with the restrictions placed on their sisters in Saudi Arabia. I'd accepted the invitation on the proviso that nothing would be censored and the Iraqi Consulate—located above a shop selling sunscreen and surfboards—in Bondi Junction, duly issued my visa on a visit to Sydney.

The five-hour flight from London to Baghdad on Iraqi Airways stretched to eight hours as I waited at Baghdad International Airport to retrieve my luggage. It seemed that immigration was allergic to camera equipment. I was taken to a room at the rear of the airport that was stacked from floor to ceiling with confiscated cameras, typewriters and other media tools of trade. Things had looked bad until a short, unshaven official wearing a brown tweed sports jacket and baggy trousers showed up to escort me to the hotel—with my luggage, including my camera bag.

Going out to explore that afternoon, I discovered to my disappointment that Baghdad was no beauty queen. It presented as a drab, concrete city, its overall grey appearance relieved only by ketchup-coloured double-decker buses. The beautiful Shi'ite mosques of Iran were nowhere to be seen: only the Khadimain Shrine, rising above the congested traffic on Bab al-Kublah Street, was at all photogenic.

In the nearby Gold Bazaar, shop windows displayed every sort of bauble, bangle, pendant, ring, and chain to distract the faithful on their way to worship.

'*Ahlan wa sahlan*. Do you wanna buy necklace?' whined a merchant in the doorway of Gold Shop Number 3.

'*La-shukran*, I am just taking a stroll,' I smiled at him.

'Come in. Siddown and have tea,' he said and removing a necklace from the window.

'For you I make price 80,000 dinar,' he cajoled and despite my protests, he slipped it around my neck.

'Good price. Buy today. Tomorrow cost 100,000 dinar.' He laughed at his own joke and a rather fat man, his stomach quivered like jelly.

I was actually looking for a carpet. The previous week I'd won a considerable sum playing roulette in an exclusive club in Mayfair, invited there by Trevor Kennedy, editor of the *Bulletin,* the now defunct Australian weekly news magazine on culture and politics.

I knew Trevor only from brief visits to his Sydney office so his call was a surprise, but his adrenalin was flowing after a night's highrolling with media-tycoon Kerry Packer. We were to dine at the club owned by John Aspinall, a close friend of the Seventh Earl of Lucan who was convicted in absentia for the sensational murder of the family nanny in November 1974, the year I moved to London.

Taught the intricacies of roulette by a wealthy Dutch lesbian on the Riviera, I'd grown to love the game and the charged atmosphere of the casino. But it remains a personal idiosyncrasy that I must play using borrowed money, that I repay whether I win or lose. I'd explained this superstition to Trevor who grandly peeled off £100 in notes before stalking off to play blackjack.

Seated at the green baize roulette table and betting 'straight up' and 'tiers', (numbers lying on the opposite side of the wheel between 27 and 33) I started to win. So much so that other players left their games to stand around to watch.

'*Faites vos jeux,*'—place your bets, announced the croupier whose black moustache and slicked back hair made him look like 'Lucky' Lucan himself.

'*Regardez ou elle met ses puces,*'—watch where she puts her chips, whispered an oleaginous Lebanese man flanked by two beautifully coiffed female escorts.

Reaching out, I placed pink chips on my favourite numbers: 5, 17, 25, 31, 33 and 35. I also dropped a chip on 'outside black', offering a smaller payout, but with better odds. The croupier flicked the ball into the wheel and for seconds, the only noise was the sharp sound of ivory spinning round on walnut wood.

'*Rien ne vas plus,*' he said. No further bets.

There was a sharp click as the ball dropped into the number 17 slot. He placed his plastic marker on the black square and raked in the losing bets as I had the satisfaction of watching him pile up my winning chips.

'*Elle a gagner de nouveau,*'—she has won again, said one of the escorts who was smoking through a diamond-studded cigarette-holder.

But Trevor had lost at cards and although it is a sacred rule that you never interrupt a winning streak, he petulantly wanted to leave. Collecting my winnings, I repaid his £100, adding another fifty in crisp £10 notes and now in Baghdad, I wanted to buy a carpet with this unexpected windfall.

Muslims have special reverence for the carpet. Bedouin use it as a floor covering in their tents, as a curtain to segregate the women's area, it is woven into saddlecloths, cushions, and prayer rugs and Surah 88, in the Holy Qur'an, even counts the carpet among the riches a true believer will receive on arrival in Paradise. I feared the Prophet would not look favourably on a carpet bought from the proceeds of gambling, but after much searching, I discovered a store stacked with rugs, sandwiched between the Aladdin Travel Agency and Sindbad Trading on el-Mansour Street.

It was almost dark before I chose an old brown prayer rug, that the trader assured me was woven from camelhair. Like the patter of a second-hand car dealer, one should never believe what a carpet merchant spins, but it was certainly handwoven and I decided its design would suit the eastern decor of my maisonette. Money changed hands, the trader rolled up the rug in a copy of the *Baghdad Times* and dispatched a boy to carry it back to the hotel with me. I felt pleased, a feeling shortly to desert me.

The journalists from the *Canberra Times* and the *Melbourne Age* arrived the following morning. Neither man had been to the Middle East and we were to be thrown together for the next ten days, when far from being an exotic experience, Iraq would become a nightmare. My every move required permission from Abu Kater and the supervision of the spotty-faced guide who'd met me at the airport, the irony being that I was less free than the Iraqi women I'd come to interview.

At first my work was interesting. I met some of Baghdad's foremost career women: Iraq's first female judge, twenty-eight year old Suad Abdul

Wahab, Mrs. Mana al-Alwasi, president of the Iraqi Women's Federation, and Dr Ibtihaj al-Aloosi, a consultant gynaecologist.

'Of course we are liberated,' said Dr Ibtihaj, an elegant woman who looked as if she had just stepped off the pages of *Vanity Fair*. 'I'm married with a family, I have an important job and I drive my own car. What else is there?'

While I was disturbed to learn that an unmarried woman who falls pregnant in a rural village can be stoned to death, I was heartened to hear of progress in urban areas. Far from being the veiled slaves of men and subjected to a life of domestic drudgery, Iraqi woman were jumping centuries of tradition. I learnt that forty per cent of students at Baghdad's Mustansirya University were women, and quite the opposite of living in bondage, they were basically free to marry the man of their choice.

'Sexual relationships between unmarried couples are prohibited, but shall we say that more and more young people have close friends,' said Dr Ibtihaj when we met at Baghdad's teaching hospital in Medical City.

'But attitudes are changing. In my country clinic, a farmer brought in his sixteen-year-old daughter who was seven months pregnant. He told me they did not want to harm her, but what could they do? Her lover had run away.'

'I advised them to keep her indoors, let her have the child, then offer it for adoption. And to my surprise, they agreed. Don't you see this is an enormous step? Previously, even in Baghdad, a single girl who falls pregnant can be killed for the family honour.'

'We are not like women in Iran where the government has rolled back social freedoms,' said Mana al-Alwasi, a lawyer, married to a pilot and mother of four young children.

'You have to know the situation here before the Ba'ath Revolution,' she told me earnestly. At that time, only three percent of women worked outside agriculture and the majority were illiterate. Today this has risen to sixteen per cent of the workforce and the Iraqi Federation of Women has 250,000 members,' she said proudly.

'The return of Imam Khomeini is not a renaissance, but an anti-revolution. He insists women wear the chador, university classes are segregated and morality police patrol the streets. Our great president, Saddam Hussein, says that no country that leaves out women can consider itself advanced.'

One of twelve children of a Baghdad pharmacist, Suad Abdul Wahab, the fair-skinned judge was still living at home and I'd wondered about her social life.

'As a judge are you fully liberated?' I asked at our meeting in a chamber of the court- house.

'Only partly because I'm still single,' she answered softly. 'But there is no clash. I switch roles easily from being a judge to doing the cooking. I am a family person, but I am also ambitious.' She gained momentum. 'Nothing will stop me doing what I want to do.'

'How do men react when they are brought before a young woman judge?' I looked up from writing in my spiral notepad.

'Sure, they are a little surprised, but they will get used to it. We have many women lawyers in Iraq.'

'Do you think you could combine marriage with a demanding legal career?'

'Why not?' She tossed her hair. 'Didn't Indira Gandhi?'

'Ah, so you can see a future Iraqi woman president.'

'Why not? Men and women are equal in Iraq's constitution. You know we had equality here before you did in England. Excuse me now. I am required on the bench.'

My interviews over, I joined the men in visiting ministries, factories, and housing communities, but of the rich heritage of Mesopotamia, I saw nothing.

'You're here to promote modern Iraq,' Abu Kater told me tersely.

At dinner on the fifth day, I voiced a desire to see Hatra, the ancient Parthian city in the Ninawa governorate, north-west of Baghdad. 'I'm not interested in you now. Just make sure you write a good story about the women,' he snapped.

I found his attitude disturbing, but when I tried to express this concern to Peter, the younger man from Melbourne, he told me not to be difficult.

'They are doing their best to be nice,' he said.

Nigel Wilson, the bespectacled, neatly dressed scribe from Canberra was apparently ignorant of the subterfuge of the Middle East. Peter was naïve. Abu Kater had told me privately he was invited because he worked in the telex room of the *Age*. 'With some good old Iraqi hospitality, he'll be more likely to push Iraqi news up front.' He made an effort at smiling.

I grew more uncomfortable as we were driven up to the Autonomous Region of Kurdistan in the historically militant area of northern Iraq. Kurds constitute fifteen per cent of the Iraqi population. They have their own language, preserve traditional customs, and the desire for a Kurdish homeland is well known, but during a live television broadcast from Arbil, the regional capital, we were forced to listen to a government flunkey.

'I am first of all an Iraqi and then a Kurd. And if you ask all the other Kurds, they will tell you we are Ba'thist Iraqis.' He beamed for the cameraman.

Assyrian records date Arbil from 2,500 BCE and in the early Middle Ages it was an important Christian bishopric. Its main attraction is an imposing citadel built over layers of previous settlements and a soaring mud-brick minaret, from the thirteenth century. We had time to see something of this historic past, but Abu Kater turned down my request and in pouring rain, he ordered the driver to take us straight to our hotel.

As we checked in, I watched tall, untidily turbaned Kurds stamping muddy boots in the foyer. If this wasn't bad enough, my room was the pits. The sheets were stained from occupation by countless truck drivers, wires hung out of the walls like the entrails of a disembowelled sheep, and pieces of brown smudged lavatory paper littered the bathroom floor.

A vigorous complaint brought a Kurd carrying an armful of sheets who was trailed by another man dragging an ironing board along the corridor. The first Kurd set about pressing what looked like a month's supply of laundry in my room. His mate collected the lavatory paper and punching open the window, he hurled it into the garden. The wiring was clearly unfathomable, but brandishing a candle from his baggy trousers, he dripped some wax on the bedside table and plunged it in with as much panache as an athlete lighting the Olympic flame.

TV INTERVIEW IN ARBIL, ABU KATER (L), NIGEL, PETER AND ME ON THE SOFA

In need of a drink after this experience, I located the bar, but there was no barman, and there were no customers, but the hundreds of cans of Swan Lager stacked on shelves against the wall made me wonder if they were expecting a West Australian rugby team.

The lager and the dinner menu were the great unsolved mysteries of Arbil: *Paper stake, Chateau Brian, Brian meet, Froot Jeely and Ratih Chiss* were written in a hand that had clearly found the effort difficult.

'If they cook as well as they spell, we haven't a hope in hell,' I said to myself and to be on the safe side, I ordered chicken soup.

The boys were seated in the restaurant chatting with Abu Kater. A waiter placed a bottle of Johnny Walker Black Label on their table. I would have loved a drink, but I drank my soup and went to bed. The night was made terrible by Kurdish dogs, or possibly wolves, howling in the garden, and tossing and turning in the still damp sheets, I voted the Horaman Hotel the worst of my travels—I hope it has since burnt down.

Next morning I rose early with the idea of photographing the citadel while the others were asleep, but Abu Kater appeared on the hotel steps. There were to be no pictures of Arbil and none of the giant oil refinery at Kirkuk, where we stopped for the Aussie boys to take snapshots of each other beside the eternal flame.

By now I was seething, but also terrified. I had hidden both passport and traveller's cheques under the mattress of my room in our hotel in Baghdad, only to forget them on our trip to Kurdistan. I hardly dared to ask whether the room was still vacant. But it was. And tip-toeing upstairs with heart aflutter, I lifted the mattress to find everything still there. Praise the Lord, I sighed with relief.

Basra was the final stop on our tour, but a flight delay left our aircraft sitting on the tarmac in Baghdad for two hours with front and rear doors open, and everyone smoking furiously. The Singapore experience had left me with a slight fear of flying, but the flight passed without incident and we landed safely in the big southern port, 55 kilometres (34 miles) upstream from the Gulf proper.

Basra lies on the Shatt al-Arab waterway formed by the confluence of the Tigris and the Euphrates flowing through the southern Iraqi marshlands. A maze of canals once criss-crossed the town earning it the sobriquet 'Venice of the Middle East,' but like Bangkok, the city had lost much of its charm when the waterways were filled for motorised traffic.

Basra is an extremely old settlement, founded in the early eighth century by the Umayyad Caliph Umar bin Abdul-Aziz, becoming a thriving cultural centre under Hārūn al-Rashīd only to decline along with the Abbasid caliphate, in the mid-thirteenth century. Then occupied by Portugal, which controlled much of the Gulf by the fifteenth century, it passed to the Ottoman Turks before being taken by British troops in 1914, and again during the disputed allied occupation of Iraq in 2003.

Nothing remained of its historic sites except for a few houses whose lattice-worked *mashrabiehs* overlooked a canal in the Shanasheel district. These enclosed balconies projecting over the street, preserve the privacy of women who can see out, but are concealed from public gaze. They also provide shade when temperatures in the delta reach 48°Celsius (118°F), accompanied by intense humidity.

I was delighted by these grand old dames, but attempting to get out of the car to take a picture, I was stopped by the driver who locked my door. When I tried to open a window to attract the boys who were already outside with Abu Kater, he locked this as well. I found his actions incomprehensible until I caught Abu Kater looking at me. Obviously he felt the Shanasheel painted a shabby face of Iraq and the driver was acting on his instructions.

We were spending the night at the Shatt al-Arab Hotel built in the

HOUSES IN THE SHANASHEEL DISTRICT OF BASRA, 1980

1930s to accommodate passengers using Imperial Airways eastern service to Karachi, via Cairo and Basra. The biplane flying boats, flown by pilots in an open cockpit and with a radio operator seated among the passengers, used to land on the river where a launch ferried them ashore.

How pleasant it would have been to reminisce with someone over cocktails. Of Basra in the old days, when big ocean-going *booms* were moored on the Shatt al-Arab, of bars filled with sailors from all over the world …. of the music of the Zunuj—black musicians from Zanzibar… of lemon-sellers pushing their street-carts along while crying '*limoun, limoun*'… of the bewitching, faintly erotic odour of dates and drains.

It was not to be. Arriving hot and upset after the Shanasheel incident, I asked the barman for a soft drink, but there was only tea or river water. A glass cabinet in the foyer displayed what Basra apparently considered were luxuries: a bottle of White Horse whisky, a packet of Camel cigarettes and a tin of that goddamn Chinese corned beef. The only local product was a box of Babylon Lion Dates, but dates are not hard to find in Basra with its wall-to-wall palms, which Ibn Battūtah had remarked on during

WALL-TO-WALL DATE PALMS IN THE SOUTHERN PORT OF BASRA, 1980

his visit to the river port in 1327: '…We travelled on waterways through an uninterrupted garden of … overshadowing palm groves to the right and left, with traders sitting in the shade of the trees, selling bread, fish, dates, milk and fruit …' I had no appetite for supper. Instead, I wrote home on a fly-spotted postcard bought in Shenasheel: it was Sunday 24 February 1980.

Back in Baghdad, Abu Kater left without a word and thank God that was the end of him. I shed no tears for the Australians either, but at least they had the courtesy to say goodbye.

The next day I took a taxi to the Iraq National Museum, founded by the British archaeologist Gertrude Bell who spoke both Farsi and Arabic. Finally I could feast my eyes on treasures from Mesopotamia. And evidently satisfied I could do no harm, the minder sat on the steps smoking a cigarette, leaving me free to explore alone.

Except for my footsteps, the museum was deathly quiet. I passed the Warka Vase, a giant alabaster vessel engraved with processions of naked men bearing offerings to Inana, the Sumerian goddess of love and war. Glass cases displayed ancient pottery and sculptures, cuneiform tablets from Sumerian and Babylonian times, and stunning stone reliefs from the palace of the Assyrian king, Sargon II at Khorsabad. Among this abundance of priceless objects, I wanted to find the golden lyre from the burial chamber of Queen Pu-Abi, who lived in the celebrated city of Ur.[25]

Excavation of the royal tombs by the famous archaeologist Sir Leonard Woolley[26] in 1929 had discovered a munificence of grave goods: a headdress made of golden leaves, extravagant necklaces and belts, a chariot adorned with lioness heads in silver, and golden rings and bracelets. The legendary lyre had been found standing upright against a wall of the pit and beside it lay the bodies of thirteen maidservants—retainers sacrificed to serve their mistress in another world.

'It would seem,' said Sir Leonard 'as if the last player had her arm over the harp, certainly she played till the end.'

Suddenly picked out by a shaft of sunlight, I saw the lyre encrusted with lapis lazuli and with the gold-bearded bull on the front representing Shamash, the sun-god. Hopeless at anything musical, I shivered with excitement as I imagined Sumerian fingers plucking its strings some five thousand years ago.

My thoughts were interrupted by the minder creeping up behind me. In order to reach Hatra before dusk, he indicated we had to leave. He was the same man who had shadowed me since my arrival. The only time he spoke during the 290 kilometre (180 mile) journey north was when we passed Tikrit.

'Saddam Hussein,' he jerked a finger at the town where Saddam was born in 1937 and where Saladin, with whom the Iraqi president liked to compare himself, had been born eight hundred years earlier.

We reached Hatra just before sunset to find we were not alone. Watched by a guardian wrapped in a sheepskin greatcoat were two people wandering about the ruins. Drawing level, they gave quick bows; a Japanese couple, they had also driven up from Baghdad to visit the historic site on the windswept steppes of the Ninawa governorate.

Hatra, originally an important caravanserai on the trade routes between Mesopotamia and the Mediterranean, grew into a permanent settlement under the Parthian empire of ancient Persia, becoming the capital of an

THE GREAT TEMPLE DEDICATED TO SHAMASH, THE SUPREME GOD OF HATRA

independent Arab kingdom around the third century BCE. Heavily fortified by a double set of walls reinforced by more than a hundred towers, the city had deflected repeated attack by Roman legions, eventually falling to Sassanid armies around 241.

Archaeologists did not visit Hatra until the twentieth century when they were astonished to find a fusion of Hellenistic, Parthian and Asian architecture, as distinct from the pure Roman style of other cities in the Middle East.

Scattered over a wide area, the ruins are dominated by a great temple dedicated to Shamash, the supreme god of Hatra. Inside, I confronted a tall statue of a woman, obviously a person of some importance, but a sign simply read: Statue of Abu, daughter of Dimion, 200 BCE. The curious aspect was the position of her right hand. It was held in the classic *abhaya mudra*[27] posture of the Buddha, emphasising the blend of religions and cultures existing in Hatra.

As night fell, I wondered where we were to stay. The big city of Mosul was not far away, but our accommodation was a spartan rest house. My room was unheated and in an effort at keeping warm, I wore the fox fur to bed and placed a floor mat over the blanket.

Half-frozen, I rose early to find the Japanese couple already seated for breakfast on a wooden table in a bare concrete room resembling a large

STATUE OF ABU, DAUGHTER OF
DIMION, 200 BCE IN HATRA

prison cell. I was very hungry, and sweet milky tea, a dead baguette and apricot jam were not very inviting before another day of travel with my minder.

'*Mumkin zebdeh?*'—is there any butter? I asked the guardian who looked tortured at having had to get up at this hour: six o'clock.

'You can hardly expect butter out here,' said the Japanese man in perfect English.

Half-starved, I was now also utterly humiliated. I admonished myself as we set off back to the Iraqi capital. Halfway there, the minder pointed at a golden dome rising above a dun-coloured city spread across the featureless plain.

'Samarra,' he said as the driver turned off the tarmac in that direction.

With Kerbala and Najaf, Samarra is one of the three sacred Shi'ite cities of Iraq. It was founded by the Caliph Abu Ishaq 'Abbas al-Mu'tasim following riots among Mamluk slaves in Baghdad and remained the seat of Abbasid government until 892. Its Great Mosque, of which only the crumbling wall and a unique spiral minaret remain, was once the largest in the world, covering an astonishing 38,000 square metres (409,041 square feet).

I had not asked to visit Samarra, whose name comes from the Arabic *sarr man ra'a*—a joy to behold—a reference to the al-Askarī shrine containing the mausoleum of Hasan al-Askarī the eleventh Shi'a imam, as well as the shrine of Muhammed al-Mahdi—the 'Hidden Imam'—whom Shi'a believe will return one day and save the world. The minder, a Shi'a wanted to pray, I concluded.

Forbidden to enter, I watched him prepare for worship, when not for the first time, I was struck by the unselfconscious devotion by those of Muslim persuasion. He performed *wudu* in strict order: rinsing his face and slicking back his hair, cleaning out his ears with his fingers, sniffing water, then blowing it out, washing his arms up to the elbows and finally his feet. Thoroughly purified, he then stood up and followed other pilgrims inside.

Left to myself, I decided the best place to photograph Samarra was from the top of the spiral minaret, but as I was walking towards it, alerted by our driver, the minder came running out of the shrine to join me. Higher and higher we climbed up the ramp winding counter-clockwise around the tower until finally, I was standing right on top, but there were no safety railings. I'd felt fine coming up. Now the line from John O'Hara's *Appointment in Samarra* flashed through my mind: '… I was jostled by a woman in the crowd and when I turned, I saw it was Death that jostled me …'

Paranoia is a terrible affliction. Derived from the Greek word *paranous*, it is a state of mind where rationale takes flight, but I'd been hounded so much in Iraq: my treatment by Abu Kater and the fact that the Iraqis hadn't expected a photojournalist in the first place. Why did the minder want to climb the minaret? Because he intended to kill me! When this conviction took hold, I was off running. And as I ran round and round down the tower, I remembered a night at Covent Garden Underground, when instead of taking the elevator, I'd run down the stairs. Down, down, all the way down, to arrive on the station platform feeling dizzy, and just like now in Samarra, more than a little silly.

My return to London coincided with the screening of the television film, *Death of a Princess*. I sank into a comfortable cane chair. Samarra seemed far away. Samarra was far away…

The brief, sad life of the Saudi Princess, Masha'il bint Fahd Āl Saūd, 1958-77 is well documented.

The granddaughter of the older brother of King Khalid, she had been educated in Beirut where she fell in love, and began an affair with the nephew of the Saudi ambassador to Lebanon. On their return to Saudi Arabia, the lovers were caught and tried under Sharia law. It states that a person can only be convicted on the testimony of four male witnesses, or in the event of no witnesses—as was the case of the nineteen-year-old princess—by admission of their own guilt in stating three times: 'I have committed adultery.' The girl's family had begged her not to confess and instead to promise never to see her lover again. When she refused and pleaded guilty, her head was struck off in a Riyadh car park: '*Princess Executed for Love*,' announced the British press.

After watching the film, I attacked the typewriter. My article stressed the gap between the emancipated women of Iraq and Saudi women whom current laws still ban from driving, or travelling abroad without a male family companion. Under the heading, *They Behead Princesses Don't They?*, the story was published in the *Irish Independent* using a pseudonym to safeguard my own neck.

'The executioner turned the sword upside down so the blunt end struck the fellow's neck. He hit him once, twice, three times, before reversing the blade and slicing off his head with a single stroke,' said a truck driver I met in Doha, forced to witness an execution in Riyadh by the notorious *mutawwai'n*—Saudi religious police from the Commission for the Promotion of Virtue and the Prevention of Vice.

***

The Iraqis had evidently been pleased with my story for on 16 July 1981, I was again waiting for bus 33 to take me to Hammersmith, and thence on the Piccadilly Line to Heathrow. On this occasion, we were not merely three, but three hundred journalists invited to cover the anniversary of the Ba'athist Socialist revolution that put Iraq on its nationalist path. I had several commissions, but the most important was to obtain a cover photograph of the Iraqi president for the Lebanese-owned magazine *8 Days*.

Saddam Hussein had been scheduled to place a wreath on the Tomb of the Unknown Soldier at 9am on the 'Glorious 17th' (the armed revolution that overthrew the government on 17 July 1968).

For some reason the foreign press was not invited to this event, but determined to get my picture, I slipped out of the hotel to find my way to the monument. I had no map, but I remembered vaguely where it was from my visit with Abu Kater. If I fail in other areas, I'm a wizard at directions. Who saved us when our Land Cruiser crashed over a dune in the Wahiba Sands in Oman? Habitually plotting landmarks, I was able to guide my driver, who lived in Muscat and had never visited the desert, to a Bedouin camp-site where I bathed our injuries with well water.

Clearly millions had been spent on bunting to brighten up the Iraqi capital, but with people rising late during Ramadan, there were few pedestrians and little traffic. After nearly an hour wandering about, I spotted a small crowd of military personnel, ambassadors, high-ranking bureaucrats and police gathered around the monument on Saadoun Street.

'You can't stand here,' said an official when I joined them.

'*Sahafia!*' I spat out the Arabic word for journalist.

THE REVOLUTION DAY PARADE IN ADDIS ABABA, 13 SEPTEMBER 1975

GODE CAMP FOR FAMINE VICTIMS IN THE OGADEN REGION OF ETHIOPIA, 1975

OTTOMAN FAMILY TOMBS IN CAIRO, 1993

MUHAMMAD AND RAOUF SAFE IN
ALEXANDRIA, AFTER DISHDABA, 1964

A TOURIST BAR IN HURGHADA, 2010

THE ONLY PHOTO FROM DISHDABA, 1964

QUEEN ELIZABETH IS RECEIVED AT RIYADH AIRPORT BY BY KING KHALID, 1979

A TRADER IN MUTTRAH SOUQ IN THE SULTANATE OF OMAN, 1975

THE SPIRAL MINARET IN SAMARRA, 1980

THE FABLED BULLS-HEAD LYRE IN UR, 1980

THE 'GLORIOUS 17TH' IN BAGHDAD BUT NO SIGN OF SADDAM HUSSEIN, 1981

TOWER HOUSES IN AL-HAJJAH, YEMEN, 1981

POOR MEN CHEWING *QAT* IN A BACKSTREET OF SANA'A, 1981

THE BEGGAR WOMAN AT THE BAHA-UD-DIN ZAKARIYA SHRINE IN MULTAN, 1997

A BLUE MAN NEAR MERZOUGA IN THE DEEP SOUTH OF MOROCCO, 1990

HIDE-AND-SEEK IN ZAGORA, 1990

A PASSAGE IN FEZ EL-BALI, 2010

Inflight on Pakistan International

16 Oct. 8

Dear Mum,

Just a note to say I will be thinking of you tomorrow on my birthday and all you have done for me during my time on earth! It has all been greatly appreciated and though you may not have thought so at times, I have always listened to your advice. Most of which has been jolly good advice to follow through the undercurrents of life.

Anyhow, tomorrow I turn 40 in Rawalpindi. Who would have predicted such a place? The weather could not be more beautiful — about 80 and fresh at night. I have been invited to dinner by the same man who sent me the cake in 1978. He and his wife are jolly wonderful friends: so I shall have a birthday dinner — in Islamabad (the capital about 20 kms. away).

p.s. A little from Julie.

PIA

The only foreign photographer, indeed the only woman present, meant a struggle to stand my ground. To move at all would have indicated weakness, so with my blue denim hat pulled well down over my eyes, I stood rigid in the rising sun. As the day grew hotter, first one general, then another, moved into the shadow cast by the monument. In dark suits and ties, the ambassadors mopped their brows, and I noticed the wreath of orange gladioli reserved for the monument was beginning to wilt.

Nine o'clock passed, then ten o'clock, and weighed down with medals, a general buckled at the knees. I too was feeling faint when at 10.20am a telephone rang in a blacked-out Mercedes. The message was evident: after keeping Iraq's diplomatic corps waiting for more than two hours, Saddam Hussein would not appear. Instead, his brother-in-law, Defence Minister Adnan Khairallah (who was to die in a mysterious helicopter explosion in 1989) joined by a grim-faced General Abdel Jabbah Shenshal, Commander-in-Chief of the Armed Forces of Iraq, placed the dead wreath on the cenotaph and we all dispersed.

Back at the hotel, I took off my dripping clothes, washed them in the bath and placed them on the windowsill. They were dry in an hour and in the bar that evening, I learnt the temperature had touched 49° Celsius (120.4°F), causing a roll of Ektachrome film to turn brown in my camera bag.

The bar was crowded with correspondents from every conceivable newspaper, both east and west, but I seemed to be the only woman and looking around, I caught the eye of a clean-shaven young Arab journalist wearing a white open-necked shirt, blue jeans and Nike trainers.

'Would you like to join me for dinner?' He came over and extended a hand. 'They serve the best *masgouf*[28] in Baghdad in the restaurant across the road. Hi, my name is Ali Abid, I work for *Al Zawra*.' He smiled broadly.

Entire families were seated under the trees eating *masgouf* with bread and salad when we arrived, but our meal was abruptly interrupted when a taxi hit two men crossing the road the impact projecting their bodies into the restaurant garden. I got up to see if there was anything I could do, but neither man had a pulse and other diners quickly picked up the bodies and tossed them into a passing taxi.

'Don't concern yourself,' said Ali when I returned to our table. A 32-year-old bachelor, he was more interested in discussing women than anything either political or cultural about Iraq.

'Iraqi girls are not as liberated as they think. It's very hard to meet them and sex is a problem,' he sighed.

'I once had a holiday in Bali where I met many Australian girls. I liked them. They were fat and we like our women fat. But now Iraqi girls all try to be thin like you. You are 55 kilos (121 pounds),' he said cheekily.

'I bet an Iraqi woman couldn't climb a minaret like I can, and carrying all this camera gear,' I told him.

'Yes, that's why I like Australian women.' He flicked the ash off a cigarette. 'They are very active.'

Sensing I was entering dangerous waters, I paid for my *masgouf* and left him to settle our drinks tab: two Sprites and three Araks.

We had now waited four days for the Iraqi president to hold a press conference, the formal preliminary to any government invitation. Disgusted by the poor organisation, most journalists had flown home. About sixty of us remained. The delay was particularly frustrating for the few freelancers and in my own case, I had only two days left before flying to Dubai to photograph development for an advertisement in *Time* magazine.

Sensing our growing irritation, the Ministry of Information arranged a bus trip for us to visit Babylon and Kerbala.

The capital of ten Mesopotamian dynasties, Babylon and its fabled 'Hanging Gardens' built by King Nebuchadnezzar II for his wife Amytis-of-Media, was one of the Seven Wonders of the Ancient World. With its palaces and monuments, many of them pure gold, and the Tower of Babel rising skywards, Babylon must have been a wonder to behold. Now, however, it was simply a small rural settlement. There was no evidence of its gardens, and Nebuchadnezzar's fabulous palace was reduced to mud-brick debris scattered along a bank of the Euphrates. I took some pictures of the Street of Processions and Ishtar's gate with its reliefs of a dragon, the symbol of Marduk, the supreme Babylonian god, but the journalists were waiting in the bus with the air-conditioning running, so I hurried to join them.

THE IMAM HUSAYN SHRINE IN THE SACRED SHI'ITE CITY OF KERBALA

In Kerbala, we moved up a thousand years to a city that witnessed momentous events in Islamic history that continue to impinge on Iraq today. There are two branches of Islam, the religion founded by the Prophet Muhammad in the seventh century. The Sunni branch believes that Muhammad's successors, the first four caliphs, are legitimate religious leaders, but the Shi'a schism only recognises heirs of the fourth caliph, Ali, the prophet's grandson, as his legitimate successors.

In the Muslim month of Muharram in 680, the Imam Husayn ibn 'Alī, his brother Abbas and their families and followers, had led a peaceful demonstration against the Umayyad caliphate on the plains outside Kerbala. In an historic battle, Husayn was killed and his head, spiked on a spear, was paraded before the successful army. Also beheaded were Abbas, Jaffer, Abdullah, Uthman, Muhammad, Abu Bak'r, Abdullah, Husain bin Ali, Abu Bak'r, Qasim, Hasan bin Ali, Oun, Muhammad, Jaffer Abdur Rahman, Abdullah, Abdullah bin Muslim and Muhammad bin Abee Sa'id—close relatives—all martyred like the Imam Husayn leaving Zulzinar, Husayn's bloodstained horse, to walk back revealing the massacre to the citizens of Kerbala.

The anniversary of the martyrdom of Husayn is commemorated annually by Shi'ite communities all over the world. Manifestations reach a climax on *Ashura*, the tenth day of *Muharram*, when processions of mourners slash themselves with whips and double-sided finger razors. I have photographed *Ashura* when 100,000 men marched through Karachi, splattering the streets with blood. I have also witnessed *Ashura* in Tooting Bec (south London) when the sound of Shi'a thumping their chests was audible a bus stop away, and the television news beams the ferocious Hezbollah paramilitary processions in Lebanon, into all our homes.

A sacred city for Shi'a pilgrims, the spiritual heart of Kerbala is the huge blue and gold tiled Husayn Shrine that is said to stand on the imam's grave. Since its construction in 684, a roll call of Muslim clerics added to, destroyed, and rebuilt the mosque: the caliphs Mansur, al-Mahdi, Hārūn al-Rashīd, and al-Mutawakkil, as well as the Safavid and Qajar shahs of Persia. An Indian sub-sect of Ismaili Shi'a Islam, the Daudi Bohras, presented the silver lattice screens around the tomb in 1939.

With people observing the fast, the streets around the mosque were silent when we arrived. There was no traffic, just a passing horse-cart carrying blocks of dripping ice. An elderly woman, exhausted by the heat, lay asleep on the pavement, while inside the courtyard, families sat in silent groups. People reading the Qur'an gave us barely a glance as, discarding our shoes, we were directed into the inner sanctum of the shrine where worshippers were pressed against the screen. Handed a black chador, I was allowed to photograph the scene, but it was one of those sensitive moments—similar to the occasion with the queen in Riyadh—when I considered the camera too intrusive.

On our way to lunch, there was an excited buzz in the bus about Najaf, the second holy Shi'ite city in Iraq containing the shrine of the Imam Ali whom Shi'a consider to be the first imam. Here, too, is the vast Wadi as-Salam cemetery where many holy men are buried and where every devout Shi'a aspires to be interred, close to Ali.

Najaf was especially tense due to the recent execution of the Grand Ayatollah Muhammad Bāqir al-Sadr, who claimed direct lineage to the Prophet through the seventh Shi'ite imam. A scholar of Islamic jurisprudence, philosopher, writer and co-founder member of the Islamist movement in Iraq, he had inevitably fallen foul of the Ba'athists, our hosts.

Following his support for Khomeini, Sadr and hundreds of Da'wa members had been executed. His sister Amina bint al-Huda's fiery discourse in the Imam Ali Mosque, urging people to rise up had also caused riots, not only in Najaf and Kerbala, but in Baghdad and Basra. al-Sadr had been released, but on 31 March 1980, the Revolutionary Command Council passed a law sentencing to death anyone connected with the Da'wa and along with his sister, he was re-arrested, tortured and hanged on 8 April 1980.

This event and the continued oppression of Shi'a in Najaf was a good story for the newsmen fed up with waiting for Saddam Hussein. More than 90,000 Iraqi Shi'a had been expelled to Iran in the past two years with Najaf reportedly the only town the Sunni president had never visited.

It was a good story, but the journalists did not consider it merited skipping lunch, instead they sat down to a table loaded with *mezze*. Standing on the steps of the rest-house, I watched *Times* correspondent Robert Fisk shoot off in a taxi and unable to afford to visit Najaf alone, I wished he had taken me along. But as luck would have it, a Palestinian journalist advised of a minibus driver willing to take a group to Najaf and I quickly rounded up six journalists: an Englishman, two Americans and three Italians, who were dressed more for a spree in Menton, than a visit to the pillar of Shi'a Islam.

We set off along the fringe of the Badiet es-Sham Desert, but rumbling along at barely 50 kmph (31 mph), we did not reach Najaf until late afternoon, the most difficult time of the dawn to dusk fast. Except for drooping horse-carriages, its streets were deserted and outside their shops, traders sat on mats waiting for *iftar*, when the town would come to life and eat.

Leaving my colleagues, I set off to look for the Imam Ali Shrine housing the sarcophagus of 'Ali ibn Abi Talib, the son-in-law of the Prophet, and the fourth caliph who was killed in Najaf in 661. Even without a guide, it was not hard to find as the gold-tiled dome dominated the surrounding flat-roofed houses. On reaching the gate, in my best few words of Arabic, I inquired of a custodian if I might go inside. I had come a long way. Would it be one of those maddening moments when I felt like tearing out my hair.

Hearing a foreign voice, a row of blind men seated against the wall started rattling their tins for alms and coming out of the shrine, a black-turbaned *mullah* inquired in excellent English whether I was a Muslim. When I said no, he snapped, 'Then go away.' It was apparent that had the government not stage-managed our visit to Kerbala, the reaction would have been similar.

Wandering through Najaf, I looked for a sign of life. The old town counted a population of some half a million people, but all were indoors and its ancient bazaar was shut. A funeral procession rounded a corner, men carrying a coffin and weeping, wailing women trailing behind— one of many faithful to expire when Ramadan falls during a Middle Eastern summer.

Retracing my steps to the bus, I found my colleagues in some distress. It seemed that no one in Najaf would sell them a drink.

'Can you help us?' asked Marco, one of the sweating Italians, who was wearing a red Hawaiian-type floral patterned shirt, white shorts, and a Panama hat. As the organiser of our trip to Najaf, I had suddenly become a mother provider. Asking the Palestinian to come as an interpreter, I went off again in search of water.

The first shopkeeper we encountered spat contemptuously on the pavement.

'*Nasrani*,'—Christian, he hissed.

'He is fasting,' said the Palestinian unnecessarily.

Finally we came upon a man seated outside a shuttered shoe shop and beside him, on an upended box, was a white enamel basin containing purple grapes. Most were withered, but I noticed, one or two bunches that looked edible.

'*As-salaam aleykum, bik kem?*'—peace be upon you, how much? I asked him.

Averting his head, the grape-seller waved a hand, whether because I was an infidel, a woman, or both, was not explained. Dropping a dinar in his dish, I selected the least unpleasant looking bunch and returned to the men. No one had located al-Sadr's old house; no one in Najaf had wanted to talk to them.

Later in London, I read Robert Fisk's exclusive report on the Najaf executions from the *Times*: '... The governor of Najaf, as I recall, leant towards me with a special eagerness. Yes, we hanged him he said, with a smile. And his sister. Legend has it, all too real I fear, that they burned off his beard with a cigarette lighter and hammered a nail into his eye before they hanged him...'

Back in Baghdad, we found Saddam Hussein was still playing a waiting game, but perhaps as compensation, he sent an official bearing gifts including a black plastic quartz clock with his photograph on the dial.

More journalists returned home. We were now only a small group intent on covering the Iran-Iraq war, started, without warning, by Iraq, on 20 September 1980. As the only person who had previously been to Baghdad, it was decided I should visit the Ministry of Foreign Affairs as our representative.

Entering the building, I inquired of the only official who had treated me courteously on the visit with Aussie boys.

'Where is Hamid?' I asked.

Standing up behind a dusty reception desk, a badly groomed security guard asked me to repeat the name.

'Hamid. I met him last time. Has he gone?'

He repeated the name to his friend.

'He's gone all right,' said the friend, and they both chuckled.

Escorted to the office of the new responsible, I was told to sit down and asked whether I wanted *sh'ay bi sukkar* (tea with sugar), *sh'ay nissf sukkar,* (tea with medium sugar), or *sh'ay sukkur kalil,* (tea with a little sugar)?

I had drunk my tea and was dozing off, when I was startled awake by a tall man in a tailored suit who shook my hand and ushered me into his office displaying the biggest portrait I'd yet seen of Saddam Hussein.

'The press may not like it, but we cannot take them to the border,' he told me earnestly. 'The situation is deadly serious. In the past ten months, we've lost 60,000 men.' Plucking a tissue from the box that every Arab official keeps on his desk, he blew his nose violently.

'Iran likes to take journalists to the front to impress them,' he continued. 'In Iraq, we have just held democratic elections so there is no need. Tell your colleagues that when the time is right, they will receive an invitation to the war.'

Ever fluid, the situation deteriorated after we left Baghdad. With his old enemy President Hafez Assad of Syria engaged in eliminating the Muslim Brotherhood, Saddam Hussein seized the opportunity to grab the offensive and Iraq launched a major thrust into Iran. His short-term objective was to annex the oil-rich province of Khuzestan and to retrieve the Gulf islands of the Thumbs from Iran, on behalf of their rightful owners, the Arab Emirates. A more far-reaching aim was to destabilise the detested Khomeini-led government in Tehran.

Despite the desperate tactics of chemical bombing and virus warfare, human wave attacks by devout Iranian fighters succeeded in driving back Iraqi positions around the time Saddam Hussein had understandably been too busy to receive us. The war no one would win was to continue until 1988, but following a new scorched-earth policy in 1982, Iraq managed to gain a slight upper hand, when the official was as good as his word.

That April, three hundred members of the international press received a letter, or a telephone call from their Iraqi Embassy, inviting them to witness the battle for Khorramshar, the big Iranian port city north of Abadan, but unfortunately for those who accepted, the invitation turned into a rout.

The advancing Iraqi infantry encountered Iranian-made Zulfiqar and British Chieftain tanks, and Baghdad Airport was closed following Iranian air strikes. Abandoned by their Iraqi minders, the foreign press had to exit the mess as best they could. The taxi-fare across the neutral zone to Kuwait suddenly tripled, while other drivers were heard to be charging vast sums to cross the desert to the Syrian capital, Damascus, a distance of 1,000 kilometres (623 miles).

I was working in Khartoum at the time, but on my return home, I found an unopened invitation to the war in my letterbox. I had ultimately left Baghdad, never having seen Saddam Hussein except for his picture plastered all over the city. As for the plastic clock, it stood on my fridge until 1994 when, in a fit of pique, a French lover smashed it to pieces.

Chapter 5

No Mocha in Mocha

I distinctly remember my first sight of a penis when a six-year-old attending kindergarten beneath St Augustine's Church in Neutral Bay. A southerly blowing off Sydney harbour was disturbing the rest hour and our teacher, a gentle, soft-bosomed lady we called Miss Rita, asked me to get up and close the banging door.

Reaching up for the big brass knob, I confronted a tousle-haired boy on his way to the toilet. He had his thumb in his mouth and a pink tadpole was poking out of his shorts, and transfixed by this unfamiliar part of the human anatomy, I allowed the heavy oak door to slam on my finger. Running back to my mat among the other children, I sobbed quietly into my little pillow while Miss Rita, unaware of anything amiss, continued reading her book, but ever since that hot afternoon in 1946, I still associate the penis with a degree of pain.

Over the years, I've occasionally wished I were a boy. Not for the penis per se, but for the freedom it allows a man, since reality for a woman traveller is that her sex presents constraints. I wanted to sail on Arab dhows like the French adventurer, Henri de Monfreid, and to follow in Wilfred Thesiger's tracks across the Empty Quarter: how wonderful to go on mountain walks like the travel writer Kevin Rushby and at sunset, to simply roll out your sleeping-bag under a tree.

'Not leave Sana'a,' announced the immigration officer at Sana'a International Airport.

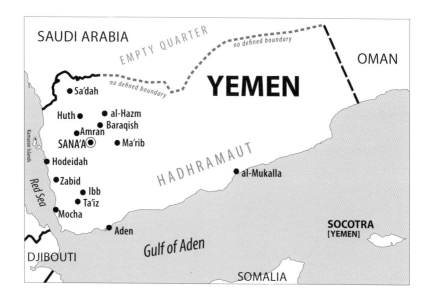

Oh dear, already a setback. I'd come to North Yemen to research some travel articles, but I couldn't leave the capital without permission and I would learn soon enough, there were some places, scattered with the ruins of ancient civilisations, where I could not go at all.

The history of Southern Arabia (present-day Yemen) centres on ancient tribal kingdoms and their struggles to control the lucrative caravan routes. Especially caravans carrying frankincense and myrrh. And while essentially traders, the South Arabian peoples were also exceptional builders of fortified cities, temples and irrigation works: the Ma'rib Dam, built by the Sabaean Kingdom about the seventh century BCE is considered one of the engineering wonders of antiquity.

This strategic part of the Arabian landmass at the mouth of the Red Sea was to experience constant invasion. The Axumites from Ethiopia, the Sassanid Persians, the Egyptian Mamluks and Ottoman Turks all occupied the country dubbed Arabia Felix by a Roman expedition in 24 BCE. Originally pagan, worshipping the sun and the moon, under the Axumite kings many people adopted Christianity, but when local Himyarite rulers converted to Judaism, this became the official state religion, until overwhelmed by Islam in the seventh century.

The domestic history of North Yemen is a tangled mix of religious and tribal conflict that continues to this day. In the tenth century, it fell under control of the Zaidi imams, a Shi'ite sub-sect embedded in the north and on the central plateau, contested by the Shafis, orthodox Sunni Muslims, inhabiting the western mountain slopes and the Tihama coastal plain. The Mamluk sultans briefly occupied Sana'a, the Zaidi capital in 1516, but expelled from the interior by the Imam al-Qasim ibn Muhammad (Qasim the Great) in 1636, the Turks subsequently only retained a toehold on the coast.

With the collapse of the Ottoman Empire in 1918, the Imam Yahya Muhammad Hamid al-Din established the Mutawakkilite Kingdom of Yemen beginning forty-four years of absolute rule when no one could enter the country without his permission, and he alone had to sanction all requisitions. The repression continued under Yahya's son, Ahmed bin Yahya on whose death in 1962, a pro-Egyptian military coup overthrew his successor and declared the Yemen Arab Republic.

This convoluted history of invasion and isolation explains the xenophobia characteristic of Yemen. It is the reason why people locked themselves away in fortified settlements on the high mountain ridges and why many Yemenis still harbour an inherent suspicion of visitors— a similar reaction to islanders, who question the motives of anyone stepping ashore on their sacred plot in the sea.

The process leading to the division of Yemen began when Britain occupied the southern port of Aden in 1839. As well as seeking a secure base on the eastern sea lanes, British interests lay in safeguarding the country's flank against Turkish expansionism. An agreement was reached whereby Britain would guarantee protection in return for the loyalty of the independent sheikhdoms and subsequently known as the Federation of Arab Emirates of the South, the region was administered as a Crown Colony from Bombay, between 1937 and 1967.

A violent liberation struggle against British rule had reached a peak when the Italian liner *Galileo Galilei* carrying 1,594 young Australians, on their way to Europe, docked in Aden on 3 January 1964.

Hanging over the rails, we were so excited by our first Arab country, an enthusiasm that quickly cooled. Huddled around a barren mountain, it was as unsightly as a place could be. It was also filthy. Wandering into the café where I was eating lunch, a goat had rubbed its bottom on the roller-towel beside the washbasin. Other girls returned to the ship with stories of 'wogs'[29] selling 'Spanish fly', while a boy from Brisbane, who'd paid a fortune for a leather camel, on discovering it was stuffed with soiled hospital bandages, hurled it into the Gulf of Aden.

When I arrived in 1980, there were two separate Yemens: the Yemen Arab Republic (North Yemen) and the Marxist-leaning People's Democratic Republic of South Yemen, declared in 1970. North Yemen, where an airport sign said NO QAT CHEWING, was one of the world's poorest countries. At this time, there was no newspaper, no tourist industry and life expectancy for women was only forty-four years.

I joined other passengers off the Yemenia Airways flight for the shared taxi ride into Sana'a. They included a woman with a blue patterned textile like a tablecloth draped over her head and two small men wearing *futas* (short, wrap-around skirts), sports jackets, silver daggers, and stacked heel shoes. On the outskirts of town, I was startled by the sight of a bare-chested foreigner jogging past in red lycra shorts. I think we all were. Further on, the scene reversed as three women in black, wearing scarlet masks, scurried across the road.

'*Funduq kebir*,' said the driver dropping me at the Sheraton Sana'a, North Yemen's first international hotel aimed at foreign businessmen. There were no tourists and calling at the Ministry of Information next day, I discovered there were no brochures, maps, or anything for visitors but Erhard Noreisch, the genial manager of the Sheraton offered to help wherever possible. That afternoon his sales manager Najib had a meeting downtown and I accompanied him for my first look at Sana'a.

'The Old City is through there. You'll be perfectly safe,' he said, dropping me at the Bab al-Yemen and driving off.

Finding myself alone in an alien world, for a while I stood there watching men pushing barrows loaded with dung and boys carrying bundles of *futas,* passing in and out of the gate. When a legless man, propelling himself along in a box on wheels joined the stream, I took a big breath and followed him through the wall.

THE OLD CITY OF SANA'A, INHABITED FOR 2,500 YEARS

A marriage of Walt Disney and Alice in Wonderland, the Old City of Sana'a was like nothing I'd ever seen. All around and above me were hundreds of fudge-coloured tower-houses whose architecture was emphasised by their height: some were eight stories tall. Their construction, the lower levels stone, the upper floors of brick using mud mortar, is a building technique inherited from Sabaean masons, the exuberant decoration being an equal tribute to local skills. Geometric patterns in gypsum highlighted every window and cornice; it was if a pastry chef had sprayed white icing in every direction. Indeed many looked good enough to eat. I passed mosques and *hammams* tucked away among buildings packed so close together, they blocked out the sun. The lintels of many doors, now below street level, indicated their age, in some cases more than a thousand years old. Donkey carts bumped along in a nimbus of dust, a thump of water pumps came from hidden gardens and from somewhere in this mysterious urban labyrinth, I heard children chanting verses from the Qur'an.

It was 5pm and the Old City souq was awakening from a torpor induced by chewing the leaves of *qat*, the evergreen shrub I'd encountered in Harar. Shutters banged open and shopkeepers arranged baskets of dates, limes, barley, lentils and spices outside in the narrow streets. I passed the foreman of the Coffee-Growers Guild weighing hessian sacks of shiny brown beans, a farmer unwrapping withered tobacco leaves, and turbaned merchants unloading baskets of dried fish trucked up from the coast.

A market depot for Yemeni farmers since time immemorial, the souq was once known for jewellery and polished gemstones, especially agate. The Jewish silversmiths had long since departed, but I passed potters, blacksmiths, carpenters and craftsmen making *jambias,* an essential accessory to male dress. In Souq al-Janabi, I watched a man shaping a dagger using a foot-driven grinding wheel. When I addressed him, he explained in halting English that the angle a *jambia* is worn indicated the status of the wearer.

'Sheikhs and *qadis,* religious scholars, wear the handle to the right. Tribesmen,' he indicated his own dagger, 'just below the navel. Old *jambia* with rhinoceros horn handle cost maybe ten thousand dollars.'

I passed shops stocking antimony, frankincense and sandalwood. Others sold incense burners, brass ewers and alabaster oil lamps. Their dusty patina made them look antique, but I decided they were genuine as with no tourists, fake Indian imports had not yet flooded in. Suddenly I was again transfixed by a penis. This one was python-sized, curling round the thigh of a spice seller who had let his *futa* slip. Eyes glazed, he was masticating *qat* like the *jambia* maker, the salt merchant and other traders in the souq. When he leant over to spit a stream of green slime into the street, the member disappeared from view.

As the sun settled behind the mountains, I left the old for the new. Aside from the Central Bank of Yemen and a glass building housing Yemenia, there was little development outside the city walls—a few small food stores and pharmacies, but no familiar shops or takeaways. I passed groups of women wearing black pleated skirts and capes walking home from afternoon social gatherings. Tribesmen strolled by linking fingers, a gentle gesture common in many Muslim countries. Outside Bab al-Yemen, a few youths sat astride spanking new motorbikes: occasionally one gunned up and raced along the street, scattering goats munching on discarded *qat* stalks. At dusk, the call to prayer, echoed from more than a hundred mosques in Sana'a. Most began on time, others were seconds out so that

MY DRIVER MOHAMMED
CHEWING *QAT*

for more than a minute the words came from every angle—*Allahu Akbar.
Ashhad-a-la ilaha-illa Allah; Ashhad-anna-Muhammad-rasool-Allah.*

To my great surprise next morning, the Ministry of Information sent
a car to show me the local sights. Its driver, Mohammed, was a typical
Yemeni, slim, short and dark and wearing a jambia on a wide, gold-
embroidered belt. Asif, the guide who spoke good English, favoured
western style jeans and gym boots. Our first stop was the Jami' al-Kebir,
one of the oldest mosques in Islam and esteemed as one of the most
important monuments in Yemen.

'Its site was chosen personally by the Prophet,' [30] said Asif. 'To ensure
its prayer niche was aligned with Mecca.'

An inscription revealed its construction as 753, but there seemed no
reason to doubt the story. Some of the capitals, cut with a cross, were
clearly filched from an earlier cathedral, built when Yemen was annexed
by the Axumite kings of Ethiopia.

We moved on to the Dar es-Shukr (House of Gratefulness), a former
residence of the imam's brother converted into a National Museum. Its
exhibits included human figurines—offerings to pre-Islamic deities—and

a bronze statue of a warrior wearing a lion-skin cloak, found at Ma'rib, the capital of the Sabaean Kingdom, (8th century BCE to 275 CE). I found the displays fascinating, but Mohammed and Asif were agitated. It was midday: time to buy their *qat* which some eighty percent of the male population chews every afternoon, costing the country millions of lost working hours a day.

'*Kum namla wa takul sukr*—work like an ant and you'll eat sugar,' said Asif quoting a Yemeni proverb. He laughed. 'But we prefer *qat*.'

The *qat* market was swarming with tribesmen picking over the bushes like a plague of locusts. Vendors were yelling out prices and buyers were bargaining as if their lives depended on it: it was a stock exchange for leaves. Mohammed scrutinised a bundle, then breaking off a rose-pink leaf tip, he popped it into his mouth.

'*Tammam*.' He gave a thumbs-up sign.

Analysis of the *Catha edulis* leaf reveals sugar, considerable amounts of tannin, and cathine, an alkaloid related to nor-ephedrine that induces a mild euphoria, giving the chewer his so-called 'kick'.

'It makes you feel on top of the world,' shouted Asif, who was debating the cost of a bunch of *shami*, the best and most expensive of some forty-four varieties of *qat* originating from different regions, but mainly from the central highlands. 'But it depresses the appetite, so now we must eat lunch.' He stood on tiptoe to look for Mohammed.

Yemen has an ageless cuisine, a melting pot of ingenuity augmented by centuries of traders and invaders adding new ingredients. *Saltah*, a soup prepared from meat, eggs, chillies and tomatoes and topped with a dollop of frothy green *helba* (made from fenugreek seeds) is eaten ritually at lunchtime by all *qat* chewers.

'The best in Sana'a is served here,' said Asif as we stopped outside a hole in a wall into which some enterprising person had stuffed tables and chairs.

Mohammed bought some bread from a woman selling it off a tray on her head and going inside, we found the only vacant table: right in front of where the chef was cooking. Perched on a rocky ledge, he was ladling steaming broth into stone bowls for a helper—using iron tongs, to carry across to the customers, all of whom were men.

A problem was the tight arrangement of the tables. This meant that the only way for newcomers to reach a seat in the rear was to walk across the tops of the ones in front. More diners entered and after hanging their *jambias* on a hook, they hopped up and strode right across our table where we were eating. The *saltah* was excellent, but I found this disconcerting and with the port-a-gas stoves turned on full blast, and everyone shouting for his order, I was relieved to pay our bill and step outside again.

'*Saltah* makes *qat* taste better,' said Asif, patting his stomach.

The streets were now eerily quiet. Rich merchants had retired to chew in a *mafraj,* the room-with-a-view on top of a house and reserved for this purpose. Poor men were slumped in doorways with their bundles of leaves and plastic bottles of mineral water. Only the juice is swallowed and stored in the cheek, a wad of masticated *qat* is an ugly sight, almost like a facial tumour.

'*Qat* makes you thirsty and you can't do it,' Asif said as we drove back to the Sheraton.

'Can't do what?' I asked. Then I understood. When the high wears off, the chewer feels morose and is unable to perform the sexual act for several hours.

The good news was that the Ministry of Information, having evidently decided I was not a spy, had arranged for me to visit Ma'rib, capital of the Kingdom of Saba—the biblical Sheba—175 kilometres (108 miles) east of the capital. I was delighted, and pleased with yesterday's sightseeing, I decided to reward the men with a bottle of wine from the Sheraton bar.

'*Sabah alkhair,*' I said, settling into the back seat of the old Mercedes. 'Here is a small present for your afternoon *qat* session.'

Accepting the bottle, Asif unscrewed the cap and took a long swig. He passed it to Mohammed who took a longer swig and returned it to Asif. It was nine o'clock in the morning and our visit to Ma'rib was doomed. I wanted to find the remains of the fabled dam whose collapse in the sixth century saw the irrigated farmland revert to dust, but Ma'rib was deserted and Mohammed, who was giggling, said he'd never heard of the Queen of Sheba.

'Bilqis?' I used her Arabic name, popular for Yemeni girls. But it was a great joke. Even Asif thought it was funny.

Across the wadi, five columns poking out of the sand recalled a fragment of altar I'd once seen in the British Museum: *Sabaean, 6th century BCE. Likely from Ma'rib*, read its caption. Could that be the Bar'an Temple, known as *Arsh Bilqis*—the Queen of Sheba's throne? I was left wondering.

Treat it as a reconnaissance trip, I told myself as we slowly weaved our way back to Sana'a. And when you return to Yemen, visit Ma'rib with a professional guide.

At the Sheraton, I was informed that Mr Noreisch had found me a ride with a businessman going to Hodeidah, the main town on the Tihama. I could use Hodeidah as a base to explore and find my own way back by bus, or taxi. I did not have permission to leave Sana'a, but who was to know?

My driver, Mr Haideri, was looking to invest in Hodeidah ahead of a new port development. A pleasant, middle-aged man, he was also rare in not indulging in the *qat* habit.

'Ha, *qat* is wicked,' he said. 'Our revered poet Mohammed Mahmud al-Zubairi has likened it to the devil. I know men who spend ten times more on the leaf than on their families.'

'How many children have you?' I asked politely.

He held up four fingers of which the third displayed a large agate ring.

'I once met a Syrian farmer with twenty-one children who told me he was angry with his wife as she wouldn't stop having them,' I said.

'Ha,' said Mr Haideri, lifting a hand off the wheel, 'but I know about this thing you wear.'

'I read the average number of children per family here is seven. And your infant mortality rate is 77.2 percent per 1000 births,' I said.

'So much still bad, poor diet and most women have no access to health care. Look.' He gestured towards the mountain peaks. 'How do you bring supplies to those villages?'

'I think baby clothes would be a good business,' I announced. 'I've seen so many women with kids in Sana'a, but there's not a single children's wear shop.'

'Ha, good idea,' said Mr Haideri. 'Bring some samples when you come back from London. I'll be your local partner. *Insha'allah.*'

We were headed towards the Haraz Mountains whose highest peak, Jebel an-Nabi Shu'ayb is 3,760 metres (12,333 feet) above sea level. The road would climb up to the central plateau, then climb again, before descending in a series of giddy bends to the coast. Although Hodeidah is only 240 kilometres (148 miles) from Sana'a, the journey was to take us all day due to twenty-three roadblocks, where soldiers scrutinised my passport.

The rugged interior of Yemen is dotted with tall stone houses either built against the mountain flanks, or perched in clusters on the misty peaks. Several I saw were seven stories tall, true medieval skyscrapers.

'Most villages have electricity, but women have to make a daily trip down to the valley for water. They go together as gossip relieves the chore,' said Mr Haideri, stopping on a ridge where far below a group was gathered around a spring.

Flat land was rare. Every piece was cultivated with coffee and *qat*, sometimes growing on alternate terraces separated by dry-stone walls splashed with scarlet dock. Other decorative flora, pink thistles, blue star-like flowers and wild white Abyssinian roses, covered the rocky hillsides. Getting out, I became caught up in a mauve shrub, coiled like barbed-wire, that Mr Haideri kindly untangled from my trousers.

As we began the descent from Upper Yemen, the sky turned sepia-coloured and after a flash of lightning, it began to rain. At first as big drops, but following a clap of thunder, the sky emptied like the Ma'rib Dam. Local farmers consider rain *baraka* (blessing), but a downpour flushes away soil from their mountain terraces.

The Tihama coast is a fusion of Arabia and Africa, although its African genes are not strictly negroid, but Hamitic from Ethiopia. People are brown, the women go unveiled, and everyone wears the high-crowned *zillah* hat against soaring summer temperatures.

'This is the first rain in Hodeidah for eleven years,' beamed the receptionist at the two-star hotel recommended by Mr. Haideri.

'I am Tefnut, the goddess of rain.' I smiled grimly because rain, along with security men, is the enemy of a travel photographer.

On occasions, after months of planning a trip and flying to the other side of the world, I have arrived to find my subject awash in floodwater. In Muttrah souq one evening, a wall of water from the wadi rolled through it like a tsunami. One minute it was ankle-deep, the next it was over my knees, and had a man not helped me into his perfume shop, I would have been washed into the harbour along with walking-sticks, kitchen pots and moneychangers.

While signing the registration book, I noticed a faded black-and-white photograph on the wall above the desk. It depicted three fishermen and a blond man standing beside a huge hammerhead shark. Tiny writing in a corner read: *Mit freundlichen Grüßen aus Rolf, Hodeidah 1960* and I wondered what Rolf might have been doing in Hodeidah twenty years ago. Could he have been an anthropologist studying the coastal tribes, or an ichthyologist charting Red Sea fishes? Or was he simply a traveller like Eric Hansen, whose yacht was wrecked off the Kamaran archipelago, at the southern end of the Red Sea in 1978.

'Room 10,' said the receptionist handing me a key.

The bed in room 10 was made up with an orange throw. The linoleum was red and the curtains were brown with dust, but the room was adequate for a few days stay and I found the shower worked. *Alhamdulillah.* Unpacking the few items I'd brought from Sana'a, I hung two cotton shirts on a bent wire coat-hanger and placed the cake of *Roger et Gallet* on the basin (my personal cake of soap is something I never leave home without).

'… From the sea, one glimpses a town, the white buildings of which lean drunkenly like so many tombs in the sand …' wrote William J. Makin, a British traveller and adventure writer who had arrived in Hodeidah by dhow in 1932.

Many of Hodeidah's waterfront houses were blitzed by a British warship in 1918, and going out to explore, I found little seemed to have changed. Every second building was a pile of rubble, but the architecture of more stalwart buildings was the traditional 'Red Sea Coast style' seen to best effect in Suakin, the old island port off Sudan. Constructed of coral-stone, several had *mashrabieh* balconies where Ottoman ladies had sat and watched the sea, but their teak doors, bleached by salt-laden winds, were now bolted with solid wooden latches.

Behind the bay, sheltered from sun and rain by palm-leaf matting, a ramshackle souq sold coconuts, bananas and baskets, donkey girths, well-ropes and camel muzzles, all woven from the munificent dom palm. Seeing my interest in these simple, but functional items, a friendly shopkeeper pressed me to accept a fan.

'*Bukra al-shams.*' He waved a hand. 'Tomorrow the sun will shine.'

Finding a small café for supper, I naturally ordered fish and apparently flattered by my custom, the chef himself brought out a blackened filet of what was possibly shark. It was delicious. Happiest by the sea, I wandered back to the hotel and climbed up to the roof terrace for a view of the Milky Way. Taurus was overhead: I recalled Freya Stark seeing the same star in her classic book *A Winter in Arabia*, of a journey she made through Yemen in the 1930s.

Next morning the sun was shining and I was guided to the fish market by a man walking past with a large kingfish balanced on the handlebars of his bicycle. Kingfish is a prize catch. Salted and dried, its flesh is sold and eaten when storms prevent the boats from putting out. Garfish, another local speciality, is split, salted and smoked on palm-frond skewers—I used to catch garfish at Lake Macquarie which mum would fry in batter, but I'm sure the Tihama way is equally nice.

The fish market consisted of a score of boats pulled up on the beach where a brisk auction for baskets of *wasif*—the whiskered anchovy used in *zahawiq*, a hot, spicy dip—was underway. A large octopus was being beaten on a wooden beam and small boys were running about collecting the fins and tails cut off sharks. A 2.43 metre (8 feet) long hammerhead—*mokarran*—in Arabic, lay on the sand: it must have taken all night to tow ashore.

As I stood watching this busy scene, I was joined by a bird-like man hopping about on a crutch. I wondered how he had he lost his foot? To a shark, when diving down to free an anchor snarled around a coral head? As if reading my thoughts, he pointed seawards and brought his fingers together. Chop! Definitely a bite of some sort.

'*Baga,*' He pointed his crutch at a pile of shiny black striped mackerel lying in one of the boats.

'*Khalb,*'—dog. He said the Arabic name for the sharp-toothed Indian halibut that shoals off the Tihama during the milder winter months. Then he touched my arm to move aside as two fishermen staggered past carrying a stingray slung on a shoulder pole. Yemenis bite the barb off smaller rays with their teeth, but this brown stingray of two metres (6.5 feet) across, had a barb the size of a walking-stick.

On the edge of the crowd, women in black *abayas* stood back from flying scales as a fisherman cleaned a barracuda. Blood and guts flowed down to the water's edge where crabs scuttled about after scraps. Scrawny cats hissed and spat over discarded fish heads and a one-eyed tom with balls the size of walnuts, pounced on a silver bream and bolted along the beach. As I turned to go, the bird-man dropped the distinctive saw-edged tooth of a tiger shark into my palm.

'*Al qarsh kebir,*'—big shark, I said.

'*Nam.*' He traced a line in the sand.

'*Shokran. Ma'asalaama,*' and giving him a double handshake, I left a similar scene played out every morning in countless smaller fishing communities along the Red Sea coast.

My program for the day was to visit Zabid, one of the oldest towns in Yemen, once celebrated for its university where the Zabidi scholar, Ahmad abu Musa al-Jaladi, lectured students on the intricacies of *al-Jabr* (algebra). The road cut across the coastal plain, an arid landscape broken only by thickets of dom palms and dotted with clusters of *tukul*-style huts swelling out of the ground like the ant hills of Australia's Northern Territory.

A few locusts hit the windscreen of the taxi I'd hired. Yemen lies on the crossroads of swarms migrating from Africa and the subcontinent, and invasions are frequent on the Tihama. In past times, families would gather in the fields beating drums and singing, 'oh, locusts, stay away from our crop'. However, if a swarm flew in, the entire village would turn out to kill, collect, to fry and eat them. My driver, a tall round-headed man, rather Ethiopian in appearance, assured me they still do.

Zabid was founded in the ninth century by Muhammed bin Zayid in order to suppress a local rebellion against Abbasid authority in Baghdad. Under the Zayidids it became a flourishing intellectual and religious centre, growing in stature under the Rasulid imams who used it as winter headquarters when Ta'iz—their mountain capital—was too cold. While my driver sat under a spreading acacia, I walked about counting the ruins of some eighty of a former two hundred mosques and religious colleges. It was just past noon and people were coming out of their houses to worship in al-Ash'ir, the Great Mosque of Zabid, where Muslims have prayed for nearly a thousand years.

Seeing my interest in the architecture, a woman wearing a shiny indigo-coloured dress, her eyes heavily outlined with kohl, beckoned me into her house in an alley behind the square. She guided me into an elaborate stucco plaster room, whose wall niches held alabaster oil lamps and vases of plastic flowers. We were joined by a third woman, then a fourth, one more beautiful than the next and clearly descended from the '… exceeding and pre-eminent beauties…' observed by Ibn Battūtah on his visit to Zabid in the fourteenth century. A servant appeared bearing a tray of hot bread smothered in melted ghee and honey, and seated on low, hemp-strung beds, we ate, dipping pieces in the syrup. We could not converse but I knew they were dying to ask about a husband and how many children I had. And seated in this genteel gathering, I remembered an Arab collecting me from Abu Dhabi airport had asked this question when I'd responded: two teenage boys and a girl—to be done with it.

'That's curious Miss Osborne.' He peered in his rear vision mirror. 'I was your driver two years ago and you didn't have children at the time.'

Calling through a window, the taxidriver caused a nervous flutter among the women. In order to get back to Hodeidah by nightfall, we had to leave for Mocha. The car door slammed shut and we set off again, driving through a landscape drained of colour in the harsh afternoon light. Ahead, men seated by the roadside scrambled to their feet, but they were not seeking a ride. As we drew level, they cocked a thumb at their mouth: they were selling black market whisky from Djibouti, across the Bab al–Mandab (Gate of Tears) entrance to the Red Sea.

Mocha is built around a shallow bay at the southern end of the Tihama. Legend attributes its growth to the fifteenth century when a local sheikh welcomed the crew of an Indian dhow with a cup of coffee. Its captain, delighted by the fragrant beverage, took on a cargo of beans and as word spread, other vessels began arriving and before long, Mocha had become one of the wealthiest ports on the Red Sea. In *Voyage de l'Arabie Heureuse* published in 1715, Jean de La Roque describes its coffee bazaar as having two great courts with covered galleries, where beans were unloaded from donkeys under the gaze of Turkish customs officers. He estimated that Mocha counted some 6,000 houses, but that not a tree remained, the timber having been used in huts for the Jews, Somalis and Danakils living outside the walls.

Yemen's monopoly of the coffee trade went into decline when the bush was found to thrive in Java and Brazil. When its harbour began silting up, British vessels—now taking on coffee for Europe—were obliged to anchor as far as 7 kilometres (4 miles) offshore. Ultimately they bypassed the port for Bombay and without employment, people drifted away. Calling at Mocha in 1934, the Red Sea trader Henri de Monfreid noted that only the governor's house, and another occupied by an Italian merchant, were in a livable state. The rest, he said was 'chaos and rubble'.

With Zanskar and Zanzibar, Mocha was on my list of places to see. I wanted it to be exotic, but it was a disappointment. Slabs of its once grand, lime-washed houses, had dropped off like rotting fruit off a tree. A massive carved door swung on rusting hinges; other buildings were buried up to their roofs in windblown sand. Alone the Sheikh Shadhili Mosque defied the decay. A cluster of peeling white domes, its minaret, once a beacon for seafarers, pointed an accusing finger at the sky. I wanted to peep inside, but the guardian was asleep on a palm mat and I didn't want to wake him. A skinny dog creeping around a corner frightened the life out of me. Mocha's own life was over.

'*Y'alla*,' I called the driver who was watching two old men playing checkers in a rundown café.

Back in Hodeidah again, the receptionist informed me of a ride to Jibleh, a town roughly half way back to Sana'a. His friend was delivering fish and poultry for a family wedding and I should be ready at 8am outside the British Bank of the Middle East.

Following thirty minutes wait, a yellow utility pulled up with fifteen jovial men in the tray and forty miserable chickens, hanging by their feet off the back. Placed beside the driver who did not speak English, on the journey I obsessed about the hens. If they needed to lay an egg, how would they manage upside-down?

Jibleh is associated with Arwa bint Ahmad al-Sulayhi, Yemen's second illustrious queen who ruled for seventy years until her death in 1138. Records left by the Sulayhid dynasty, an Ismaili branch of Shi'ite Islam, describe her as being tall, fair and voluptuous, and possessing a keen knowledge of the *hadith* (a record of the sayings attributed to the Prophet). One of Arwa's first acts was to relocate the capital from Sana'a to Jibleh. The arched bridge at the foot of the hill dates from her reign; she founded schools for girls and encouraged farming. Her tomb in the Arwa Mosque is a place of pilgrimage, in particular for Daudi Bohras, the wealthy Ismaili community from Gujarat who donated the screens for the Husayn shrine in Kerbala. A party was leaving as we arrived: I recognised the men by their white gold-rimmed caps. They were returning to Sana'a and their tour leader said there was room for me in their minibus.

'Where have you been?' asked Asif in the Sheraton foyer. 'We are waiting to take you to Sa'dah.'

I had already asked the ministry for permission to visit Sa'dah, an historic town on the border with Saudi Arabia, a request they'd refused. Central authority ended just north of Sana'a and the Zaidi tribal federations in the Sa'dah governorate were a law unto themselves.

'We'll say we went to Wadi Dhar,' grinned Asif.

Expatriates I met that evening advised against going to Sa'dah. A British diplomat had apparently had his vehicle hijacked during a picnic trip to al-Hajjarah and causing huge embarrassment, Bedouin had nicked the Chinese ambassador's car while he was inspecting a new section of the highway, financed and built by China.

'If you do find a way to go, leave your valuables behind,' advised a British midwife.

We set off next morning, but only 16 kilometres (10 miles) north of Sana'a, we confronted the first checkpoint where several dusty, but brand new cars bearing Jeddah Port Authority clearance plates were parked—stolen vehicles, smuggled into North Yemen and impounded by the army. As Asif conferred with the soldier, a beaten-up truck came rattling down the road from the direction of Sa'dah.

'Ask the driver what lies beyond the hill,' I called out to him.

There was a short exchange before the men looked at me and laughed, except for the soldier who was scowling.

'He said that bandits hold the road this morning. Mohammed and I can go on, but you are unlikely to return.'

After this abortive effort, I was even more determined to visit Sa'dah and back in Sana'a, I heard of a travel agent called Abu Taleb.

'He's the only person who can get you there,' my informant told me. 'His drivers are from the area.'

Abu Taleb's man arrived punctually at six. Aged about thirty-four, Fuad was a powerfully built Bedouin wearing an ankle-length *thobe* with a cream turban, and his *jambia* handle was set with a piece of turquoise. Not the sort of bloke to meddle with, I decided before hopping into a new Toyota Land Cruiser.

With no traffic, we made good progress up the black ribbon road. Fuad, who came from Amran, estimated our arrival for 11am, a bad light for photography, but to get to Sa'dah would be a miracle. I made notes in my spiral pad as with some fifty words between us, Fuad and I attempted to converse. Clearly briefed on my need for accuracy, he announced, then repeated, the names of the villages we passed: '… al-Marner, Thula, Thula, and on the left, Bani Maymun …' whose houses crowned a hill like burnt sugar lumps.

The sight of this rocky outcrop jolted me back to a day at Royal North Shore. We had just started an operation when the surgeon had taken my hand and plunged it into the patient's abdominal cavity.

'Feel this, nurse,' he frowned over the top of his mask and reaching around in the scarlet basin, I'd felt a hard, cauliflower-like growth.

'Cancer,' he growled and barking at the registrar to close up, he'd stripped off his gloves and stalked out of the theatre.

CONFISCATED VEHICLES AT THE ARMY ROAD-BLOCK NORTH OF SANA'A

As the sun rose higher, people began to appear: women fetching water, farmers slashing sorghum, and a boy herding sheep who suddenly dashed across the road after a lamb, causing Fuad to brake suddenly.

Seventy kilometres (43 miles) from Sana'a, we reached Raydah, where remnants of Yemen's former population of some 45,000 Jews still live. Houses now resembled miniature forts. Passing vehicles had no licence plates and their drivers sat in an odd hunched manner over the wheel. Driving a truck, a boy aged about eight overtook us. Too tiny to sit, he was standing on the seat, dropping out of sight to change the gears.

'Even the blind drive in Yemen,' Asif had told me.

In the treeless landscape, I looked for somewhere to go to the loo, but squatting behind a rock, I found myself watched by a turquoise-blue chameleon. It studied me with one eye, flicked out its tongue, then rolled it back like a coiled spring. Yemenis call it *al-fukhakh*, the hisser, and believe its breath will make your teeth fall out.

On the move again, Fuad jerked a thumb at the cloud-ringed massif of Jebel Shaharah, stronghold of the old Zaidi imams. I wanted to make a detour to see its ancient hanging bridge, but he shook his head—the mountain was held by dissident tribesmen.

Farther north the buildings abruptly changed from stone to mud. Watchtowers popped up from emerald patches of cultivation and grapevines tumbled over crenellated walls. We stopped for me to peer into a garden filled with quinces, figs and pomegranates, three of the seven fruits mentioned in the Qur'an (others are grapes, dates, bananas and watermelons).

Located on a plateau west of the Empty Quarter, Sa'dah was an historic halt for incense caravans. It was also an important tanning centre and enjoyed a reputation for making iron tools and the earthenware pots still used for cooking *saltah*. In the late ninth century, the Zaidi imam al-Hadi ila'l-Haqq Yahya, summoned from Medina to settle a tribal dispute, stayed on in Sa'dah to found the Zaidi imamate which persisted until the revolution. His shrine, located in the courtyard of al-Hadi Mosque has an aperture for pilgrims to breathe his saintly air.

Like other early towns in Southern Arabia, Sa'dah is enclosed by a medieval wall entered via four gates. We joined traffic flowing through Bab Najran: donkey-carts, pick-up vans and on this occasion several camels, to enter a dusty square flanked by offices and cafés filled with tribesmen. Told to get out while Fuad looked for a parking spot, I found myself in a man's world. Overflowing from shops into its crowded streets was every type of weapon from a 'Tommy Gun' to a Kalashnikov. Gunsmiths sat cross-legged under faded parasols with heaps of arms spread out at their feet and everyone carried a gun. A boy, aged about twelve, brushed past me carrying a chrome-plated AK-47 as casually as a tennis racquet. Other merchants were selling holsters and daggers and among the crowds, I noticed men trailing black shoulder-length locks, like the wild-haired Sufis of Pakistan.

Suddenly I was overwhelmed by fear. It wasn't just the problem of getting around this rough, though fascinating country and the stress of coping with obtuse officials, but of always being alone. I stumbled along oil-stained alleys lined with mechanics and shops selling generators and tools. Every car was a white Toyota Land Cruiser. Where was our own? Now I found myself in a street of moneychangers whose grubby glass counters were stuffed with crumpled bills sent back by Yemeni labourers in Saudi Arabia. A donkey road- accident victim hopped by on three legs, the fourth swinging like a broken windscreen wiper. There was not a woman in sight and every man resembled Fuad. Thoroughly upset, I eventually found my way back to the square where he was puffing on a *shisha* in the front row of the biggest café. Did I want a coffee?

'No way. Let's get out of this horrid place.' I said firmly.

We were hurtling back on the highway to Sana'a when a solitary armed tribesman flagged us down near Raydah. Sauntering across, he peered in the driver's side as Fuad opened the glove box, then snapped it shut. Walking around to my side, he leant into the rear where I'd hidden my cameras under the seat. Then apparently satisfied there was nothing worth taking, he stepped back, took a long look at me, and nodded his head. Not a word was spoken. I felt my armpits prickling and a little further on Fuad spat out of the window.

It was now time to leave Sana'a, and after interviewing Mr Noreisch, I caught a Yemenia flight to London where my roof garden was in bloom. Covered in delicate pink flowers, the clematis had shot up and the blue iris had held out for my return. Thank you.

I spent most of the following year researching books on Yemen in London and Paris. And to emphasise my interest in tourism, I sent a dummy guidebook, along with my articles, to the Ministry of Information where my interview with Mr Noreisch—published under the headline: *Remove the Cars and you're Back in the 15th Century*—caused an uproar. My application for another visa at the previously cordial Yemen Arab Republic Embassy was refused, but having put in so much effort, I was not to be easily deflected.

Visiting Khartoum to produce *Two Niles,* the flight magazine of Sudan Airways, I decided to outwit them. Yemen could be the next destination feature, and the embassy, unaware of the fuss in Sana'a, willingly issued a visa and I flew in on an ageing Sudan Airways Boeing 707.

On this visit I was booked at the Taj Sheba, North Yemen's second international hotel where the welcome was warm by contrast to my chilly reception in the Ministry of Information.

'Mr Noreisch has gone and you shouldn't be here,' I was told in no uncertain terms.

'Where is the dummy of my travel guide?' I asked.

No one knew.

I returned to the hotel wondering what to do. I hadn't visited Ta'iz, the medieval Rasulid capital of Yemen; I hadn't had a proper look at Ma'rib, and I hadn't been to Wadi al-Jawf, historic centre of the Kingdom of Ma'in and conduit for the wealthy incense caravans from the southern Hadhramaut. You're here now. Make the most of it, I told myself before setting off next morning with a British salesman—met in the Sheba bistro—who had business in Ta'iz.

Mr Graze was boring company, but the scenery on the drive was superb, the emerald vista of Ibb with peasants riding donkeys through hugely branched candelabra, reminded me of La Palma. In Ta'iz, we both checked into the Mareb Hotel. Mr Graze left to find his local contact and I went to interview the manager, a man, rather well-fed for a Yemeni, most of whom are gaunt from chewing *qat*.

After discussing tourism in his office, he offered me a drink. 'You can get anything here for the asking,' he said, removing a bottle of whisky from a drawer in his desk.

Weary after the journey from Sana'a, I was in bed by 9pm when my room was suddenly lit up like a night tennis court. Emerging from behind the curtains, a naked man had stepped on the floor switch of the standard lamp and clearly shocked by his silly faux pas, he shot out, and all I saw of him were wobbling buttocks disappearing down the corridor.

'Did you get a look at him?' asked the night receptionist.

'Unfortunately he was too quick,' I replied and lighting a cigarette, I noticed my hands were shaking.

'I am extremely sorry to hear of the incident.' The manager's oily voice snaked through the line. 'Can I do anything to help?'

'Nothing thanks, but as my door was locked, I don't understand how he got in, or where he could have left his clothes.'

After double-checking my door was locked, I eventually fell asleep only to dream of other misadventures: the cat burglar who broke into my hotel room in Palm Springs; the thief in the Gambia who stole everything I had—money, wristwatch and cameras. There was also the Masai woman in Dar es-Salaam who threatened to stab me in the eye, accusing me incorrectly, of taking her picture. That occasion was really frightening.

Rising shortly after the dawn prayer-call, I got up to play Miss Marple. Tip-toeing down the fire escape at the end of the corridor, I opened a door to find myself not on the first floor as I'd expected, but in the manager's office. So this was where he'd left his clothes and using a master key was able to enter my room, but alas I couldn't report the incident since I was not supposed to have left Sana'a. Packing my bag, I paid the bill and left without a word. No day could start better than in a safe place to stay and I also decided to be more cautious. My behaviour was normal by western standards, but it is impossible to know what an Arab thinks—especially of a woman who accepts a drink.

Putting the incident behind me, I stepped out into Ta'iz, a big town overflowing the surrounding hills and edging up the side of the glowering face of Jebel Saber. My new hotel was located in a street lined with shops selling televisions, radios, fans, irons and other hardware and curious about the prices, I entered a store with a sign Aden Enterprises above the door.

'How is the weather in Cardiff?' said a singsong voice.

I spun around. But there was no one there. Just tall packing cases of Italian refrigerators. It uttered again and above me on a mezzanine, I spied a turbaned man puffing on a *shisha*, just like Lewis Carroll's caterpillar. Removing the stem from his mouth, he introduced himself as Mr Najib al-Shamsi, who had spent ten years running a shop in Wales.

'The British called Aden a hell-hole, but I couldn't bear the rainy Welsh winters.' He gave a little shudder. 'Ta'iz is full of Adenis. We came north when the communists took over. Tea or coffee?' He rang a bell.

'Our family owned an import business in Steamer Point, as it was known in colonial days. I remember my father running things up the mountain to the Imam Ahmad in Ta'iz. He had a fondness of perfume and liquorice all-sorts and for years the palace remained as it was on his death. Redolent with musk and attar of roses, slippers under the bed and toothpaste on his brush. Most Yemenis use a *miswak* from the toothbrush tree, but not the Imam Ahmed. His was a Wisdom bristle.'

Our coffee arrived with a plate of *halwa*. My spirits were rising. Mr al-Shamsi was a perfect gentleman. His neat grey beard must have been trimmed by the Geo. F. Trumper of Ta'iz,[31] and he wore his *jambia* upright. 'Would you like to be accompanied to the souq?' he inquired politely.

I certainly would and we set off, an incongruous couple, tall Australian and diminutive Yemeni, using his cane to point out items of interest.

We passed spice and grain merchants and other traders selling honey in sticky plastic bottles.

'Beekeeping is an old tradition in Arabia. There are more than a thousand hives around Ta'iz,' said Mr al-Shamsi. 'We eat honey on bread and in sweetmeats. It is also used against sunburn, for diarrhoea and other ailments.'

Hard-boiled eggs, dried fish and smoked sheep's milk cheese—a local speciality—were sold in other shops. Of course there was *qat*, but here traders were women from the Jebel Saber.

'With their husbands working abroad, they have complete control over growing and selling the bush,' said Mr al-Shamsi as we climbed steep alleys where handsome unveiled women were doing a brisk trade in leaves.

Several displayed indigo facial tattoos and I noticed they wore gold instead of silver, an indication the *qat* business was profitable. One handed me a sprig which I pretended to chew before spitting it out behind a wall. Jonathan Raban has described the *qat* habit as being similar to chewing privet hedge. Other writers such as Kevin Rushby, whose first edition of *Eating the Flowers of Paradise* carries my photograph of *qat* chewers on the cover, became addicted to the leaf. I wonder if he still is?

Mr al-Shamsi took out a gold fob watch from his jacket. It was Friday. He had to pray. I watched him tap-tapping along until he merged with the other worshippers going into the al Ashrafiyeh Mosque,

That evening I found two tourists in the hotel restaurant. The first I had seen on either visit to Yemen, they were male, middle-aged and sipping soup.

'We're birdwatchers from Kent,' said one, his broad grin revealing a gap in his teeth.

THE FRAGRANT SPICE MARKET IN TA'IZ, FORMER RASULID CAPITAL OF YEMEN

'I'm Herb and this is Norman.' He indicated his sandy haired companion.

'We've been doing avifauna checks on the Tihama,' said Norman. 'The rest of our group has left, but we want to do some spotting on the plateau. You're welcome to come.'

I joined Herb and Norm in the lobby next morning. They were wearing khaki safari gear, multi-pocketed gilets and canvas hats. I was in brown linen trousers and a cream high-necked shirt, as worn by Meryl Streep in *Out of Africa*. Our taxi-driver was wearing jeans with a sleeveless sheep's wool jacket and a black baseball cap with Baltimore Orioles on it.

'*Siddiq*—friend America,' he said, pleased I had noticed.

The rugged central plateau abounded in birdlife. Creeping about with expensive Luger binoculars, the men identified amethyst starlings, shrikes, warblers, jays and Arabian babblers and hopping around the euphorbia, Herb called out the name of each bird—roller, rock pigeon, weaver, waxbill—for Norm to record in a logbook.

'Look!' He whistled through his teeth as a beautiful bird alighted on a fig tree. It was a shimmering paradise fly-catcher, that our driver—deftly miming the action—explained will nip off its tail in order to confuse a predator.

After an hour bird watching, the men spread out a tartan blanket and sat down with a thermos of tea. It was too soon after breakfast for me and I wandered off along a track where a woman was climbing up from the ravine. She wore a smock over black harem trousers, embroidered at the ankles, gold bracelets, and a piece of muslin wound around her head securing a bunch of marigolds. A goddess of the coffee terraces, showing no sign of astonishment at our meeting, she walked up and kissed my hand all in a single movement, and continued striding up the hill.

Back in Sana'a, I continued to research anything I could lay my hands on, which was very little. *The Ring Road Rag*, a pamphlet published by the British Council was useful, but time was passing, and I still hadn't visited Wadi al-Jawf, a wild, unmapped region abutting on the Empty Quarter.

'To omit the Minaean Kingdom from a guide on North Yemen is like writing a book about Jordan without mentioning Petra.' I attempted to explain its significance in Yemeni history, but the Ministry of Information would not hear of me going there. I argued and pleaded, but they stubbornly shook their heads. I had to remain in Sana'a until my flight back to London.

Discreet inquiries revealed that travel to al-Hazm, the ancient heart of the Minaean civilisation, was only possible with an armed escort. Apparently even the Yemen Hunt Oil Company with a concession in the region, allowed for vehicles being hijacked, and for Bedouin taking an occasional pot shot at its engineers. However, my luck was in when I met Tom Sherman, its burly Texan manager, during Friday's buffet lunch at the Sheba pool. Listening to my interest in al-Hazm, he offered to take me to Wadi al-Jawf as his guest, but we had to leave at dawn so the security officer posing as front office staff, would not know where I'd gone.

'Daylight in the swamp,' Sherman growled down the line at 5am.

Away in thirty minutes, we headed out on the Ma'rib road where 145 kilometres (90 miles) from Sana'a, he braked at a single petrol pump where our heavily armed escort was waiting.

Dipping his Stetson at them, Sherman gunned the Land Cruiser onto a sidetrack, crashing it over rocks the size of coffee-tables. As we clocked speeds of 120 kph an hour (75 mph), I realised I was being put through another test: we were to drive like this, windscreen wipers working against the dust, for a further five hours.

'Base camp, babe,' he said as we finally pulled in beside six trailers parked beneath a ridge where an army tent offered token protection.

'Coffee,' he stepped up into the mess and following him, I found myself surrounded by photos of naked women. In London, they would be considered merely distasteful. Out here they assumed a threatening aspect and I flinched at one of a woman fingering her genitalia. Whatever did the locals think?

Happily humour was provided by a larky cook, a toothless patriarch with a desert face. When I expressed an interest in taking his picture, he opened a cupboard, unclipped a Kalashnikov, and standing on the trailer steps, he sent a hail of bullets into a distant soft drink can. Yasser was clearly a character and I was disappointed to learn he could not accompany us, but evidently his tribe held a grievance against another farther up the wadi. Instead, a teenager holding his own AK-47 climbed in and we were off again, followed by a backup vehicle with our escort.

Our destination was the 'Fly Camp' near the head of Wadi al-Jawf, but barely an hour out of base camp, we became bogged in sand drifts and muttering about it being a good spot for a hijack, Sherman ordered us to get out.

'Lost a vehicle here last week,' he grunted.

Pulling down my hat, I scanned the wadi for any sign of life. There was only a camel browsing on a tamarisk, but walking away from the men who were frantically digging out our vehicle, I came upon a stream where a young shepherd was grazing sheep.

'*Ahlan wa sahlan,*' he smiled in a friendly manner, although instead of a crook, he too was carrying an AK-47.

The spring was gentle in the rough surroundings. I watched a brown skink sunning itself on a stone and electric blue dragonflies skimming the surface, but bending down to wash my face I was stopped in mid-action.

'Bilharzia, babe,' shouted Sherman, who'd evidently been watching.

Underway again, arid-zone scrub closed in like fog and when four armed Bedouin stepped into the road, swerving around them Sherman drove even faster.

The youth sat in silence with his gun between his knees and studying his lean, sardonic features in the mirror, I decided that he made me feel ill at ease. Instead of helping with directions, he'd ignored us. Was he leading us into a trap? So far, Bedouin had only pilfered vehicles and equipment, but I didn't fancy becoming another Madame Claustre: the French archaeologist kidnapped by rebel forces in 1974 and held hostage for seventeen months in the Tibesti Desert in Chad.

As I considered her ordeal, two figures appeared on a watchtower ahead, and removing their turbans, they waved them vigorously as we approached.

'*Wakif!*'—stop! The youth uttered his first words.

Ignored by Sherman, he boldly tapped my shoulder and when I turned around, he drew a finger across his throat.

'Stop here and it's a long walk back,' growled Sherman, putting his foot down on the accelerator so that we were almost flying.

In another hour, we reached the field site where tribesmen squatted around a huge piece of sounding equipment. On seeing me, they stood up and shuffled over for a closer look, but needing a bush, I asked Sherman to ensure no one followed.

It was extremely hot. Attempting to do my hair, I found it snapped off in the comb. I slapped some moisturizer on my face and gave myself a squirt of *Diorissimo*—my favourite perfume at the time. It was a bit of a waste, but like the British dressing for dinner in the jungle, it would help keep up morale.

'Hit the road,' said Sherman after inspecting the site.

'Can we go back a different route?' I wanted to know.

Swigging a bottle of warm mineral water, he took it out of his mouth and said two words: 'Bandits babe.'

With local Bedouin alert to our presence, we made a detour back via al-Mansaf, a fly-spot settlement built of mud on the last memorable occasion that Wadi al-Jawf was in flood. Getting out to photograph the houses, I watched a woman breaking firewood. Evidently so poor she didn't even possess a saw, the rock she hurled at a branch bounced off and struck a dog. Ignoring its terrible howls, she aimed again but on seeing me, she dropped the rock and rushed inside and a veiled face had appeared at an upper window.

'*Y'alla,*' yelled Sherman.

I gave the woman a friendly wave, but as we drew away, she pointed at something glistening on the ground. My gold watch had slipped off and was lying in the sand. Jumping out, I snapped it on my wrist, blew her a kiss, and we were off again with red dust spewing out behind.

Apparently I'd passed this latest test, for at 4pm, while still some way from Sana'a, Sherman offered to show me Baraqish—my reason for wanting to visit Wadi al-Jawf in the first place.

Early scriptures place the construction of Baraqish, or Yathul, to about the fifth century BCE and while archaeologists considered it likely to be the best-preserved site in Southern Arabia, few had seen it as local tribes had refuted any attempt at excavation. Yemeni legend says that under siege by warring tribes, the starving Ma'eenis inside the fortified town managed to survive on supplies brought in through a secret tunnel; but a dog, exiting through the entrance, had revealed the site, enabling the invaders to storm in.

'Ain't brought no one here daughter,' drawled Sherman of the fabled city etched like a cardboard cutout against the pewter-coloured sky.

For a moment, I simply stood and stared at the enclosing wall, topped with the crumbling remains of an original fifty-seven watch-towers. Scrambling in through a gap, I then entered a museum of collapsed houses, civic buildings, the rubble of a great temple likely used in Minaean worship rites, and the scattered bricks of a silo, an indication that long ago, the region was fertile. My sandals crunched on flint-stone chippings as I walked about, stopping here and there to pick up pieces of scored earthenware. On straightening up, I noticed the youth was watching, then still clutching his AK-47, he turned and urinated against the ancient ramparts.

'Just a normal working day babe,' said Sherman, crushing a hairy, yellow camel spider under his boot.

Deposited at the Sheba at eight that evening, I caught sight of a wild-haired woman in the mirror. It was me.

Where had I been, the night receptionist wanted to know?

'Baraqish,' I said, flushed with excitement and, whispered around the foyer, the name was my downfall.

'... Nowhere have I experienced more strenuous travelling than in Yemen...' writes Wilfred Thesiger in *Desert, Marsh and Mountain.* Neither had I. The wild ride up Wadi al-Jawf had taken its toll and, lying in bed in the Sheba, I recalled other occasions of ill health on my travels: pneumonia in Casablanca, food poisoning in Dubai, dysentery in Delhi, and the awful accident in Luxor when my legs were sliced open by the metal step on a horse-carriage. It was not a nice feeling to be sick and all alone.

Two days after our trip to Baraqish, I was called out of bed by Yemenia.

'Please come and bring your passport,' said the female voice.

'We want to facilitate your departure with Sudan Airways,' smiled Mohamed Al-Haimy, the bantam-sized airline chairman, when I reached the office. 'Please give us your passport, so we can pass your details to immigration.'

Three more days passed and still unwell, I remained in bed writing up notes. My flight was imminent, but there were no messages in my pigeonhole and as my passport had not been returned, I called Mr al-Haimy's secretary.

'I'm leaving tomorrow,' I told her 'but I'm still without my passport.'

'It's with Hamid. A car will take you to his house,' she replied.

It was five o'clock when we arrived at one of the tower-houses and the driver pointed upwards at the *mafraq,* a climb of six storeys up—up—up that left me breathless.

Inside the room some fifteen men were reclining on mattresses arranged around the walls. All had cricket-ball cheeks and the bulging eyes of the *qat*-stoned. The carpet was littered with leaves, branches, plastic bags and empty water bottles and a brass spittoon was half-filled with green expectorant. Sunlight filtered in through pink-and-yellow fanlights and from this height, there was a splendid view of Sana'a, but photography was not on my mind. As I stood there unacknowledged, a man I'd never seen before casually pulled my passport out of his jacket and stepping over the vegetation, I grabbed it like a lifebelt.

THE YOUTH OUTSIDE THE RAMPARTS OF BARAQISH, 1981

Back in London, I continued writing my guide to this bizarre, but interesting country and determined to start a business in Sana'a, I decided to contact Mr Haideri about launching a baby-wear boutique. Too poor to invest in the 1970s Dubai land-grab, I would seize the opportunity now.

I bought booties, nighties, pink dresses and blue bodysuits, Mummy's Little Hero T-shirts, I Love Daddy bibs, scratch mitts, shawls, and a large pack of nappies. Everything I supposed a baby needed to survive. They remained stacked in my bedroom waiting for winter to pass in Sana'a, and now that I was ready to check my manuscript, I made an appointment at the embassy in Mayfair.

'You cannot go back to Yemen,' said a stony-faced consul. And that was that.

It was a busy Saturday afternoon when I caught a bus to Boots in Richmond where I had purchased the babywear goods.

'I would like to obtain a refund please,' I told the manager of Customer Services.

'We don't change baby clothes,' she said loftily.

'But here's the receipt. They're not even unpacked.' I held up the large plastic bag.

'It's our store policy,' she replied firmly.

'Baby is dead.' I looked her straight in the eye. 'Dead,' I repeated for emphasis.

'Oh, I'm so sorry madam.' Her cheeks flushed slightly pink.

'In that case of course you may have a refund.'

I have never returned to Yemen.

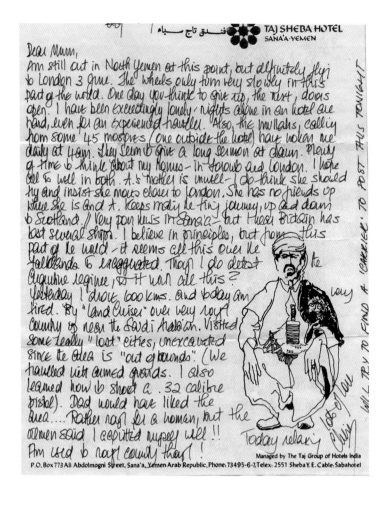

Chapter 6

May you Never be Tired

In sorting through my letters to mum—she kept every one—I've found many references to loneliness and while happy with the life of my choice, there was a huge difference between nursing and travel writing.

At Royal North Shore I'd lived and worked among hundreds of colleagues. Some were good mates. Most were unknown. But they were there. There was always someone off-duty with whom to share coffee and a 'ciggie'—we all smoked in those days—or to slip out of Vindin House for a meal. Travel writing is a solitary occupation. Missing home and dining alone are inevitable downsides to the profession, and while grateful for having developed a capacity to be independent, I find that a birthday with no one to celebrate, exacerbates the sense of social isolation.

I've awakened on 17 October in London, Paris, Rome, Amsterdam, Nairobi, Dublin, Moorea, New York, Marrakech, Muscat, Provincetown and Algiers. I have also seen out three birthdays in Pakistan: my thirty-ninth in Peshawar, my fortieth in Rawalpindi and my forty-first in Sukkur, an historic town on the Indus River in Sindh. In Sukkur I decided to plan ahead. I would rise early and buy sweets for the houseboat children and while normally skipping lunch, today I would order something special in my room (it was Ramadan, so I couldn't eat in public.)

'Catfish *masala*,' I told reception. 'And please send an electrician to fix my fan. Or the airconditioning. Neither is working and it's rather warm.'

In a few moments, a man wearing overalls had appeared at the door.

'Electric,' he said, and coming in, he switched the fan on. Off-On-Off, and spinning the blades (the cage was missing), he declared 'fan heat', and balancing it on his shoulder, he carried it out.

A second knock was a waiter with lunch. Taking the tray, I placed it carefully on the bed and dragged up a chair, but before I could take a mouthful, there was another rap on the door. It was the electrician again. This time he kicked off his sandals and stepping over the tray, he stood on my pillow, placed a foot against the bedhead, and yanked the airconditioner off the wall, splitting the wooden frame and showering my lunch with dust balls.

'Check,' he said, dragging it into the corridor.

Moments later he was back again with the fan.

'Wire,' he announced and plunged a screwdriver into the wall socket.

'Don't do that,' I shouted, picturing an incinerated corpse.

'Problem fix,' he flicked the switch, and starting up like a turbojet, the fan blew my birthday curry all over the bedspread.

Pakistan is like a *rilli*, a handmade patchwork quilt of many coloured cottons and embroidered threads. Even hundreds of tiny mirrors are sewn into the pattern. I first visited the country in 1978 to write an article for *Middle East Travel*. Pakistan was a popular destination for Gulf Arabs who came to shop in Karachi and to hunt bustard in the southern Punjab. Lodges and hotels were being built for them and in return, the sheikhs funded schools and hospitals: a convenient arrangement for the Arabs, less so for the bustard.

Other commissions took me back to Pakistan when I discovered a country rich in historic sites, from the ruins of the Indus Valley communities, to the shrines of eminent Sufis where other than pilgrims or scholars, I was inevitably the only tourist. I found the average Pakistani an amenable sort of chap—I use the masculine since I rarely encountered women on a personal level—and despite occasional grim sights, I was charmed by the wit of the literate, and the graciousness of the poor. At Karachi Airport, when one of my suitcases wouldn't close, an observant porter had whipped out the rope supporting his trousers and strapped it around the lid.

In 1980, I was commissioned to write a book on Pakistan by Longman Group, the distinguished British publishing house founded in 1724. The same house had published my second book on Jordan, but this was a far bigger project in a geographically dramatic country where travel is restricted by climatic extremes. Towns on the plains endure sizzling temperatures and monsoon rains, while snowbound for six months a year, the Northern Areas are also subject to serious landslides. I decided that autumn (October-November) was the best time to visit and starting in the North-West Frontier Province (NWFP) and ending in Baltistan, the research, writing and publication took approximately three years.

Sharing a border with Afghanistan, the NWFP is historically one of the world's most unruly frontiers. Not simply on account of the rugged terrain, but due to the fearsome reputation of the Pathans, a people of Persian origin whose territory—Pashtunistan—was divided by the British contrived 2,640 kilometre (1,640 mile) long Durand Line, drawn through the mountains in 1893.

Pathans belong to one of the world's largest tribal societies comprising scores of different tribes, sub-tribes and clans whose leaders sit on a *jirga* council which arbitrates over endless cups of heavily sugared tea. The Pathan code of ethics—*Puktanwali*—is incumbent upon every member of the tribe. Hospitality is paramount. So, too, is the guarantee of a safe passage for any stranger travelling through tribal territory. Revenge follows an 'eye for an eye' and may extend to flaying an enemy alive—the experience of many a wretched Russian soldier. Feuds are a way of life, the need for vigilance being reflected in the traditional Pashtu greeting— *Starai Masahi*—'May you never be tired'.

My introduction to this lawless area was in a Sydney cinema we called the 'fleapit'. My father—a fan of Lauren Bacall—had taken me to see her and Kenneth More starring in the 1959 adventure film *North-West Frontier* whose poster depicted the Khyber Mail. Now twenty years later, I was about to catch the legendary train, scheduled to depart from Peshawar Cantonment at 9am and to arrive at Landi Kotal, the end of the line, three hours later.

My companion was Habib Afridi, a member of the Adam Khel clan of the Afridi tribe whose territory covers the Khyber agency. He was a lovely man of almost pastoral gentleness and I found it hard to accept that the Afridis had struck such terror in British soldiers stationed on the frontier, but attacking Landi Kotal in 1897, they had defeated the Khyber Rifles Frontier Corps and it required 35,000 British soldiers to recapture the strategic site.

For our day out, Habib was wearing a grey *shalwar kameez* (the long shirt and baggy trousers worn by men in Pakistan) while I had teamed a floral shirt purchased at the Galleries Lafayette in Paris with khaki trousers. And naturally I was wearing my hat. However we had not chosen a good date for our journey up the Khyber. It was the start of a religious holiday and hundreds of tribesmen were returning home to their remote

THE KHYBER MAIL IN THE FAMOUS PASS IN THE NORTH-WEST FRONTIER, 1979

compounds in the barren hills. Boarding at Jamrud, I was swept along in an arsenal of Pathans waving guns and hawkers brandishing cigarettes, sugarcane and hard-boiled eggs. Chickens, even a cow, were bundled on board as we pulled out of the station, with me seated in the LADIES ONLY carriage pretending I was Lauren Bacall and Habib riding with the driver in the front locomotive.

Our five carriages were pulled and pushed by two steam engines from the 1920s. Two were needed because unable to turn in the narrow gorge, the front one had to run back to gain momentum when the rear engine acted as prop. In one place, the ascent was so steep that all the passengers leapt off, scrambled up the rocky hillside and re-boarded fifteen minutes later when we steamed into the station above. The train traversed thirty-four tunnels between Jamrud and Landi Kotal, the summit of the pass 1,067 metres (3,501 feet) and seated in darkness with soot pouring in windows I was unable to close, I reflected on my previous rail journeys: the Chittagong Mail in Bangladesh, the Nairobi to Mombasa Night Express and the Indian Pacific crossing were memorable, but none matched the Khyber Mail. In the longest tunnel, a prankster pulled the emergency cord, no doubt to frighten me the only woman on board, but as we ground to a halt, the joke was on him. At the last stop, I'd jumped down from my carriage and ran along the track to join Habib in the engine and we could see each other by glowing coals in the furnace.

Landi Kotal is the historic gateway to India. Alexander the Great, Mahmud of Ghazni, and Tamerlane all passed through here, but it was now simply a marketplace for goods smuggled in from Dubai, and a warehouse for the prodigious poppy harvest from the Tribal Areas. Its roads were strewn with broken packing cases, and a stench of raw sewage from open drains was mixed with the mystic, slightly tarry odour of opium. I was covered in coal-dust, but no one paid me attention in its smoky opium dens where addicts were sucking heroin through pipes stuck in soft drink bottles. Did I want a puff, asked a man, removing the stem from his mouth?

'Scotch keeps my motor oiled, but drugs are for dummies,' I told Habib who didn't touch the stuff.

Capital of the NWFP, Peshawar is the last stop in Pakistan for travellers headed west on the Grand Trunk Road from Delhi. I was booked at Dean's Hotel whose polished floors and mahogany furniture symbolized the Victorian era. Shown the guest book, I noticed that Muhammad Ali Jinnah, King Nadir Shah of Afghanistan, and Rudyard Kipling, were among its former distinguished guests. After dinner of mulligatawny soup and leftover Sunday roast I retired early and slept until six when I was awakened by squeals in the garden. Had the *chowkidar* (watchman) seen a cobra? Opening my door, I found Imran Khan, the Pathan cricket star signing autographs on the verandah—he had slept in the room next to mine.

As in other towns in India, the British had worked and socialised in the cantonment area of Peshawar, well away from the hoary old Qissa Khawanni bazaar thronged with tribesmen wearing bandoliers and women hidden under their tent-like *burqas*. Smelling of fried chapli kebabs, the bazaar still resembled this description by a Victorian visitor in 1815:

'... The streets were crowded with men of all nations and languages... Dried fruits, and nuts, bread, meat, boots, shoes, saddlery, bales of cloth, hardware and readymade cloaths, and posteens, books, &c. were either displayed in tiers in front of the shops, or hung on hooks from the roofs …'

Many of the shops still looked medieval and while cafés screening Hindu movies had put paid to professional raconteurs in the 'Street of the Story-Tellers', the *chai-kannas* brewing tea in huge copper samovars remained a colourful part of life.

Habib and I were sipping tea when we were joined by a tired-looking man who introduced himself as Dr Ghayyub Hussain Ayub. He had trained at Bangor General Hospital in Wales and was now a surgeon in Parachinar in the Kurram Tribal Agency jutting into Afghanistan.

'I've just removed a broken plastic parrot from a boy's axilla,' he said wearily. 'We treat dozens of people injured by booby-trapped toys dropped from Russian helicopters—frogs, dolls, necklaces. Would you like to visit my hospital? You would have to wear a *burqa*.'

'My height would be a giveaway,' I said.

'*Tik da*,' he agreed. And drinking a second *chai*, he joined the flow of passers-by.

Peshawar was an historic halt for caravans plying the Silk Route, the network of roads winding across Central Asia from the commercial centres of the Middle East, Russia and China: skins, cotton fabrics, bronze weapons, glassware, and ivory going east—carpets, tapestries, porcelain and especially bales of silk—coming west.

'This shop still sells Czarist wares,' said Habib bending his tall frame to enter a dimly lit basement cluttered with icons, candlesticks, amber necklaces, and gilded furniture all covered in layers of gritty, frontier dust. Hearing our voices, the elderly shop-owner shuffled over to a Victorian cast-iron safe and after fiddling with its lock, he carefully removed a delicate floral-patterned plate.

'From Everyday Service of Memsahib Catherine.' He turned it over revealing the stamp: Imperial Porcelain Factory of St Petersburg.

Habib gave one of his slow smiles. 'He's had that plate for years,' he said. 'Nobody can afford it.'

We were in Sethi Mohalla whose grand *havelis* (mansions) once belonged to the prosperous Sethi merchant family who maintained offices as far away as Samarkand and Shanghai. It was quiet here after the racket of traffic outside the city walls and hearing the trill of birdsong, I glimpsed a tiny brown bird flitting over the rooftops.

'A nightingale,' said Habib. 'People put out sugar to attract it to come to their windowsill and sing for them.'

I soon learnt this romantic side of the Pathan does not extend to women whose lowly status remains the raw side of life on the frontier. In marrying a Pathan, a woman becomes his possession and if her husband forbids her to leave the family home—that is her lot. I met a forty-two year old woman in Chitral, who had never been outside her garden.

The northern wedge of the NWFP, Chitral is walled off from Afghanistan by the Hindu Kush whose name is believed to mean 'kill Hindus', a reference to the harsh terrain where many travellers have perished crossing between Afghanistan and India. On an earlier visit, I had come upon a group of armed mujahideen riding horses across a stream splashing down from Tirich Mir, the highest peak 7,708 metres (25,289 feet). In his book *A Short Walk in the Hindu Kush* Eric Newby describes his surprise at meeting Wilfred Thesiger, a man more associated with burning lowlands, on a mountain path. '...You'll stay the night with us. We're going to kill some chickens...' Thesiger told him. [32]

'How do you manage when Chitral is snowbound?' I asked my driver, the son of the woman who had never left the family compound.

'Rust,' smiled blue-eyed Sher Afzal whose fair complexion underlined a belief that some locals may have Greek DNA, attributed to the 64,000 infantry accompanying Alexander into India in 327 BCE.

Instances of fair hair and light-coloured eyes are not uncommon in north-west Pakistan. In Brumboret Valley near Chitral, we passed a tall, blonde woman herding sheep. She was a member of the Kalash, a pagan tribe that on rejection of Islam, had retreated to three isolated valleys where they remain to this day, living close to nature, worshipping totems and making ritual sacrifices—a male goat to Mahandeo by men, a nannygoat to Jestak, by women. Cut into the hillsides, their small stone-and-walnut timbered houses are windowless—doubtless for warmth—cooking is done on an open-hearth, bed is a heap of animal skins, toilet entails a squat in the great outdoors. And if such basic living conditions are not hard enough, each month Kalash women must endure segregation with others in a similar condition in a special menses house that no one may enter for fear of contamination: relatives leave cooked food at the door.

All the women—some tall and fair, others short and olive-skinned—wore elaborate costumes that stood out like fancy dress against the rugged backdrop. To their main garment—a long, black wool gown, embroidered at the hem and hitched up into a tasselled belt, they add strands of red, white and blue china beads and matching earrings, but their crowning glory is a black hat, topped with purple pom-poms and trailing a hood encrusted with more beads, metal buttons, coins and cowrie shells.

Sher had warmed to my interest in their habits. 'A comb is considered unclean.' He pointed out a girl plaiting her hair under the willows. 'So it is kept under a stone by the stream.'

I'd read about the Kalash women's penchant for a primitive make-up made from melted-down goat horn and approaching the girl, I held out a tube of lipstick brought for this reason. Uncertain what it was, at first she refused to take it but after watching me paint my own lips, she snatched it and scurried off up the valley. Soon another girl appeared and reaching into her gown, she handed me some freshly cracked walnuts, but all I had left to give away was a small cake of soap off the flight from Peshawar.

Turning it over, she looked up at Sher for an explanation.

'Soap,' he said and squatting down beside the stream, he demonstrated how to wash her hands.

'Soap,' she repeated in a lilting voice, but it slipped through her fingers and was borne away by the current. I still see her look of disappointment.

The Northern Areas comprising a portion of Chitral, the former princely state of Hunza and the old agencies of Gilgit and Baltistan is the meeting place of the world's most formidable mountain systems—the Himalayas, the Karakorams, and the Hindu Kush. While petroglyphs indicate a Buddhist presence in the fifth century BCE and Mahmud of Gazni had marched through the Khyber Pass in the early tenth century, it took Islam a further three hundred years to penetrate the region. In some remote valleys, the old folk still believe there are only four peoples in the world: the Tibetans, the Kashmiris, the Hunzakuts and the Chinese.

Until the completion of the Karakoram Highway in 1986, the only way into the Northern Areas was by Pakistan International Airlines Fokker Friendship service from Rawalpindi, a zigzag flight through narrow mountain passes when windshear is one of several hazards.

'How do you follow this route?' I asked the captain who'd invited me onto the flight deck.

'Well, it's very hard. We don't have navigational aids and the weather...' his voice trailed off.

'Oh, don't say that,' I pleaded. 'My hair will stand on end which is quite difficult since you can see it's very curly.'

'Well, I'm frightened too,' he said. 'The Americans say we're mad operating this route, but we've done so for thirty-four years without loss of life.' He glanced out the window to check our clearance from the mountains.

'Are you enjoying it?' grinned his co-pilot. 'It's very dangerous.'

'We're coming in,' said Captain Khan, putting on his earphones. 'I'll give you a prize if you can see the airstrip. Look, we're flying straight at that spur. No, don't sit down, but hold on. See we just missed it.' He laughed.

Gilgit's flight monitors had been drinking *chai* and chatting to departing passengers, but on spotting our aircraft over Bunji, they rang a bell to clear the runway of livestock and as we completed a tight turn, they rang it again to alert two vintage fire engines that trundled out to meet us. It was a perfect landing, but invited to sign the Visitor Book, I noticed the names, including my own, were written in shaky hand.

The western gateway for expeditions in the Northern Areas, Gilgit's dozen stores stocked icepicks, freeze-dried rations and spare parts for the 4x4s jolted to pieces on the mountain tracks. A single souvenir shop displayed old coffeepots, rugs, musical instruments and traditional rolled goat-hair berets. Its owner, however, had something else to show me.

He plonked a dirty plastic bag of coins on the counter. 'Antique,' he said. Turned up by his cousin's plough.

Copper with an inky green patina, they certainly looked antique and although I'd been offered many fakes—Roman vases in Tunis, rubies in Rangoon, Buddha statues in Bangkok—I bought three for curiosity value and back in London, to my surprise a numismatic expert at the British Museum declared they were from the Kushan Empire *c.* 248-256.

'That is King Kanishka in front of a fire altar on one side, and Shiva with Nandi the bull-god, on the other,' he told me.

Next morning I found Gilgit transformed by a polo match that was causing as much excitement as a World Cup football final. The streets were chock-a-block with badly parked jeeps, and people were streaming out of town to the polo ground where I joined them on a low stone wall to watch what looked like a free-for-all on horseback.

'In England you change horses each chukka, but our tough ponies see it through till the end,' said an enthusiastic man with two small sons, one of whom was so excited, he had wet himself.

Encouraged by an exuberant band, people barracked for their team. Just how a goal was scored didn't seem to matter: at one point, a man's arm was apparently broken and a little later, a horse dropped dead.

'The important thing is to move casualties quickly,' said my friend as a cavalry charge through the goalposts saw everyone, me included, leap for our lives.

That evening in Gilgit's Chinnar Inn, I drank my last drop of whisky. The import of alcohol is forbidden in the Islamic Republic of Pakistan, but I'd managed to smuggle in a bottle among my underwear. Now with nowhere to leave the empty, I went onto the balcony and hurled it into an adjacent wheatfield: come harvest time, I knew the farmer would be thrilled to find a bottle for his apricot oil.

Hunza, the 'Apricot Capital of Pakistan,' lies in an amphitheatre of snow-capped peaks, 90 kilometres (62 miles) north of Gilgit. My interest in visiting the valley was to investigate its reputation as a sort of Shangri-La whose people are said to have discovered the elixir of life.

'The people are Ismaili Muslims. Their capital, Karimabad, is named after the Ismaili spiritual leader Prince Karim, the Aga Khan,' said my guide, Riaz Khan, whose uncle was the last *thum* (ruler) of Hunza.

Karimabad's grey-rock houses seemed as though they were stuck on the mountainside with superglue and unlike the A-frame architecture of alpine resorts, their roofs were flat for drying millet, corn and apricots.

In the nineties, it became a popular base for trekking with many hotels, but when I visited there was a single guesthouse with no heating and the taps were frozen.

'I must wash.' I mimed the action to the bearer-wallah who went outside and returned with a bucket, filled from the dripping glacier. Dinner was equally spartan: potato curry and paratha[33] washed down with 'Hunza Water', a mildly alcoholic beverage that locals brew from fermented mulberries.

I awoke to mists drifting up from the valley and people wrapped in blankets pattering along to their fields. A shepherd playing a flute walked past and I spied a tiny old woman stumbling up the path with tins of sloshing water. Taking them, I nodded for her to lead the way and while puzzled by this unexpected gesture, she continued climbing up to her stone house facing the icy tooth of Mount Rakaposhi 5,800 metre (19,029 feet) across the valley.

Invited in, I noted her possessions: a bed-roll, a white china cup, an enamel plate of apricots, and pinned on a wall a picture of Tower Bridge from a 1967 London transport calendar. Squatting on her heels in ill-fitting shoes, she cheerfully responded to my questions, via a bright-eyed boy who'd popped in on his way to school.

'She live up in summer and down in winter. All Karimabad move up-down, or down-up, on same day,' he said, skipping off.

A toothless 104 years old, the lady was a member of the Hunza Centenarians Club. Having no contact with the outside world, she was unaware that eleven years before, man had walked on the moon. Or that Zulfiqar Ali Bhutto the prime minister of Pakistan, had been hanged by General Zia al-Haq in Rawalpindi.

By 10am Riaz had located a dozen people, each one more than one hundred years old including one woman who said she was 310. She directed us to a house where rosy-cheeked elders were seated on a carpet drinking tea from a rose-patterned thermos flask. One wrinkled faced man, his blue eyes twinkling, wanted to know how old I thought he was.

'That's Wazir Ali Murad, aged 108, the oldest man in Karimabad,' Riaz whispered.

'I've heard their longevity is linked to a diet that includes lots of apricots. Another theory suggests it might be particles of gold in the water. Can you ask?' I whispered back.

After a brief exchange in Burushaski, the isolated language of the northern agencies, Wazir Murad fired back a response.

'Our great age is because we are cut off from urban life. But the new highway is changing things. It's our custom to offer apricots to visitors, but now the tourists want to pay us. And our young men are returning from this place called Dubai with new ideas. Why do I need a radio? I've lived one hundred years without hearing the news.'

More old people entered the room. Seven of us were now seated on the carpet drinking salted tea. A girl carried in chunks of corn bread spread with yak butter and apricot jam and Begum Mehrab, the only woman, passed around a plate of walnuts.

'Wazir Murad is the oldest man and the others are 92, 100, 101 and 102,' said Riaz of each man in turn.

I'd suddenly felt uncomfortable at discussing age, and suggested that Riaz might invite them to guess my own. 'Very young, about twenty-five', smiled the Wazir, draping an arm around my shoulder.

The 101 year old gentleman who was wearing a fine cream cloak, guessed I might be thirty, but peering into my face, Begum Mehrab declared I was thirty-five. Announcing that I'd turned forty the previous week brought mutterings of disbelief, but learning I was single caused murmurs of consternation, followed by a respectful silence at such misfortune. More walnuts were passed around and several women, wearing the embroidered Hunza cap, popped their heads around the door to stare at me.

'Women in Hunza work much harder than the men,' explained Riaz as we walked down to our jeep. 'They must carry water, fetch wood, cook, raise the kids, and help with the harvest. I don't think you'd like the life.'

'What do you mean?' I asked.

'Because the Wazir has requested I tell you he's looking for another wife.'

'I'm a plains person,' I said and picking up a stone, I hurled it into the Hunza River.

I've always loved rivers. The north coast of New South Wales, where we spent family holidays is blessed with waterways such as the Tweed, the Richmond and the Clarence. In fact the first poem I ever learnt was about a river from Robert Louis Stevenson's collection *A Child's Garden of Verses*. An original edition, published in 1946, lies open on my desk as I recall my travels through the riverine plains of the Punjab.

The name Punjab, from the Persian *Panj-ab* (five waters) refers to the Chenab, Beas, Ravi and Sutlej rivers, tributaries of the mighty Indus whose banks sustained advanced civilisations long before the birth of Christ. Historians remain unclear as to what caused the demise of these communities, but for whatever reason, invaders queuing to enter the fecund agricultural land of the Punjab included the Aryans, Persians, Greeks, Kushans, Hephthalites, Afghans, Arabs, Sikhs, and ultimately the British whose imperial legacy in Lahore, the provincial capital, is second only to its magnificent Mughal heritage.

I was billeted at Faletti's, an old British India hotel with slowly rotating ceiling fans and perky mynah birds hopping about its lawns. Ava Gardner had stayed here in 1955 while making *Bhowani Junction* when Lahore Railway Station became 'Bhusawal' in the film of John Master's novel of the turbulent last weeks before the partition of India. Room 55 has been named the 'Ava Gardner Suite' in her memory.

My first day coincided with Eid ul-Adha[34] and I elected to photograph *fajr* (morning) prayers in Lahore's great Badshahi Mosque, built by the Emperor Aurangzeb in 1673. My guide Liaquat Gill, a plump young official from the Pakistan Tourism Development Corporation (PTDC), had chosen to wear a new cream *shalwar kurta* (a straighter, more formal shirt than the *kameeze*) and men and boys, also wearing new clothes, streamed into the mosque along a path lined with beggars, among whom was a disabled man, spinning himself around on a metal garbage-bin lid.

At 7am a long, resonant call signalled the start of worship and the congregation of 50,000 assembled in the vast courtyard performed the prayer positions in perfect unison: standing, bowing, standing, kneeling, seated, kneeling, seated, looking to the right, looking to the left: Peace be upon you, and the mercy and blessings of Allah.

EID UL-ADHA PRAYERS IN THE BADSHAHI MOSQUE IN LAHORE, 1980

A cannon announced the end of exaltations and people stood, embraced, then surged forward to retrieve their footwear at the door. Caught in the crush, Gill and I were startled when all the buttons popped off his new *kurta* and bounced down the steps—the blind, scrabbling in the dust, thought someone had thrown them coins.

The flowering of Lahore occurred under the Mughals, a tribe of Turkish lineage from the eastern Caucasus whose rulers were renowned for their refined taste in architecture, a love of gardens, and of Persian literature, whose dynasty lasted until 1858. Within the ancient city walls they constructed a vast citadel complex—rather like a medieval version of a gated community—enclosing audience halls, pleasure gardens, parade grounds and the royal apartments of the four greatest emperors: Akbar, Jahangir, Shah Jehan and Aurangzeb.

Inside the fort, I found myself in another world, although one battered by occupying Sikh and British armies. Gill pointed out the Diwan-i-Aam where the emperor had reviewed parades numbering hundreds of caparisoned elephants and near it, the Moti Masjid, a charming little white marble mosque used by the *zenana* women of the royal apartments.

At the Shish Mahal I was lost for words. A crystal belvedere that had overlooked the Ravi River, it was built by Shah Jehan for his great love, the Empress Mumtaz Mahal and their personal courtiers. Fretted marble-work screens had concealed its occupants from view while allowing in gentle breezes during the fiery Punjabi summer. I ran my fingers over its walls inlaid with diamonds, rubies, and semi-precious gems and was dazzled by sunbeams striking thousands of tiny mirrors set in the ceilings. Closing my eyes a moment, I imagined an elaborate scene with musicians and poets reciting *ghazals*[35] and the emperor, surrounded by doe-eyed courtesans, drinking from a wine cup carved from pale nephrite jade. I decided there and then, that if I could be whisked back to any point in history, it would be to a Mughal court—preferably that of Shah Jehan—and on opening my eyes again, I was astonished to see a peacock strutting across the quadrangle, as peacocks must have done at that time.

Emperor from 1628 to 1658, Shah Jehan was also the genius behind the nearby Shalimar Gardens, a supreme example of Mughal landscaping incorporating pavilions, waterfalls and terraces descending to a marble

EMPEROR SHAH JEHAN
(1592-1666)

tank. Its fountains were turned off when we arrived so I tipped the guardian to ensure they would be playing at 4pm—a perfect light for photography.

'*Chaar bajaay,*'—four o'clock. I had Gill repeat it twice, but returning at the given hour, we found one of Lahore's poor old *tonga* horses collapsed by the gate under a cartload of chains.

Laughing at my apparent interest, the owner had detached the cart and with an assistant pulling on its bridle, the horse struggled up and it was reattached. I'd seen some grim sights in the NWFP—pit ponies with holes in their backs from carrying bricks, pye-dogs stuck together, being pelted with stones—but this blew my fuse.

'Enough,' I shouted and we marched the man into the nearby Shalimar Circle Police Station.

'To pay a fine,' barked the sergeant opening the register and recording my complaint with a scratchy pen. 'Charge overloading.' And jumping up, he ran around his desk and belted the man on his ear.

The old horse was still there when we returned, but none of the onlookers had thought to give it a drink. Gill borrowed a bucket from a man pressing pomegranate-juice, a boy was sent into the gardens for water and as I glanced in, I saw the fountains were playing but by now, it was too dark for photography.

Gill and I later visited British landmarks all over Lahore: Aitchison College where Imran Khan received his schooling, the great ox-blood coloured University of the Punjab, the neoclassic Lahore High Court and the town hall where the bronze cannon from Kipling's *Kim,* stands on a plinth on The Mall. Then on my final afternoon, I set off alone to explore the Anarkali bazaar whose network of lanes were a contrast to the pencil-straight Mall.

Crowded and dirty, but utterly fascinating, the lanes were lined with thousands of shops and mini-markets within the bazaar.

Some sold spices, others sweetmeats, vegetables, ironware, textiles, footwear, handbags—literally everything ever made by God, or man. I passed wedding stalls selling floral shields, coloured lights and boxes of *mehndi* for applying designs to a bride's hands and feet. There were straw and rope shops with brooms, woven stools, and *charpais*—the matting beds used by the poor—embroidery shops, charcoal shops, shops displaying plastic lamps filled with goldfish, and others selling discarded hospital bottles for use by *hakims* (street healers). There were locksmiths, keysmiths, knife-grinders, tailors, tea-wallahs, men roasting corncobs, boys peeling water chestnuts and others making *paan,* a chewy mixture using areca nut wrapped in betel-nut leaves that stains the mouth the colour of a blood orange. When I stopped to ask directions in the women's market, I was seized upon by a group of animated women buying embroidered *dupattas* (a long scarf worn over the head to protect modesty) and invited for a lassi, I was asked to relate the entire Osborne family history—what my father did and what was I worth—so that I did not reach Faletti's again until after dark. I believe they were *hijras*[36] from the 'red light' district of Lahore.

The following day, Gill and I and Shefi our driver, embarked on a road trip through the Punjab in an old PTDC minibus. Our plan was to head south to Multan, to cross the Indus River to Dera Ghazi Khan, and to travel down the west bank to Jacobabad.

'Why do you want to visit Jacobabad?' Gill wanted to know. 'You'll be the first English person to go there since General Jacob.'

'Australian,' I corrected him.

'Ah,' he said, 'Dennis Lillee.'

By now I've lost count of all the towns seen on my travels. If I was writing a guide, I explored them religiously. Others simply got a nod. Still others remain treasured places whose memory remains as vivid today as when I was there: places such as the Swahili island of Lamu and Macau, an exotic cocktail of Portugal and the Orient in the South China Sea. Then serendipitously in the Punjab, I came upon Multan, a place of haunting spiritual beauty, rooted in dazzling Sufi shrines.

Sufism, 'the mystic thread in the warp and weft of Islam,' is based on a mode of living directed towards attaining a relationship with the Divine. Aesthetes strive to achieve this communion through various methods such as meditation, music, poetry and the whirling advocated by Maulana Rumi in thirteenth century Turkey. Originating in Persia, Sufism quickly attracted *murids* (devotees) in India, notably in the Punjab and Sindh.

Once part of Sindh, Multan was known to Hindu ancients as *Omphalos* (navel of the world) and in their biggest temple sat a huge idol with a ruby eye. The travelling Tang dynasty monk, Hiuen-Tsiang, noted that the deity was cast in gold, and that pilgrims travelled from far and wide to offer *puja* there. Following the Muslim conquest of Sindh in the early eighth century, the temple was destroyed and Multan became a centre of Islamic jurisprudence and culture, attracting historians and poets, along with eminent Sufis and their disciples. Visiting Multan in 1808 during his tenure as Lieutenant-Governor of Bombay, the Scottish statesmen Mountstuart Elphinstone noted the amazing number of old 'Musalman' *masjids* (mosques) graves, tombs and shrines that '... would seem to justify a belief that one lakh, or 100,000 saints, lie interred within the vicinity ...'

It was impossible to miss the shrines. They were everywhere I looked, but the richest repository adorned Multan hill, among them the mausoleum of Sheikh-ul-Islam Hazrat Baha-ud-din-Zakariya, who introduced the extremely pious Suhrawardiyya order of Sufi mysticism to Multan in 1222.

As my gaze roamed over the majestic burnt-brick building, I noticed a woman seated among other beggars at the gate. I'd never seen such a face. Leathery brown and cracked like a dry riverbed, it peered out from beneath a thin, grey blanket covered in flies. She looked almost antediluvian, the tough, rural life having exacted a heavy toll on her haughty features. I then saw her hands. For days I'd searched for a marvellous pair of hands to say the *tasbih*—the Muslim version of the rosary—and pulling out a string of turquoise glass prayer-beads from my pocket, I asked could I take her picture?

'*Gi*,' she agreed and her withered fingers began counting off the ninety-nine names glorifying Allah: *Ar-Rahman* (the All Compassionate), *Ar-Rahim* (the Merciful), *As-Salam* (the Source of Peace) I heard her whispering.

'She may keep them,' I said, to a murmur of approval from the crowd.

Most of Multan's shrines which include the masterful mausoleum of Sheikh Rukn-e-Alam, the 'Pillar of the World', are constructed of bricks interspersed with garters of glazed tiles—blue on blue, cobalt on azure, verdigris on indigo and turquoise on white—the historic colours of Islamic art. The mausoleum of Shah Shamsuddin Tabriz, a Sufi luminary from Baghdad is an equal tribute to ancient tile-makers. So too the shrine of Shah Yusuf Gardezi, an Afghan mystic whom legend says rode into Multan on a lion, using a live snake as whip. Inside I found its walls embellished with floral murals—rare in Islam—and seated in a corner poor women *murids* were counting the names of Allah, using bean seeds.

Suddenly I was filled with angst. Should I have given the beggar woman more than just a string of beads? Good-natured Shefi drove us back to the Zakariya shrine, but other beggars had taken up places and she was not among them. But as we turned to go, Gill had uttered a cry. There she was. The wily old thing had already sold my *tasbih* and was seated under a mango tree, counting out rupee notes.

Old Multan, packed with wooden houses of the purest Indo-Islamic architecture, remained in a time warp. Its bazaar was crowded with groups of women shopping for its famous hand-stitched wool shawls, *tongas* and carts pulled by big Brahmin bulls almost outnumbered cars, and sipping *chai* on a chair placed outside a textile shop, I realised what was nagging me: Multan reminded me of Marrakech in the 1960s, before its discovery by tourists.

Between research in Pakistan and writing in London, I'd received several invitations to parties hosted by Mr Qutubuddin Aziz, then Minister at the Pakistan Embassy in Knightsbridge. Although Mr Q.A. was himself a devout Muslim, the whisky flowed and guests were an eclectic mix of people flushed out of London and the Home Counties. One person I met was Sir John Biggs-Davison, a Conservative MP who had served as District Commissioner in Dera Ghazi Khan, in the southern Punjab. Our brief conversation was why Gill, Shefi and I were headed for DGK, but before leaving Multan, I had to photograph the Pak-Arab Fertiliser Company for an Arab investment magazine.

We finally located it outside the city limits, but there was no one on the gate to seek permission to enter.

'Drive through,' I instructed Shefi. 'We'll find someone inside.'

With no response to my knock, I opened a door on a large room, furnished with brown velvet drapes, deep armchairs and a television beaming a cricket match.

'Everyone must be sleeping off lunch,' said Gill creeping in behind me.

Suddenly the place was in uproar. A security guard was running across the courtyard followed by an intensely angry middle-aged man in khaki uniform with a cream cravat knotted at his neck.

He stormed into the room shouting. 'Trespassing. You're under arrest!'

'Arrest?' I said. 'I'm merely seeking permission to photograph the production plant.'

'Operating plant?' he spluttered and to Gill he ordered 'Sit down over there. What is your rank? A-B-C-D? Speak up young man.'

'D,' said Gill, sinking into a chair like a deflated balloon.

He turned on me. 'And who are you?' he fumed. 'It doesn't matter. You'll both go to jail for trespassing.'

'We're not going anywhere without afternoon tea,' I announced.

'Ah, tea. Yes.' And remembering traditional courtesies, he picked up a bell and rang it very hard.

'Bearer! Tea for three.' He bellowed the instruction.

'Can't hear the cricket score,' I said staring intently at the television.

'Cricket? You're interested in cricket?' and crossing the room, he turned up the volume.

'West Indies all out for 302,' I said. 'It's hotting-up now. Let's see what Pakistan can do in reply. I hope Imran is as good with the bat as he was with the ball. Five wickets, eh.'

And that solved that. We finished afternoon tea with the colonel (ret) and after a chat about spin bowlers, we left the Pak-Arab Fertiliser Factory without any photos, but free to continue our journey through the Punjab.

I was in my element on the flat, alluvial plains between the Chenab and the Indus. Dark-green mango plantations lined the road, camels with tinkling knee-bells plodded past, and I counted half a dozen shimmering kingfishers sweeping the canals for insects. Near Muzzafargah, Shefi stopped for me to photograph the Desert Canal and walking over the bund, I encountered a middle-aged man, wearing horn-rimmed glasses, seated

WOMEN HAD A LONG WALK FOR WATER AT THE DESERT CANAL, 1980

in dripping underwear. Getting off the Kashmore bus to wash his clothes, he'd been left behind—and it was most kind, most gracious of me to offer him a lift, but his *shalwar kameez* was still drying on a tree.

The original Dera Ghazi Khan had been swept away in a flood which I found hard to imagine in this bone-dry part of the Punjab. It was now a busy town with sugar and flour mills, textile and cement industries, but to Gill and Shefi, DGK meant only *nihari*—a rich, meat dish from Mughal kitchens for which local restaurants enjoyed a reputation. Buying a mango I sat eating it beneath the crumbling shrine to Ghazi Khan. Where was I to wash my hands? The problem was solved by a thoughtful shopkeeper who sent his son across with a little pot of water.

'Poetry readings and a marriage relieve the monotony of such a place,' said Gill when we were on the road again and as if by magic, a procession of fifteen ox-carts came rumbling towards us. They were carrying rural women to a tribal wedding and bringing up the rear was the bride-to-be riding on a decorated tractor.

By late afternoon I was concerned about accommodation. I can cope with most situations by day, but at night I must have somewhere clean and comfortable to rest my head: heaven forbid I should be like Dervla Murphy in her book *Full Tilt* '... I hadn't taken off my clothes, or slept in a bed for ten days ...'

'There's a resthouse in Choti,' a cyclist called out to Shefi. 'But it doesn't have a bed.'

'Let's try the Water and Power Development Authority house,' said Gill. 'It's for government officials, but you're a lady becoming distressed.'

'*Gi,*' said the WAPDA-wallah. 'It has a bed and water, but there's no electricity.'

'Any port in a storm,' I declared but needing to get up in the night, I found the room invaded by hundreds of mustard coloured frogs and in the light from my torch, they began hopping about like a scene from an Alfred Hitchcock movie. At least they're not tarantulas, I told myself—that would be truly terrifying.

Our ultimate destination was Jacobabad, a town named after Brigadier General John Jacob, Commandant of the 2nd Scinde Irregular Horse, who had been sent out to restore order among the tribes in 1847. I had no problem photographing the brigadier's grave in Jacobabad's small Christian cemetery, or that of his horse Messenger in the grounds of the Red Cross hospital, but further pictures were impossible. The arrival of a foreigner in Jacobabad was an event of imperial dimension and wherever we stopped, a huge crowd surrounded our dusty old bus.

'We can't come all this way without getting photos.' I smacked my hat on the mudguard to emphasise the point.

Shefi suggested I should try taking a photograph from the balcony of one of the houses, but I found the trees planted by Brigadier General Jacob were bristling with men who had shinned up for a view of me. Coming downstairs again, I drew a line in the dust and instructed everyone to stand behind it. Using his stick, a dwarf beat anyone back who disobeyed, but the mood was light-hearted—the tall, angry woman with her cameras was more entertaining than the Annual Horse and Cattle Show.

My patience had finally peaked in Jacobabad's bazaar selling ethnic crafts and guns made from car parts in the Tribal Areas. Each time I tried to take a picture, a young tribesman had jumped in front of my camera and on a third occasion, in retaliation, I slapped his face—a blow for Pakistani women—but I still feel uncomfortable about the incident.

Back in Lahore, it was clear that I'd reached the end of my tether. The boiled eggs were raw, the toast was cold, and the pot of tea was weak. I'd so much looked forward to a civilised breakfast at Faletti's that a hissy fit was the result, and detained for photographing the Lahore High Court that morning, I burst into tears. The hot trip through the Punjab had been too stressful: I needed to be able to make hot-buttered Vegemite toast and to sleep in my own bed, wrapped in my goose down duvet.

The day before my flight, Gill and I visited other places of interest— the tomb of the Emperor Jehangir, Lahore Museum with its friezes of Gandharan art, and Hazrat Mian Mir, the mausoleum of another great Sufi mystic where we found a crowd gathered around a frail woman in soiled clothes lying in the courtyard. Her eyes were sealed with pus and bending down to feel for her pulse, I thought she had expired.

'She has nine children. Her husband is a bricklayer who has brought her here for the saint to effect a cure,' was Gill's explanation as the man picked up the woman like a rag doll and carried her inside.

'You can't take pictures,' shouted a *mawlānā*[37] who was reading the Qur'an in a corner of the shrine.

'Let her be. She must learn about our beliefs,' responded a well-dressed man who was scattering pink rose petals on the tomb.

With no desire to create a scene, I approached the woman again whose arm fluttered weakly against the bricklayer who was stuffing ashes in her mouth.

'Peasants believe ashes are a cure-all,' muttered Gill looking concerned.

'She's hysterical,' pronounced the *mawlānā* coming over.

'No, she's very ill,' I said. 'I'm a nurse and I can see she's dying.'

'If you're a nurse, do something. Give us a diagnosis,' he told me.

Bending down again, I pinched the woman's jaundiced skin. The poor soul was severely dehydrated, most likely from a virulent strain of dysentery.

'Get her to hospital, or she will die.' I glared at him.

'How can you predict death? You are not God,' he fulminated.

'Take her to hospital,' I said, feeling in my pocket for taxi money and wondering once again whether I was doing the right thing. The bricklayer wouldn't be able to afford the treatment and I pictured her lying on a concrete floor in a crowded Out Patients in Lahore. One or two people have called me tough, but one must be strong to cope with such sad situations.

Thy soul has to be as the ripe mango fruit;
Its golden pulp soft and sweet for others' woes
And as hard as that fruit's stone for thine own sorrows.[38]

Home again, I confronted the ennuis of domestic life: a clapped-out boiler, three dead plants on my roof terrace and the end of an affair. *Saxum volutum non obducitur musco* : no one has been willing to support my peripatetic lifestyle: I was a witness to life, but without a witness to my own.

***

In autumn 1981 I flew to Karachi to research Sindh whose name—*Sindhu* in Sanskrit—refers to the mighty Indus River nearing the delta after its 3,219 kilometre (2,000 mile) journey from Tibet. Sindhis range from the Indo-Aryan tribal peoples known as Jats and the Mohana fishermen of the Indus, to the urban elite of Hyderabad and Karachi, but the most typical Sindhi is a hard-working peasant, invariably mortgaged to a wealthy landowner and living in clusters of mud-dwellings alongside his animals.

Karachi, the capital of Sindh, is a vast metropolis spreading inland from the Arabian Sea. A fishing community, it grew into a port under the Talpur rulers of Sindh but its real-time growth began when Sir Charles Napier became governor in 1843. Napier drained its swamps and erected a court house, a provincial assembly building, a bazaar, clock-tower and other monuments of British administration—even a Victorian folly—Frere Hall, a galleried library honouring Sir Henry Bartle Frere, the Chief Commissioner of Sindh in 1850.

Apart from this august colonial heritage, I found little endearing about Karachi whose sores erupted beyond the end of Chundrigar Road as streets of shabby tenement blocks strewn with garbage picked over by crows, dogs, and the poor. Sporadic riots, underlying Karachi's volatile character, are embedded in old grievances between native Sindhis and *Muhajirs*, Muslim refugees who settled there after partition. A city at war with itself, today Karachi combusts on a regular basis, but in 1981 the economy was booming and I felt quite safe walking about the shopping area surrounding the Empress market. There were no dress restrictions. My uniform remained cotton shirts and trousers that I deposited at a small laundrette which doubtless sent them to the *dhobi ghat,* a huge outdoor washing area by the Lyari river.

Wearing my sun-dried clothes, I visited the tomb of Muhammad Ali Jinnah who led the movement for a separate Muslim state in India, and on Sunday I took a taxi to the wealthy suburb of Clifton whose beach is a popular outing for inner city dwellers. The beachfront was thronged with families admiring stalls selling plastic flowers, shell jewellery, and other colourful objects. I strode barefoot along the sand, saying thanks, but no thanks, to camel rides and kite flying, no thanks to going crabbing, no to bunder-boating, to nuts in newspaper cones and to sweets in cellophane bags. And no again to having my picture taken by a beach photographer bearing a Polaroid camera.

'Karachi is different to the rest of Pakistan,' I was informed by a youth wishing to practise English. 'We are better educated than people in the NWFP and Baluchistan.'

'I've been to the Frontier and I'll be going to Baluchistan after Sindh,' I said.

'Be careful in Sindh,' he warned. 'Dacoits[39] hide in the trees, especially in Dadu district, and when a bus passes underneath, they jump down and rob its passengers.'

Equally concerned about dacoits, Begum Noon,[40] the chairman of the PTDC, had organised a guide who would double as translator. Adeeb, a twenty-six year old history graduate, was looking for a bride. She must be from a good family and share my interests which are cricket and English crosswords,' he informed me on our journey to Thatta, the ancient capital of Lower Sindh.

In medieval times, Sindh's wealth centred on its river ports; upstream Sukkur and Thatta, a thriving delta port, famous for textiles, and elaborately carved Hindu merchant houses. Fate caught up with Thatta in the seventeenth century when that arm of the Indus silted up and about this time, the European industrial revolution cost the livelihoods of some 40,000 weavers in the handloom business. Similar to Mocha in the Yemen, people abandoned their houses, and left in search of work. In the derelict bazaar, Adeeb showed me a group of once splendid buildings leaning against each other like tired old soldiers. All were in an advanced state of collapse.

On my first night in the countryside, I stayed in a simple resthouse beside Kheenjar Lake, a little way north of Thatta. It was a lovely balmy evening, one of those occasions when I wished I had company. As I gazed across the water, the only sound was the creaking oars of a passing boatman. The frog chorus struck up at dusk, but due to the high step up to my bungalow, I felt safe from visitors.

'Hippopotamus are unable to bend their knees, so they can't step over,' Joy Adamson had laughed as we strolled arm-in-arm, in her lovely garden overlooking Lake Naivasha. I'd gone to Kenya in 1973 to interview Mrs Adamson, the world-famous author of *Born Free*, the story of Elsa, the lioness. At this time the lake had a sizeable hippo population and to stop their nocturnal raids, she had laid logs across the end of her lush, green lawn.

On our way again next morning, mesmerised by the flow of the flat, dry landscape, I found my mind drifting back to events remembered, even as a child. Naughty things like filling Julia's pram with sand and locking Miss Petersen, our flame-haired English teacher in the school lavatory. I was jolted alert by Adeeb saying the driver wanted to pray and we'd pulled over beside a small mosque standing by the roadside.

Waiting in shade of the building, I discerned a knot of people on the horizon and drawing nearer, I saw they were carrying a *charpai* on their shoulders. We'd come upon a rural funeral. A score of sweating men shambled up and unloading the corpse, they lined up behind an imam who came out of the mosque to say the *salat al-janazah*—the Muslim funeral prayer seeking pardon for the deceased.

'A WOMAN HAS DIED IN CHILDBIRTH,' SAID ADEEB, 1981

'A woman has died in childbirth,' said Adeeb as grave diggers started chipping away at the sun-baked earth. 'It will take them hours to dig a big enough hole.'

As we were walking back to the car, the driver called a warning. He'd spotted an *echis* (saw-toothed viper), an aggressive snake that strikes with such force, it may launch itself at a victim. A camel-rider was bitten on the forehead by an *echis,* he recounted to Adeeb.

I was more concerned about snakes than dacoits in Sindh. The World Health Organisation estimates that some 20,000 persons die annually of snakebite—many in Pakistan. But snakes were on our agenda. Adeeb knew of a Baluch *nawab* who was said to be able to cure the sick, via the unorthodox method of a snakebite. He lived in Tajpur near Hyderabad, our destination.

A tall, fierce-looking man wearing an orange kaftan received us at a village house where several people lay curled up on mats in the yard.

'I've heard of your ability to cure the sick and as we're in the area, I thought to visit. I hope this is all right,' I told him.

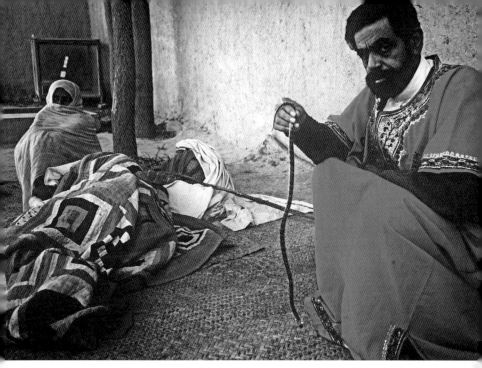

THE *NAWAB* AND HIS PATIENTS TREATED BY SNAKE-BITE, 1981

'Yes, I can even cure people suffering from leukaemia,' he said. 'I control the amount of venom by compressing the poison sack.'

Ushering us inside a living room, he handed me testimonials from grateful patients.

'I've treated 126 sick people. Only four have died. The rest went on to recover,' he continued.

'As an expert, which do you consider is the most dangerous snake?' I asked.

'The *peehan* of the krait family,' he replied in excellent English. 'It's venom first blinds, then as the blood clots, the victim suffocates. I experimented on a dog which died in five minutes.'

'But aren't your patients frightened?' I pressed him.

'Initially they're afraid. But when they begin to feel better, they want to be bitten again.'

He frowned. 'Aren't you scared of snakes?'

'No,' I said. 'I grew up with snakes in Australia.'

Going outside he returned carrying several snakes that he dropped on the floor. Adeeb looked terrified as they slithered around the furniture legs, and while certain they couldn't be venomous, I quietly pulled up my feet, an action that seemed to irritate the *nawab*.

'Come and meet my favourites,' he said, beckoning us onto the porch where wooden boxes were ranged against a wall.

'This is an *echis*. I will pay £10,000 to anyone who dares to hold it,' he said of a buff-coloured snake coiled behind chicken wire. 'That is a *naja-naja* (cobra). Death from respiratory failure in fifteen minutes.'

'And would you like to hold *this!*' Opening the door of a third cage, he thrust a fat brown snake into my hands.

'Bravo! You didn't flinch,' said Adeeb when we were on the road again.

'Snakes have been associated with healing since time immemorial. A serpent-entwined rod associated with the Greek god Asclepius remains a symbol of medicine. I know. I'm a nurse,' I replied arrogantly.

Adeeb shuddered. 'I personally would rather die.'

We spent that night in Hyderabad, the northern capital of Sindh, founded by the Kalhora dynasty in 1768, the year Captain Cook left Plymouth for the Southern Hemisphere.

Adeeb was staying with an uncle in the glass bangle business and for once I found my hotel was full. The Hyderabad First Eleven was playing a college team from Karachi and when the Karachi boys filed into the dining room, the questions had tumbled out. Could I brief them on Europe? Did they keep the crown in England? The captain inquired on behalf of others. Then prompted by team-mates, the leg-slip stood up and recited some lines by Shah Abdul Latif.

'Ah,' said Adeeb next morning. 'Shah Abdul Latif is our greatest Sindhi poet. His verses are the staff of life for everyone from students to peasants. When close to death, it is said he performed his own ablutions before pulling on a shroud and ordering the musicians to play until his last breath.'

Poets, *pirs* and *fakirs* are woven into Sindhi culture like the patches in a *rilli*. In Sehwan Sharif is the mausoleum of Lal Shabaz Qalander, a revered twelfth century mystic, of the Qalandariyah order of dervishes

MOHAMMED ALAM CHANNA, AT ONE TIME THE WORLD'S TALLEST MAN, 1981

who wander the countryside wearing only a rough woollen raiment and carrying a begging bowl.

Sehwan was not on our itinerary, but Adeeb persuaded me to visit his shrine and as I stood aside a door to allow people out, a man had emerged and straightening up, I thought he would never end: it was Mohammed the Beanstalk.

'Big isn't beautiful,' said Mohammed Alam Channa who stood 251 centimetres (8 feet 3 inches) tall.

'The constant staring keeps me a virtual prisoner here. When I do go out, I need two friends to protect me from crowds. The *tonga*-wallahs are another problem. Either they refuse to take me, or they charge me twice as much. It's very expensive being tall.' He spoke in a soft, sad voice.

'Ask what he weighs?' I told Adeeb as we spoke an ante-room in the shrine.

'400 pounds,' sighed the giant[41] who was twenty-six years old. 'My brothers and sisters are normal height. So was I until the age of ten when I began shooting up.' He twisted and untwisted fingers as thick as sausages. Did he eat giant-size portions of food I wanted to know?

'Naa,' chorused his two helpers who were listening. 'He eats no more than any of us.'

'The governor of Sindh gave him a security job in Karachi, but there was never any peace,' Adeeb translated as Mohammed spoke again. 'Strangers used to wake him up at all hours to see how tall he is. So now he's back in Sehwan working as a servant of the shrine.'

On our way to the resthouse where I was now spending the night, I realised that in my excitement at meeting Mohammed, I hadn't had a good look at the mausoleum.

'It's Thursday. There's *qawwali* (Sufi devotional music) every Thursday evening,' said Adeeb. 'So it's not a problem to go back.'

The giant was nowhere to be seen when we returned to the shrine that had become a hive of activity. Lining the entrance were stalls selling *pakoray* fritters and ghee-rich sweetmeats, and beggars holding out their tins. Many poor peasants—Hindus as well as Muslims—believing the saint will hear their prayers, had packed the courtyard where six musicians were playing a *dhammal,* a lament, in praise of the deceased Qalander.

The tapping on a *tabla* was accompanied by a harmonium, sharp clapping and chanting. As the rhythm picked up, a tall Sufi pounding a huge double-sided barrel drum, jumped up and began whirling, his long black locks flying out around him. Transfixed by the sight, an onlooker rose, then others—including women—and with arms outstretched and perspiration pouring down their faces, they whirled around and around then giving a wild yell, they fled into the night.

'Christ,' I said to myself. 'That scared the shit out of me.'

A day late, we reached Mohen-jodaro to a smell of wood-smoke from evening fires. I was the only guest at the PTDC inn whose manager cooked me a tomato omelette and bemoaned the lack of tourists to the celebrated site.

The British writer Jonathan Raban maintains that 'spells of acute loneliness are an essential part of travel' and that night I struggled with an ability to be self-contained, but a profound loneliness enveloped me like a shroud. My poorly lit room had no radio or television (don't be ridiculous), and in a hard bed under a threadbare blanket, I lay awake thinking of the souls of the dead out in the ruins.

Mohen-jodaro—a Dravidian word for 'Mound of the Dead'—was one of the most advanced settlements in the Indus Valley civilisation four to five thousand years ago. Excavations have unearthed a city planned on a grid system whose long, straight streets were lined with three-to-four storey houses, each with an individual drainage system. There were wells, and there was even a state granary, but who ruled Mohen-jodaro remains a mystery, although a vast bath sunk in a spacious courtyard, indicates likely use in purification ceremonies by a priestly sect.

Exhibits in a small museum including terracotta figurines of buxom women indicate this may have been a mother goddess, and the chess sets, seals and images of tools and animals reveal the ancient citizens were skilled potters. I was amazed by miniature oxcarts identical to those rumbling along the roads and on meeting the curator, I saw his face was straight out of Mohen-jodaro. Tannin-coloured, with prominent cheekbones and a narrow forehead, he was unlike anyone I'd seen in Sindh—until I met the Mohanas who claim direct descent from the Indus Valley peoples.

In 1981, some four hundred Mohana families lived on houseboats on the Indus in Sukkur, a number reduced by the catastrophic floods of 2010 and 2011. As I had planned on my birthday, I went off to distribute sweets to children playing on the riverbank. Applauded by an audience of little girls, little boys were running nimbly across the backs of buffaloes standing up

WITH MOHANA KIDS ON MY 41ST BIRTHDAY IN SUKKUR, ON THE INDUS RIVER

to their ears in water. The children's cries of joy at this wonderful game, and the dull clonk of underwater 'buffalo bells,' are an enduring memory of my forty-first. This and a young boy called Mohammad Damman, who invited me onto his family's *kashti* (houseboat).

About 18 metres (60 feet) long, it was as solid as a Dutch barge, its most characteristic feature being a bluff-nosed prow to deflect the shock, in event of striking a sandbank. Bedding was rolled up neatly in the prow and to my surprise, a tiny galley was stacked with rose-patterned chinaware once used by British civil servants manning the canal posts. Mohammad's mother, a slip of a woman wearing a thin pink sari and bright green *dupatta,* squatted on deck preparing *iftar* (evening meal after dusk) of rice and *palla,* a herring-like fish eaten by Mohanas since the dawn of time.

'When bad weather stops them fishing, their pet birds do it for them,' said Adeeb pointing to several great white egrets and grey herons perched on a plank suspended from the gunwale. Each bird had a string attached to one leg, allowing it to dive, but not to escape with a fish. At that moment an Indus River dolphin surfaced off the prow surprising Adeeb who had never seen one. 'They are very rare,' he said. 'In the past, the Mohanas used trained otters to herd them into a net where they were killed for oil in their lamps.'

'*Muhke tawansa jaam pyar ahey,*' chirped young Mohammad as we said goodbye. 'He loves you a lot,' said Adeeb. 'I would consider you myself if you were ten years younger. And a Muslim.'

'But I don't do crosswords,' I replied.

Back in Karachi I was booked on a morning flight to Gwadar, a small fishing village on the Makran Coast of Baluchistan. Foreigners were not allowed to visit the area that was ear-marked for development, but Begum Noon had wangled permission—a stay limited to just four hours, between flights.

Until Sultan Said bin Taimur sold it back to Pakistan in 1958, Gwadar and district belonged to Oman, a legacy evident in the features of many Makranis, who like people on the Tihama coast of Yemen, trace their ancestral roots to Africa. A Greek admiral, sailing along the coast during the retreat of Alexander the Great, had dubbed them *Ichthyophagi* (fish-eaters), a name that sticks to this day.

'Everything eats fish. Even the dogs,' said the District Commissioner's driver delegated to whizz me around Gwadar whose sandblasted, mud-walled houses with matting roofs were packed together on a vast bay flanked by hammer-shaped promontories.

Slim, bare-chested fishermen wearing ankle-length *lungis* were plugging seams on their boats with kapok and shark oil. Others unloaded fish into baskets strapped on camels waiting patiently on the rippled grey-sand beach. An overpowering stench, remarked on by A.W. Hughes in a *Gazeteer of Sind* in 1876, came from silver carpets of sardines spread out to dry, but curiously there were no seabirds. On the other hand Gwadar swarmed with slinking, swollen-bellied cats.

The one person I wanted to meet on my lightning visit was a Catholic nun who ran a clinic for leprosy patients. I found her in a one-room flat behind the bazaar. It contained only a camp bed, a metal wardrobe and a table on which lay a Bible and an English-Urdu dictionary.

GWADAR ON THE MAKRAN COAST OF BALUCHISTAN, 1981

'I intended to stay a year, but like the man who came to dinner, I'm still here,' said Sister Helen, an elderly bird-like lady originally from Massachusetts.

'I've been here ten years now, but it's kinda dull and it gets very hot in summer,' she continued. 'Will you take tea? Along with soap, dressings and disinfectant, the sisters in Karachi send me a weekly food parcel of tea and jelly jam. Fish? No, I hate it. I eat biscuits, bananas and, once a month, a chicken.'

Sister Helen and a cheerful, bushy-bearded Baluch paramedic cared for 179 leprosy patients registered with the clinic. As Helen was putting drops in the cloudy eyes of an old date farmer, a woman wrapped in a purple chador arrived in a donkey cart. Leprosy had eroded both her hands and toes and I guessed her age correctly, as thirty-five.

'She is ostracised by her family, so we look after her as best we can,' said 'Doctor' Mehdi, unwrapping dirty bindings revealing a deep, even hole in the sole of her left foot.

'That's not leprosy,' I said.

'Rats,' said Mehdi, swabbing the cavity with peroxide. 'She sleeps on the floor and at night her feet are gnawed by rats.'

I was shocked. Although my flight was due to depart in forty minutes, taking Mehdi with me, I rushed out of the clinic and into the bazaar.

'*Charpai*,' I yelled running past stalls of dried fish, sandy dates, plastic sandals, and rotting apples. 'We must buy her a bed!'

Handing the equivalent of six dollars to a woman with a gold padlock in her septum and with Mehdi clutching the *charpai*, we sped to the woman's shack. I unrolled the *charpai* and Mehdi banged in its legs, but there was no time to fetch the woman to try her new sleeping arrangements: the plane was on the airstrip with its engines running and racing out, I climbed on board.

It was a soft evening beside the Arabian Sea in Karachi. I watched fireflies in the jasmine switching on and off like fairy lights on a Christmas tree. Mosquitoes from the mangroves had not yet driven me inside the Beach Luxury Hotel where I ordered grilled prawns in the garden bistro.

'*Jinga* from Gwadar,' said the waiter.

'I've just been to Gwadar,' I said, but he obviously didn't believe me.

***

Quetta, the inland capital of Baluchistan, was my penultimate stop in Pakistan. The PTDC had telephoned its Lourdes Hotel to ensure my room was clean and having arrived on flight PK 311, I found staff had taken the instructions to heart. Every item of furniture stood in the garden. Carpets were being beaten on a line and an ancient heater was filled to overflowing with kerosene. I put a biscuit jar containing glass-fish I'd bought in Sardar bazaar, on the top to warm the water, and pulled on a jumper against the chilly night. A log fire crackled in the dining room where I was to be served the same evening meal, every day of my five-day stay: soup, kebabs, and crème caramel.

Baluchistan's ethnic population comprises many different tribes chief of whom are the Bugti, Marri, Mengal, Rind, and the dark-skinned Brahui who claim descent from the original Dravidian population.

The average Baluch is a powerfully built fellow whose greatest pride is a beard, sometimes 30 centimetres (12 inches) in length. Naturally

A POWINDAH MIGRATION THROUGH THE BOLAN PASS IN BALUCHISTAN, 1981

aggressive, like the Pathan, he is equally hospitable, and although blood feuds are common, few people greet each other with more tenderness. On my first morning, I saw two ferocious-looking men give each other a triple kiss in Jinnah Road, the main street of Quetta, but I was equally aware that the same men would not hesitate to have a woman buried alive for sullying the family honour.

A severe earthquake in 1935 had flattened Quetta killing 35,000 people. Being relatively new, it therefore lacked the crusty ambiance of Peshawar, but the broad, tree-lined boulevards and an ambling pace of life made it seem like a large country town. And the people were equally friendly. Entering the Habib Bank to change some traveller's cheques, I was charmed to be offered tea (in a cup and saucer) in contrast to Islamabad, where a teller had said I could not change money.

'Why ever not?' I'd demanded.

'Because you're an individual,' was his perplexing explanation.

Thirty years ago there was not much to see in Quetta. I visited the bazaar overflowing with nuts and fruits, especially apples, and wandering about, I found the 'Street of Partridge Sellers' stacked with cages of small grey birds with sharp beaks.

In the absence of entertainment, quail and partridge contests were eagerly followed by the poor: the better-off played squash in the Quetta Club. At night there was nothing to do, but I had my book. On this trip it was *Tracks,* the account by Robyn Davidson of her nine month crossing of Central Australia with four camels and a dog for company. '... The trip was easy ... she writes. ' ... It was no more dangerous than crossing the street...'

Switching off the light, I accepted I was not up for that sort of journey: my own travelling life was hard enough.

Next morning I set off to travel down the Bolan Pass, a rugged slash in the Brahui Mountain Range in central Baluchistan. Sibi, at the eastern end of the pass, was one of the few places considered safe to visit, for apart from a risk of kidnap by dissident tribesmen, accommodation outside Quetta was limited to rough *muzzaffar-khans* (travellers' inns).

My notes speak of a crisp, autumn day with the Bolan River, resembling a turquoise ribbon, snaking its way around sand-coloured rocks, and of poplars along the banks shedding showers of golden leaves. There was little traffic. Just Pakistan's flamboyantly painted trucks, embellished with flowers, lions, and quotes from the Qur'an, and farther out, the spectacle of *powindah* nomads plodding south to winter pastures in Sindh.

Baluch migrations from Persia have historically followed the Bolan route to the sub-continent and at one point, we stopped for me to photograph a group of stragglers. A black-turbaned tribesman was leading swaying piles of blankets, balanced on camels, that I assumed were his wives. Ragged children clutching puppies and dragging goats brought up the rear. Suddenly the man had halted, and with one hand on his rifle and the other outstretched, he strode purposely towards me. Had he confused my tele-lens for a gun barrel?

Hurtling down the bank with the cigarette he'd requested, my driver saved the situation. 'Give him the packet,' I told him. 'We'll buy more in Sibi.'

We reached Sibi in mid-afternoon to find it humming with activity. Here a knife-grinder, there a man crushing sugarcane juice, and everywhere tailors pumping antique treadle machines. The driver said that Sibi was the hottest town in Pakistan. So hot you could boil tea straight from the tap. But I wasn't listening. Threading their way through the *tongas* and cyclists were groups of tall, dark and incredibly handsome men. They were Marri and Bugti tribesmen wearing huge turbans, baggy trousers, and tunics slashed open to the chest. Every man was a dark-haired Adonis. Some had ringed their eyes with kohl; others sported a single gold earring. It was a Baluch version of the paseo. Except that there were no women. What would they be doing in Sibi on a Friday evening?

'Meeting friends for *chai*,' said my driver.

Baltistan was the end of my travels in Pakistan. Where is Baltistan? It's a good question for *Who Wants to be a Millionaire?*

A remote mountain agency lying in the far north-east corner of Pakistan, adjacent to Xinjiang province in western China, it was known to Chinese ancients as Tibet of the Apricots because of the abundance of this fruit that grows there. Formerly Buddhist, its feudal rulers adopted Islam during the Mughal era, but its more recent history relates to the division of Kashmir in 1947—Ladakh going to India and Baltistan remaining in Pakistan.

A Tibetan influence is evident in the people who speak a classic form of Tibetan and while of Caucasian origin, many display Mongoloid features and their coppery coloured complexions are weathered by a tough, outdoor life. Short, and frequently stooped from carrying heavy loads, they cultivate barley, wheat and millet on rare flat pieces of land in a savage environment. Without the sure-footed yak, it is unlikely many Baltis would survive: yak milk is rich in fats, yak butter is added to tea, yak fat is used as oil in lamps by the poor, and its skin is made into coats, and used as bedding.

It is difficult to estimate the size of Baltistan since much of the landscape is almost perpendicular. Covering 26,000 square kilometres (10,040 square miles)—roughly the size of Sicily—it consists of five valleys surrounded by some of the world's highest peaks, including the formidable K-2, 8,611 metres (28,251 feet).

Everywhere are towering mountains and the sound of running water. I had seen the Indus flowing serenely through Sindh: here it was a swollen grey torrent, thrusting around boulders and surging through chasms. To cross, people squatted in a cut-off box that is pulled over on cables from the other side. There are also fragile footbridges, but the Baltis seemed unconcerned by danger. In one spot we passed a man perched like a bird on suspension wires. On hearing our jeep, he casually looked up from whatever he was doing without a safety harness, 356 metres (1,000 feet) above the river.

'Making repairs madam,' my driver explained.

Hassan Khan was my favourite of the many drivers who ferried me around Pakistan. About twenty-eight, he had crinkle-chip hair, a wiry frame and a sharp wit. No better driver existed to tackle the brutal mountain tracks when our adventures were considerable: he even stopped me falling into the Shigar River when I was trying to photograph a far-off peak.

The Shigar joins the Indus in Skardu, Baltistan's tiny high-altitude capital that overlooks a gargantuan rock, like Cheops pyramid, jutting out of the river. The view of the valley is one of the most dramatic sights in Pakistan, but I soon discovered that around every bend lay a view to die for—if only it hadn't been such an arduous trip to get there.

It was an all-day drive to the Shigar Valley 32 kilometres (20 miles) east of Skardu, but autumn was indeed the perfect season. Golden under ripening crops, the fields were crisscrossed by canals fed by snowmelt and the trees drooped with apricots, peaches, pears and nectarines. Among the box-like shops in Shigar village, I found a mosque of pure Tibetan architecture, possibly hundreds of years old. Dassu, at the head of the valley is where expeditions set out for K-2 base camp, a fifteen-day trek across the Baltoro Glacier rumbling out of the Karakorams. Lieutenant Henry Haversham Godwin-Austen who mapped K-2 in 1860 writes: ' … Peak K-2 appeared of an airy blue tint surrounded by the yellower peaks of K-1, K-3 and others, all over 24,000 feet[42] in height. Other minor peaks by the hundreds thrust up their heads…'

The route to Khaplu Valley was another enthralling journey through alpine desert dotted with sedge and tundra-type grasses. Small hamlets dotted the mountainsides: we passed teams of *dzo* (a yak-cow cross) crushing the harvest, and farmers walking along the road beneath bundles of thatch resembled Strawman from the *Wizard of Oz*. The imposing, if dilapidated, fortress of the Rajah of Khaplu dominated the valley, and while poking about here for a photograph, I encountered a child who reacted with horror, dropping the lilies it was picking, and fleeing down the hillside.

'Thought you were a fairy, madam,' Hassan laughed, and going into Khaplu's small bazaar, he returned with our lunch: potato-stuffed dough wrapped in pages from the *Gazette of West Pakistan,* Dp.2, 1958.

I had flown to Skardu, but was to leave for Gilgit again via the Karakoram Highway, entering Pakistan over the lofty Khunjerab Pass 4,693 metres (15,397 feet) from China. A huge project, building the KKH meant blasting a route from here through the mountains to Abbottabad in the Punjab, a distance of 800 kilometres (500 miles). We passed work gangs clearing avalanches with garden spades, and bulldozers pushing gargantuan boulders off the road and into the Indus. At one point blocked by a landslide, Hassan suggested we should wait in a works shed where a man, covered in grey dust, was slumped in an office chair. He was Mr A. A. Butt, Chief Surveyor, Mile 10, Skardu-Gilgit section.

'Welcome, please,' said Mr Butt swivelling around, and I observed a tension behind his eyes.

'I have migration,' he touched his head. 'All the blasting. Big problem. Last week six men buried under scree. Yesterday Chinese engineer blown into Indus. Please honour with one aspirin. To help migration.' And standing up, he poured us tin mugs of vile butter tea.

My plan had been to visit Rama Lake and to spend the night in Astore— 'excellent trout fishing and good resthouse madam'—said Hassan, but the 56 kilometres (34 miles) corrugated track from the Jaglot turn-off had become a bone-shaking five hour drive. Adding to our discomfort was my insistence that we stop for a walker whose uncured yak-skin jacket left everything in the jeep—my hat included, stinking of rancid fat.

'Bunji last place for madam to wash,' declared Hassan as the road climbed upwards from the river gorge and straightened out across a bleak, high-altitude plain. The great ice-mass of Nanga Parbat that I'd seen from the plane hove into view, then just ahead of us, a plume of smoke spiralled up from the tree-less landscape. A Frontier Works Organisation truck containing six soldiers had rolled and was burning furiously.

'Do something!' I yelled to several drivers of other vehicles who stood by watching the accident. But nothing could be done. No one carried water and the Indus was now a thousand metres below.

I was desperate to reach Astore after this experience, but arriving at dusk we confronted a *chowkidar* who refused to unlock the rest-house. Where was our permission letter? We didn't have one …

A damp mountain village with nowhere to sleep was my nightmare come true. Dismayed I sat in the jeep watching a large red rooster crowing out its lungs on top of a wood pile. But how fortune can change in the blink of an eye as from out of the fog walked two tall, blond men wearing the distinctive blue beret of the United Nations Peacekeeping Force. Astore lay on the Kashmir Line of Control—they were Swedish observers—and yes, I could stay the night with them.

Their cabin had a roaring log-fire, SAS posters stuck on the walls, and wildflowers arranged in cut-off tins of Tuborg. A hot shower followed by dinner of grilled trout, mashed potato, pickled gherkins, and a sweet tapioca and raisin soup awaited. A bottle of wine was consumed and I slept like a top.

'The trout grow huge—up to 10 kilos (22 pounds),' said Major Bernstone of Rama Lake next morning. 'But you can't go down. We are on heightened alert.' He strapped on a pair of binoculars for daily patrol.

Reaching Jaglot again we rejoined the KKH following the Indus sending spray high into the air where it crashed against rock-walls. In one spot, an innovative farmer was growing a plot of wheat watered by the mist and, just beyond, Hassan stopped so I could climb down and photograph the river thundering through a chasm.

In the unstable landscape, my every step shot rocks into the river, but I finally jumped down onto grey, alluvial sand, dotted with colossal boulders. It was a good loo spot but, on squatting down, I noticed a set of pugmarks leading into a cave. The breeze had not yet smoothed their edges and with mounting horror, I caught a tangy feline odour.

'Snow leopard,' I screamed, but my cry was lost in the roar of the river and looking down from above, Hassan simply waved.

'Lots of wild animals around here, madam,' he said when I arrived panting, and semi-hysterical, back on the road. 'Leopard, ibex, wolves.' Leaving the gorge we drove across a grey, stony plateau where *chikor* (snow partridge) ran wildly off the road, as if reluctant to fly. Finally, across the valley there was Gilgit, lit up by golden rays of sun, and the surprise of Aileen who had flown up during a forty-eight hour lay-over in Rawalpindi. She was seated comfortably on the verandah of the Chinnar Inn with Riaz Khan from Hunza.

'We could see your jeep like a tiny speck winding round the mountain,' she stood up and gave me a hug.

'How was your flight and did you bring some Scotch?' I said all in one breath. 'The sun's not yet over the yardarm, but I could do with a shot.'[43]

DAWN

Karachi Wednesday, November 9, 1983

'Guide to Pakistan'
presented to Zafar

ISLAMABAD, Nov 8: The Federal Minister for Information and Broadcasting, Raja Mohammad Zafarul Haq, was presented here today a book, "An insight and guide to Pakistan" by its author Christine Osborne, an Australian writer and photographer.

The book is photo-guide on Pakistan since its creation in 1947. The book also makes detailed references to history, geography and wildlife and examines Pakistan's rich cultural heritage.—APP

Chapter 7

The *Marabout* from Taroudant

In 1964 when I first set foot in Morocco as a young backpacker, I was captivated by the desert and mountain scenery and the pageantry of traditional life. This amour fou has never entirely cooled and in a lifetime of travel, I still consider this rugged, individual, shoulder of north-west Africa—*al-Maghrib al-Aqsa*—to be one of the most exotic places on earth. Just an hours drive inland from Atlantic beaches is the hot, red *bled*[44] dotted with dramatic, sunbaked *ksour*—fortified Berber villages—and a medieval world long vanished from Europe. Here I discovered my imagined land of Aladdin and his magic lamp—in fact the sorcerer of the folktale was himself from the Maghreb.[45]

My acquaintance with Morocco began in Tangier, birthplace of the celebrated Berber globetrotter Ibn Battūtah, who set off on a pilgrimage to Mecca in 1325, and ultimately travelled as far east as China.

Seen from the deck of an old ferry plying the Straits of Gibraltar, Tangier resembled a pot of milk that had boiled over onto grey-stained ramparts enclosing a médina (old Arab town) rising in tiers to a hilltop kasbah. The word 'kasbah' had sent a frisson of excitement down my spine and stepping ashore, I caught a scent of jasmine sold by blind men waiting in the port, along with taxidrivers, faux-guides, drug dealers, moneychangers, porters and pimps. Literally everyone was there, just as crowds had gathered for approaching sails in former times.

Tangier's strategic location, on a headland at the entrance to the Mediterranean, historically attracted foreign interest. Carthaginians, Romans, Portuguese, and Spanish—even the British when it was included in the dowry of Catherine de Braganza on her marriage to Charles II—all once occupied the town. In 1923, the League of Nations, concerned by German ambitions in North Africa, designated it a tax-free International Zone where each signatory—seven European States and the USA—established a legation creating a baffling bureaucracy for local citizens. By 1945 Tangier counted eighty-four banks and ten post offices, with some hundreds of bars and brothels catering to the freewheeling lifestyle of its estimated 60,000 foreign residents.

Tangier had lost its privileges in 1956, but when Ruth and I arrived—my diary says it was the 22 June 1964—it still numbered many expatriates seduced by its enigmatic charm, cheap drugs, and for many, the boys. A Who's Who of writers—either resident, or those who had sojourned there—would include André Gide, Albert Camus, Tennessee Williams, William Burroughs, Jack Kerouac, Truman Capote, Allen Ginsberg, Gore Vidal, and Paul Bowles, known as—the 'Father of Tangier'—whose haunting novel *The Sheltering Sky* defined Morocco for the armchair traveller.

Inspired by the cameos of every day life, Bowles found Tangier a perfect place to write. 'Everyone is always leaving tomorrow,' he is reported to have told Paul Theroux. But he never left and, except for visits to Paris, Rome and Acapulco, rarely did Woolworth heiress Barbara Hutton who lived in a palace in the kasbah.

Ruth and I did not encounter any celebrities. Instead we met Jimmy, a short, olive-skinned *Tanjawi* returning from a trip to Spain. Jimmy guided us to the Pension Mauretania above a café in the Petit Socco in the heart of the médina. Our room was small—shower and WC along the hall—but we stayed a week, chaperoned by Jimmy, who seemed to be flush with money whose source we never established.

Our days began with a swim in the Baie de Tangier, the long beach linking the port and Le Vieux Montagne where many British lived in houses surrounded by scented cottage gardens. Jimmy came too. 'Eyes are watching,' he muttered as he sat on the sand to mind our clothes.

In the médina we ate our first couscous—a golden mound of wheat grain, topped with juicy chunks of lamb, marrow, and chickpeas. And it was here, in a tiny bar beneath the kasbah, that we smoked out first pipe of cannabis, or *kif* as it is known in Morocco.

Everyone was smoking in the Café Baba. About midnight an elderly musician, accompanied by others tapping terracotta drums, began plucking an *oud* (Arabian lute) and two boy-dancers with kohl-ringed eyes and jingling bracelets, had commenced dancing among the tightly packed tables. As one sashayed past, Jimmy stuck a 50 dirham note—an overprint of a 5000 franc note from the protectorate—on his sweating forehead. The youth responded with a high-pitched, quavering sound made with his tongue: Jimmy called it ululating. It was hot—even at this hour—and several pipes of *kif* had left me dizzy.

'That's Sidi Hosni—Barbara Hutton's palace,' said Jimmy, leading us onto the tiny balcony for air. He pointed to a building below, half-hidden behind high white walls festooned with purple bougainvillea.

'At her annual ball, she sits on a gold throne, showering guests with rose petals. You know she had seven husbands, including Cary Grant.' He raised an eyebrow.

Barbara had the gateway to the médina enlarged to allow access for her Rolls Royce (she had two—according to Jimmy—one white, one black) but this had not disturbed its character.

Each afternoon we explored its narrow streets and, accustomed to wide roads in rural Australia, we were intrigued. Lined with thick-walled, terraced houses, they zigzagged this way and that, sometimes leading us through spooky passages, or stopping dead, so we had to go back. Others ended at steps ascending to an upper level, or opened onto a cobbled square with a public fountain. Higher up was a view of Tangier over flat roofs with washing flapping in a breeze off the bay. No one bothered us—we were known as 'Jimmy's wives.' The only upset occurred in the Thursday market on the Grand Socco. The Rif mountain women wrapped in white *haiks*, red-striped shawls and wearing Mexican-style sombreros had made a striking picture with their pots of honey and tubs of yoghurt, but one hurled an egg at me when I took out my camera. Fortunately she was not a good shot.

The Grand Socco was a popular subject with many artists including the Australian Orientalist Hilda Rix Nicholas[46] who visited Tangier with her sister Elsie before the outbreak of World War I. Always lively with traders and shoppers, it separates the médina from the Ville Nouvelle, the new town built during the French protectorate (1912-56) and Tangier's heyday as an 'interzone' (the title of a collection of stories by William Burroughs, who lived in a pension on the rue Magellan).

Many of the street names—the rue d'Angleterre, the rue d'Espagne, and the rue Hollande, are a legacy from this time. We used to buy faded postcards in the Librarie des Colonnes on the Boulevard Pasteur, and retire

THE RIF MARKET ON THE GRAND SOCCO IN TANGIER, 1964

to the Gran Café de Paris to write home of our adventures. It never dawned that the café-terrasse—of which it was the biggest on the boulevard—is the preserve of Moroccan men, and the sight of Ruth and me seated in this bastion of male society must have shocked local women whose traditional place of social exchange is the *hammam*.

At the poste restante one day, I received a crumpled aerogramme from mum. Her neighbour, a retired minister of the church, had a brother living in Tangier whose name was George Greaves. Jimmy knew George and it was arranged to meet in Madame Porte's Salon de Thé, reputed for its delicious cream cakes and the crispest, driest of martinis.

I recognised George at once. A bulky, gentleman with a speckled beard, he was seated at a centre table with his hands crossed on a cane.

'A journalist? Is that what they think?' He chuckled. 'My years in Tangier were spent working for the British Secret Intelligence Service. I used the cover of a stringer for the *Express*. That's likely where the family got the journalist idea.' Snapping his fingers, he ordered tea.

'In the old days Tangier was a hotbed of activity—gun-running, smuggling, prostitution, spying. The main listening post was El Minzah Bar—get Jimmy to take you there. I had no cover. Lived on me wits. Had they known what I knew, I would have been shot. He emitted a hooting laugh. 'Everyone was crooked. The Spanish general in Tetouan had three pictures on his wall: one of Hitler, one of Franco, and a third of Mussolini. The Deuxième Bureau used to pay its agents in cocaine. Drug smuggling is today's racket for stupid bastards. You can buy a ton of hashish, but the seller will inform the police.'

AUSTRALIAN SPY GEORGE GREAVES,
LONG-TIME RESIDENT OF TANGIER

Suddenly he looked wistful. 'Barbara used to give terrific parties. If you didn't receive an invite you were dead, dear. But most of my vintage are dead. Harry the German giant who disappeared in Algiers, Jack-in-the-Box—a double agent—and the Spanish nobleman found in bed with a boy. I'm the last one—today Tangier is for tourists.'

If the difference between a tourist and a traveller is a question of time, Ruth and I were definitely travellers. We travelled slowly—a week here, a week there—but nothing as slowly as Victorian journey-women obliged to travel on horseback, or in a variety of bumpy carriages. From Tangier, we had no problem hitchhiking, via Casablanca to Marrakech, given a lift by Miss Moordaff, an English nurse driving a Morris Minor.

Marrakesh is a natural halt for travellers crossing the High Atlas from the north, and for traders heading up from the southern oases. In the eleventh century, it was made a permanent settlement by the Almoravids, a Berber dynasty whose empire also included vast swathes of the Iberian peninsula. In the twelfth century, the Almoravid sultans were overthrown by another

THE DJEMAA EL-FNAÂ SQUARE IN THE HEART OF MARRAKECH, 1984

Berber dynasty, the Almohads, an austere tribe from the mountain village of Tin Mal. The great Koutoubia Mosque, named after the *kutubiyin*—sellers of manuscripts—who once set up stalls outside, was built by the Almohads who maintained courts in Seville as well as Marrakech. The iconic rose-red ramparts around the médina, a mixture of water and earth from the surrounding Haouz plain, also date from this time.

In the médina we soon attracted a companion—Driss—a twenty-year-old *Marrakchi* who spoke good English (his father was a professeur). As with Jimmy, we spent a happy week together and for me, in particular, none of the tensions existed that would arise later when I began travelling in a professional capacity.

Marrakech was the joy of innocence and discovery, and an almost rapturous delight at its great covered souqs offering an emporium of exotic crafts. There were shops stacked with wrought-iron grills, brass lamps, and terracotta pots. There were shops piled ceiling height with carpets and rugs. Others sold traditional jewellery—Hands of Fatima, Berber pendants and the silver fibula (brooch) worn by desert nomads. There were big shops filled with painted furniture and small shops specialising in shimmering scarves.

'Yellow for men, red for women,' said Driss of the Souq des Babouche, an entire block of shops selling soft-leather slippers. My notes say it was a Thursday afternoon—the busiest time of the Muslim week—and the *kissaria* (central market) was thronged with women shoppers wearing blue, pink, mauve, and purple djellabahs, and black scalloped veils.

Leaving the souqs, we found ourselves on the Djemaa el-Fnaâ, a vast square also seething with activity. It was like a Cirque du Soleil of acrobats tumbling, child-boxers sparring, snake-charmers swaying, musicians drumming and water-sellers ringing bells. Scribes, fortune-tellers, henna artists—all were there. There was even a dentist brandishing a pair of pliers—the cheapest way to extract a painful molar for the poor.

In this colourful crowd tight circles of people were gathered around professional raconteurs.

'Storytellers offer an escape from the *bled*,' said Driss. 'Their tales are just as fascinating as those in *Alf Layla wa-Layla* (One Thousand and One Nights), but they are unknown outside Morocco. Even outside Berber society. That man in the brown djellabah is Omar the Wise. He is telling the tale of the *Hedgehog who Wanted to Sing*. I've heard it many times and while hedgehog is a rural delicacy, it is one of the most popular stories on the Djemaa el-Fnaâ.'

In another part of the square, we encountered a monkey scrambling about a mat on which was a jar holding different coloured quills. On seeing us, it ran across, plucked one out and placed it at my feet.

'A red quill means you will enjoy radiant health, marry a rich man and bear him ten kids,' said Driss. 'And the man says that will be five dirhams.'

I gasped. Ten children. And five dirhams was the cost of lunch.

'Two,' responded Ruth.

'Two?' Driss coughed. 'Then he says she will never marry.'

'Three, then—trois dirhams.' I held up three fingers.

The man gave a lopsided smile. '*Ça va—trois, mais seulement trois enfants.*'

Our favourite pastime in Marrakech was to make a carriage-ride in the relative cool of dusk. Giving the horse a sugar-cube (saved from mint tea) we would trot off—on a circuit of the ramparts, to the Bahia Palace, to the Saadien tombs, to wherever took our fancy. A favourite place was the Menara Gardens planted with citrus fruits and olive trees and with a decorative pavilion where the sultan used to entertain his favourite concubine. I have a now faded photograph of me, standing by the pool, holding hands with the Menara *gardien*.

One evening, tiny writing in my diary indicates it was 4 July, Driss arranged a dinner for us at his aunt's house, deep in the médina.

'*Ahlan wa sahlan*,' said aunty at the head of a line of household women—there was no sign of any men.

We were ushered into a courtyard filled with orange trees, and invited to sit on gold velvet banquettes. A child servant brought a kettle of water and a bowl to rinse our fingers and another wheeled out a traymobile of foods. Everyone then withdrew as we ate our way through baked pistachio-stuffed tomatoes, olive and radish salads, tender lamb brochettes, roast chicken smothered in smoked almonds, and couscous. The banquet ended when the child maids reappeared to serve us sliced oranges sprinkled with cinnamon and tiny gold-rimmed glasses of mint tea.

Next morning we were on the outskirts of Marrakech hitching a ride to Fez. A dented red Chevrolet, driven by a military man—medals and all—dropped us by a road-block roughly halfway there, but there we sat. For three hours, peasants and donkeys were the only passers-by and when the bus from Marrakech rolled up, a gendarme insisted we climb aboard.

'*Pas de billet, vous êtes les bienvenus*,'—you are welcome, no need to pay. He touched his cap.

Our haversacks were thrown on the roof among rolls of linoleum, bicycles, ladders, bundles of clothes, crates of pigeons and a bleating sheep, and squeezed in the back among a team of woodcutters, we travelled steadily into the Middle Atlas. Farmers scything fields of wheat straightened up and gazed as we passed. At one point the bus stopped where a boy stood with a black horse and a rich man wearing a cream djellabah and a red fez, got down, mounted it and galloped off. Alighting for the night in Khenifra—a town of carmine-coloured houses with pea-green shutters, we were mobbed by villagers. The arrival of foreigners was clearly special—one man said if we chose his hotel, he would pay our bill.

On the road at 7am, we were picked up by a man with curling eyelashes and glittering gold teeth. Abdul Aziz was going to Fez. He worked in a bank and his cousin Salma—one of the first female graduates from university in Rabat, the Moroccan capital—would act as our guide.

If we'd been mesmerised by Marrakech, we found Fez even more fascinating. Built in a bowl of hills, its médina, known as Fez el-Bali, is filled with haunting images, some little changed since the eighth century.

The growth of Fez began under Moulay Idriss II (791-828) and with the construction of the Kairouine Mosque whose celebrated university was attended by Ibn Battūtah, the Moorish geographer Leo Africanus, and other luminaries from the Islamic world. Even Christian personages—Pope Sylvester II whose interest was Arabic numerals, is said to have studied at the Kairouine before becoming pontiff in 1003.

When the Merinids—a nomadic tribe from Algeria—overthrew the Almohads in the thirteenth century, they built a new city—Fez el-Jdid—while continuing to lavish attention on the médina. The Merinid sultans built magnificent *madrassas* (religious colleges) for students coming to study in Fez along with grand *funduqs* (hosteleries) for visiting merchants. There were hospitals—even one for storks—a sacred bird in Morocco—and the writings of Leo Africanus indicate there were eighty fountains, one hundred *hammams* and one hundred and fifty public conveniences in the tightly packed, walled city.

Abdul Aziz dropped us near Bab Boujeloud—the main gateway into Fez el-Bali—where we met his cousin. Salma was wearing a bold green djellabah and black high heels, as inappropriate for the cobbled streets as our own flip-flops, but she knew her way around.

'Fassi society considers me scandalous for having a boyfriend. But *je m'en fou*—I don't care,' she declared as we set off walking down the Talaat Kebira, the main artery descending into the médina.

'On left is fourteenth century water clock. Opposite ancient latrines. Men only. No one coming. Take quick look at stucco ceiling.' She gave a furtive smile. 'That is *funduq*,' she pointed out a three-storey building. 'Stables for horses. Rooms up top. Fez once counted two hundred hosteleries. All now warehouses and shops.'

As we followed her, friendly traders invited us to dip our fingers into barrels of honey, to chew a piece of nougat, or to try a pickled snail. The man selling snails had fallen asleep, and crawling out of a box, snails were dropping down with soft plops. They were everywhere—shouldn't we wake him up, Ruth wanted to know? Salma shook her head. She was our age and despite Muslim social restrictions, she seemed much more sophisticated.

'This is where I meet Amal,' she announced in the Souq el-Henna where a perfume blender dotted our wrists with *oudh*,[47] a costly and exotic scent much prized by Arab women.

'*Labas*,'—how are you? She greeted a woman selling candles outside the *zaouia* of Moulay Idriss who died at the age of thirty-five in 828. 'Pilgrims visit for *baraka*,' (blessing), she slipped a coin in an aperture in the door.

The shrine was surrounded by scores of cubbyhole-sized workshops. We passed comb-makers and knife-grinders, potters, and tailors, and men embroidering *hadiths* on patches of black velvet, using spun gold thread. Sweating workers in the dye market draped swatches of steaming wool across a cobbled alley with pools of yellow, red and green. Here, deep in the médina, we walked through passages originally measured against the width of a loaded mule, some so narrow the walls were rubbed shiny by centuries of animals trotting through.

'Everything well organised,' said Salma as we waited for a cobbler to repair her shoe that had broken a heel in the tanneries. 'Each trade occupies same spot allocated by the *mutasib* (prefect) of Fez a thousand years ago. Strippers, scourers, saddlers and coppersmiths—like you see over there—all belong to ancient syndicates. 20,000 workers registered with Weavers Guild in Merinid times.'

We were enthralled, but souqs have always had this effect on western travellers. Jean de Thévenot, a French visitor to Syria in the seventeenth century, wrote of a parade of craftsmen in Aleppo. It included, he wrote, shoemakers wearing cone-shaped hats, eight men carrying a float on which two boys were making sandals. Next came a float with gold spinners actually spinning gold, and in order of Muslim social hierarchy, processions of coffee sellers, carpenters, smiths, and barbers.

On our final afternoon in Fez, we had tea at the Palais Jamaï, a magnificent Hispano-Mauresque building, built by the Grand Vizier of Morocco, and acquired as a hotel by the ONCFM[48] in the 1930s. Accustomed to cheap pensions, we'd never seen such opulence—vast brass chandeliers, decorative cedar doors, the finest *zellij* (tile) mosaic fountains and a terrace overlooking the médina where pigeons rose and dipped around the minaret of the Kairouine Mosque. If someone had suggested that I would one day stay in such a place, I would have said they were mad.

Ruth and I lost contact back in England and I was left wondering whether our experiences had been a shade too colourful. Especially our adventure at the Red Sea. I spent the rest of the 1960s waitressing in London, teaching biology in Mombasa, working at the Club Méditerranée in Sicily and Moorea, and always writing about my travels.

In 1989 Collins (now HarperCollins), commissioned me to write a guide for the independent traveller to Morocco. I'd been a frequent visitor through the years, but unlike the hospitality of the PTDC in Pakistan, the Moroccan National Tourist Office (ONMT) was uninterested in my project. I would have to manage alone.

***

I packed carefully for the journey. In went hat, jeans, and bikini. And in went gifts. It has always been my policy to take gifts—a ladybird radio that moved its wings up and down when you turned the dials had delighted Shefi in the Punjab—tools for a farmer living on Mafi'a Island in the Indian Ocean; a tea caddy for a woman in Cairo's City of the Dead—in Havana I gave the room-maid my brand new jeans. *Qibla* prayer compasses were my choice for helpful people in Morocco, and I threw in biros for the kids.

I decided to begin in Tangier for an important personal reason. On counting up, I found to my surprise that I'd visited fifty places in the footsteps of Ibn Battūtah who eventually returned home in 1354 and at the request of the Merinid sultan, dictated an account of his journeys in the *Rihla*[49]—one of the world's earliest travel narratives. Although I'd visited Tangier on several occasions, I was unaware that he was buried there.

'Il est quelque part vers la casbah.' The woman in the tourist office looked up from reading *Le Journal de Tangier.* He is somewhere up near the kasbah. Ask when you are there.

Leaving her office, I walked along the Boulevard Pasteur, past the Gran Café de Paris to the Grand Socco where I stopped to ask directions, but no one knew what I was talking about. Hoping for better luck in the médina, I confronted a man carrying a fragrant basket of mint and pronouncing the name—*Ibn Battūtah*—very carefully, I asked did he know the whereabouts of his tomb?

Putting down his basket, the man stuck a finger in each ear. He was deaf—*mais,oui*—he knew exactly what I was seeking and setting a brisk pace, he led me uphill, until suddenly there it was: the *koubba* of Tangier's most famous son, an unremarkable stone structure crushed between houses and identified by a simple plaque : *TAMBEAU IBN BATTOUTA* (sic).

Above the dome, a woman was pegging out washing just like the laundress in Benjamin-Constant's memorable painting—*Drying Clothes.*[50]

'Le gardien n'est pas là pour vous laisser entrer,' she called down. Only the guardian had a key, so I couldn't go inside, but touching it I made a wish. It had seemed appropriate.

On this occasion, I stayed at the Grand Hotel Villa de France near St Andrew's Anglican Church whose cemetery contains the graves of several British expatriates.

Eugène Delacroix, seduced by the exceptional light in Tangier—*'la lumière, est tellement douce'*—had stayed here in the 1830s, as did Henri Matisse and Hilda Rix Nicholas whose paintings suggest they shared the same models. I requested Room 35 where Matisse had painted the view of the kasbah[51] but there was no telephone and the basin was blocked. And in the dining-room a maître d'hotel wearing bell bottom trousers and a jacket shiny from years of ironing, stood by like a vulture. When I requested *harissa*—a chilli sauce—to enliven my couscous, he plonked down a bottle of tomato squeezy.

Package tours to Tangier had become popular during the 1980s and confronted by scantily clad tourists, locals had become cheeky. A favourite ploy was to separate a straggler from the group and cajole him into buying a carpet. Entertainment was provided by bad belly-dancers performing in faux-Moroccan restaurants and the man who'd once offered a date in the market, now cursed when I popped one in my mouth.

Nothing, however, could spoil the memory of my visit with Ruth and having located Ibn Battūtah, after a lot of walking I found the Café Baba that happily—I might even say miraculously—was still the same as on that exotic summer night. Its walls were turmeric-coloured from nicotine, but the balcony had not fallen off: three men were sitting out there smoking *kif* through long-stemmed clay pipes.

'It's the oldest bar in the médina,' said owner, Abdulgani Owfi, who was nicotine-coloured himself. 'Originally fishermen came here to mend their nets. But now everyone has been. The Rolling Stones and the Princess of Sweden—Kofi Annan came in last week and drank a mint tea. We often saw Madame Barbara too. She gave money and sweetmeats to the poor.'

Morocco's most mouth-watering sweetmeats shop is in Casablanca. The salesgirl was rather crabby as I sailed up and down its counter, oohing and aahing at the displays arranged like works of art. Along with Maghrebi favourites such as honey-dipped *briouats,* and almond-stuffed *gazelle horns* were marble cakes, chocolate-logs, jam rolls, and apricot tarts, meringues, eclairs, and petit fours. It was as if the city's flamboyant architecture was replicated in the sugary creations of the Pâtisserie au Soleil. There was even a pavlova.

Ruth and I had only nightstopped in Casablanca. To us it was just a big European city and not how we imagined Morocco. What we hadn't realised is that Casablanca is equally part of the history of Morocco as the imperial cities, the contribution to its heritage being French—the vision of General Hubert Lyautey, the first Resident-General of the protectorate. Instead of demolishing the old waterfront médina to make way for essential services, Lyautey commissioned the construction of a Ville Nouvelle outside its walls; a town of palm-lined avenues, elegant municipal buildings and a Gallic corniche curling around the rocky coastline.

This time I was awestruck by its period buildings. Along the Boulevard Mohammed V—the heart of 1930s Casablanca—the facades of grand, if weathered banks, shipping companies and apartment blocks sprouted heads

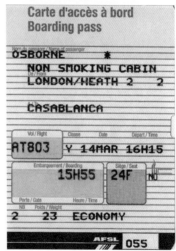

of Pan, bunches of grapes, and other fanciful friezes. Cupolas, steel balconies and loggias caught my eye and in dimly lit arcades, I found mosaic tiled walls and marble floors—even clanking wrought-iron elevators. Dropping a letter to mum in La Grande Poste, entered beneath soaring Moorish arches, I decided that of all the towns in Morocco, she would like 'Casa' best. It had a whiff of European culture in contrast to the bucolic *bled.*

'I'm sure Chris will marry a black man.' I once heard her tell a friend. 'She's always going to these strange places—Djibouti, Morocco, Sierra Leone.'

'Casablanca has some of the finest restaurants outside France,' said Clive Chandler, a long-time resident of the big Atlantic port and owner of Olive Branch Tours, Morocco's oldest travel agency established in 1958. I'd met Clive, a mild-mannered, middle-aged Englishman at the London World Travel Market when he'd generously offered the use of his car—a Peugeot 503—that was parked at the station when I arrived by train from Tangier. On my last day, we lunched at Au Petit Poucet, a small bistro once popular with the likes of Edith Piaf and Albert Camus. I chose *cerveaux au beurre noir* (I love brains) and as a change from couscous cooked by Fatima, his maid, Clive had ordered *confit de canard*.

'Bon appetit.' He filled my glass with a Gris de Guerrouane, a fine rosé from former French vineyards around Meknes. 'And remember to visit the British Embassy in Rabat to explain what you're doing.'

The Moroccan capital was thankfully a short run for my first experience of Moroccan roads. Clive had instructed me to stay well over from grands-taxis—'likely to shear off your wing-mirrors'—and to treat anyone walking—'child, adult, or donkey'—as potentially insane, since there was no telling when they might dash across the road without looking.

I spent several days exploring the city with an archaeology student, met in its Andalusian gardens. A thin strip of a youth, El Ghazi showed me Bab Oudaia, the great Almohad gateway into the kasbah, and the Hassan Tower, planned as a great mosque by the third Almohad sultan, Ya'qub al-Mansur, but never completed.

'*C'est dommage que vous partez demain,*'—it's a shame you're leaving tomorrow, he said outside the British Embassy.

'I was a ray of light in your life,' I laughed.

'*Pas un rayon—un laser!*' he replied.

'On no account should you drive to Ketama,' said the ambassador, tapping a pen with barely concealed impatience.

'How can I write a guide to Morocco and omit the Rif on account of a few *kif* smugglers?' I had smiled politely, although reminded of my experience in Sana'a with the Ministry of Information.

'If you insist on going, your fortunes are not guaranteed. Several foreigners languish in jail through folly in this area. Nor is your safety assured in the Western Sahara.' And he stood up from his desk. A sign that it was time to leave.

In my hotel that evening, I met two sisters on holiday from Algiers who were catching the morning bus to Meknes, where I was headed.

'If you'd like to come, I'm passing Meknes,' I told them.

'We are six brothers and three sisters,' said Rabia the older sibling, settling in beside me. 'Habiba here is a pharmacist. I am a professor of sociology. Sister three is a musician. One brother is an engineer. One works in a bank. One is a teacher, the fourth is a businessman, and another is a nuclear physicist.' I believe she said the sixth was a forensic scientist, but she spoke so rapidly I could hardly concentrate on my driving.

'When travelling, you must always wear gold,' she continued breathlessly. 'After performing the *hajj*, I bought everyone gifts—crystal models of the *ka'aba,* bottles of sacred water from the *zamzam* well—then Saudia lost my luggage. But I had gold. Instant cash.'

As I left them in Meknes, She bent down to my window. 'To get rich, you must write a book like *Les Oisseaux se Cachent pour Mourir,*' she exclaimed. Then followed by her silent sister, she was off so quickly I hadn't time to tell her that Colleen McCullogh, the author of *The Thorn Birds,* had once worked in x-ray at Royal North Shore.

Meknes was capital of the Alaouite sultan, Moulay Ismail a cruel despot with inflated ideas who ruled Morocco for fifty-five years (1627 to 1727). A great admirer of the French court at Versailles, he set about building a local equivalent, the Dar el-Kebira, comprised of twenty-four palaces, linked by streams and gardens, where he accommodated his wives and concubines, and the 888 children he is alleged to have sired. '… females look through the iron latticed windows, and take the air, which, in the summer, is perfumed with the smell of violets, jasmines, roses and wild thyme…' wrote a visitor of the compound.

Unfortunately Moulay Ismail's grand creations, his palaces, walls, granaries and stables for 12,000 horses used on the great *harkas* (marches) have not stood the test of time because unlike the marble creations of his peers—the Mughals—they were built of adobe, and the Middle Atlas receiving a good rainfall, means they have simply melted away.

I was spending the night in Sidi Harazem, a small town named for a twelfth century scholar who taught at the Kairouine Mosque, but my arrival had clashed with his *moussem,* a combination of religious festival and country fair. The hillside around his *koubba* was crowded with visitors eating nougat and clutching large toy animals, but curiously I was the only guest staying at the only hotel. This should have indicated a good night's rest, but just as I shut my eyes, a staff party erupted overhead. Loud music, dancing feet and female shrieks continued until morning, and ready to leave at 7am, I found reception in darkness and the front door locked.

'*Est-ce quelqu'un en service?*—anyone there?' I shouted several times and on getting no response, I opened a window, threw my suitcase into the garden and jumped out after it. The gate was open and the watchman was asleep in a chair. At the sound of the car he started up, but I was on my way to Ketama, the centre of the *kif* trade.

Before long I was glad of my early start. The road was rough and as I drove further north, it became ever more circuitous. I passed girls carrying bundles of firewood and in one spot, I stopped for a boy carrying a sour-smelling tub of *smen,* a preserved butter made from sheep's milk, used in Berber cooking.

In the foothills of the Rif, fields of marijuana replaced cereals and vegetables. For an hour or so, I passed nothing else, until I found myself driving through dark forests where I encountered the first *kif* hustlers. Sighting the Casablanca licence plate, they stepped out—miming a crumbling action with their fingers—accompanied by a shrill whistle to indicate they had something to sell. As I approached Ketama, a Mercedes parked in a woodland clearing, flashed its headlights and pulling out, a second car containing five hooded passengers, escorted me to the Hotel Tidighine, the largest building in town.

'Business, madame?' they inquired as we all got out together.

'*Merci,*' I said and hurrying inside, I inspected the hotel, then without even pausing for a café-caisse, I left for my nightstop in al-Hoceima. Soon it had started to rain and while wanting to get the hell out of the Ketama region, I stopped for three Berbers in dripping djellabahs. They only spoke Tamazight—the language of the Rif—but I understood they'd been to Souq el-Arba—the Wednesday market—and were immensely grateful for the ride. On getting out, the oldest man placed two figs in my hand.

A busy summer resort, out of season al-Hoceima was deathly quiet and almost as soon as I arrived, I fretted about the journey back. Studying the map over dinner (a fish *tajine* followed by two figs), I sourced a secondary route via the coast. I would visit the town next day and leave at dawn on the following—*kif* sellers would not be early risers, I decided.

Wearing a big hooded djellabah to disguise my gender, I left just as the *lamparo* boats were returning from a night's fishing. Fog made driving difficult and the convoluted route through the bony ribs of the Rif was truly terrifying. The only person I passed—a farmer leading a sheep—jumped in surprise of a car at sparrow's fart. But the hustlers were still asleep as I'd anticipated.

Back in Casablanca, Clive advised that he needed the car. This was a blow, but returning a favour, Michel Benisty, the director of Europcar—agreed to provide a little white Renault 4—popularly known as the 4L (pronounced 'Quatrelle')—for my journey south to Agadir and the Western Sahara.

'Since you're writing a guide, you must try a *hammam*,' was Clive's parting comment. 'Bath-day is a big deal.' He chuckled. 'You'll find one in the old Portuguese stronghold of El Jadida.'

I'd often encountered Portugal on my travels—in Goa, Macau, Mombasa and other outposts of the *Império Português*, and the Portuguese also left fingerprints along the Atlantic coast of Morocco: a fort in Azemour, the 'Castle of the Sea' in Safi, and massive marine battlements in Essaouira, but the most striking evidence of their activity is the *Cite Português* in El Jadida, where they resisted Berber attack for two hundred and fifty years. Inside the citadel, I walked streets lined with houses, once ox-blood—a popular colour in Portuguese colonies—now faded to a dusky pink. Everything was there—a church, a synagogue, a hospital, a prison and a vast subterranean cistern, a mysteriously beautiful structure with a vaulted, almost ecclesiastical roof, used as a backdrop by Orson Welles for scenes in his 1959 production of *Othello*.

Orientalists such as Jean-Léon Gérôme and Rudolf Ernst have depicted the *hammam* as a place of sensuality in their paintings, and while it does act as a place of social contact, its prime function is a public bathroom for those who do not possess one at home. Locating one in a backstreet of El Jadida, I entered an ante-room where a matronly woman gestured I should remove my clothes. She snapped the elastic—except for my knickers.

Handed a towel and a pot of *sabon beldi*—a soap made from the pulp of black olives—I followed her to a second room where steam spiralled up through a hole in the dome and a score of fleshy ladies were chatting, laughing, and dousing themselves with buckets of water. Finding a stool, I attempted to emulate the procedure, but tipping back my head as they did, I threw it up my nose. And looming out of the fog, a *tayaba*[52] added to my discomfort, as using a sandpaper glove, she set about shaving off layers of skin and pummelling my body as though she was kneading dough.

'*Arrêtez s'il vous plaît,*' I shrilled and handed another timeworn towel, I was shown to a third room where a young woman was relaxing with friends and relatives.

'*Mariage,*' the word was whispered for my benefit of the bride-to-be who had suffered her pubic hair being plucked out as part of a long purifying ritual for her husband. On her wedding night she would be roughly penetrated, and in rural communities, a rag flourished to indicate she was intact—poor little thing. Giving a tip to the *tayaba,* I left the *hammam,* relieved that I would never have to endure such rites of passage. But even as a youngster, I'd decided that marriage was not for me. I was born to travel—it was as necessary as brushing my teeth.

My notes on the Doukkala plain south of El Jadida, describe a landscape covered in plastic cloches and rustic farmhouses surrounded by hedges of prickly pear. Of roadside stalls selling flowers, of farmers offering boxes of ruby red tomatoes, of fishermen holding up spindly spider crabs that are said to walk up to 160 kilometres (100 miles) during the migration season, and sadly after such a trek, are caught and eaten.

It was an easy run to Oualidia, a small community overlooking a vast lagoon where the ocean flushed in and out through a cleft in the cliffs. Men were fishing, and a boy was collecting *oursin* off the rocks. I don't eat sea urchins. To me their little pink mouths are rather anal, but with oysters and spider crabs, they were on the menu at the basic Hippocampe Hotel whose proprietor said the Duke and Duchess of Devonshire—owners of Chatsworth House, a grand sixteenth century, 120-room mansion in Derbyshire—had holidayed there. He beamed with pride—Her Grace had passed the time painting in the garden.

South of Oualidia, I stopped for a dear old woman pushing a bag of flour in a rickety wheelbarrow. She was as excited as Mrs Bonke had been in Arba Minch, kissing my cheek and all down my arm—kiss, kiss. Deposited in Essaouira, she insisted on scratching her name (Amina) in huge symbols in my spiral notebook. But she could write. *Alhamdulillah.*

Phoenician sailors were the first visitors to Essaouira, a town of splashed white houses with Hockney-blue shutters tucked behind a seawall lined with cannon. The reason for their dangerous voyage this far south was to harvest a marine gastropod from islands anchored off the harbour mouth. A purple mucus secreted by the mollusc was prized for textiles because it was colour-fast, and towards the end of the first century, a settlement was established on behalf of Imperial Rome—'Tyrian Purple' togas were the height of fashion, but at great cost for the mollusc since 12,000 animals were required to produce just 1.5 grams (0.005 ounces) of dye.

If Essaouira was founded on the back of a snail, under Portuguese occupation, it became one of the most important entrepots on the coast of West Africa.

The manifest of January-July 1806 from the 'Barbary port of Mogador' as it was then known, lists almonds, beeswax, skins, raisins, dates, olive oil and gum-sanderac along with 5,366 pounds of elephant teeth, 556 pounds of ostrich feathers, and 2,860 pounds of thyme. Imports included 9,000 tapestry needles, 18,696 looking glasses, 406 dozen silk handkerchiefs, plus four cases of the Torah for its Jewish population. Today Essaouira relies on sardine-fishing and tourism, especially windsurfers chasing the powerful north-east trades.

To escape the wind, I descended from the battlements to the woodcarvers souq where craftsmen were carving items from blocks of *thuya*—a treacle-coloured native hardwood that is coveted for its speckled lustre. A resinous aroma replaced the salty air and I reflected how smell and hearing—as much as sight—are an integral part of experiencing different cultures.

I only have to smell a Damask rose to remember my visit to the gardens of Shiraz, burial place of Hafiz, the fourteenth century poet beloved of every Persian. In fact smells convey memories to me far more swiftly than sight—cloves to the plantations of Zanzibar, stale air and sweat to steerage class on the *Pierre Loti* when I sailed down the Red Sea that stinking hot summer, and the seraphic scent of smouldering frankincense to the souq in Salalah, run by female descendants of the sultan's African slaves. A blind person could travel throughout Morocco on the sounds and smells—on the hammering of coppersmiths, on the clickety-clack of nesting storks, on the bittersweet notes of *al-Ala*,[53] on the sharp scent of jasmine, and the oily odour of grilled sardines,

Agadir, the regional capital of the south, is Morocco's major fishing port, whose harbour is packed with trawlers as tightly as sardines in a tin. '*Mille bateaux*,' grunted a fisherman and I'd wondered about the small silver fish. A shoaling species, it cannot be farmed like, say, cod or barramundi, and hunted since Roman times, how long before *Sardina pilchardus* becomes extinct?

At 11.40pm on 29 February 1960, Agadir was struck by a massive earthquake killing 12,000 people, mainly residents of the hilltop kasbah, whose sugar-cube houses collapsed all the way down to the port. The town had been rebuilt at sea level, and while it was too pristine to have developed a patina, it had become a popular tourist resort on account on a long golden-sand beach.

Arriving from Essaouira on a warm April day, I decided to take a break from inspecting hotels for a swim, but stretched out on my beach towel, I was not left in peace. Did madame want to buy an embroidered kaftan, a metal teapot, or a Berber wedding blanket, and finally a voice asked did madame want a fuck?

Taking the hat off my face, I sat up.

'*Qu'avez-vous dit?*' I demanded of a handsome youth who'd evidently taken to pleasuring women tourists. As I watched, he approached a middle-aged *hausfrau* who leapt up, as if bitten by a crab, and off they went together.

That afternoon I sighted the youth again in a café. He was surprised when rather boldly, it must have seemed to other customers, I sat down at his table.

'Hi, I remember you from the beach,' I said.

'*Avez-vous reconsidéré?*' He used the polite *vous* rather than *tu* that was droll in the circumstance.

'No.' I replied. 'I was interested in how you earn a living.'

'*Je suis du bled*—no work,' he said. 'One day I marry good Moroccan girl. But first I need *flous.*' (money).

'*Combien des touristes ont fait vous servez?*' I spoke in French, lest English ears were listening.

'*Je ne sais plus.* Today one *Allemande.*' He tapped the teaspoon against his glass.

'You like plaisir? Give what you want. Some pay. Some buy clothes.' He spread his legs to show me his jeans.

I stood up abruptly, dropped some coins on the table, and wished him well. Banish the thought. Besides which I was leaving early for Goulimine and the Western Sahara.

Once an important halt for the gold, ivory, and slave caravans from Mauritania, Goulimine was now simply a line of buildings strung out like dusty beads on the plain. The biggest edifice was a Flour Mill—painted in large white letters on the silo—but good heavens—it had an ONMT whose officer, Sheikh Ma el-Ainin Mohammed Laghdaf, said he was a grandson, one of several hundred, of the Saharan Blue Man Sheikh Ma el-Ainin who'd rallied tribes against the French and Spanish from the desert outpost of Smara.

'I'm researching a tourist guide,' I told him. 'I'm on my way to Tan Tan.'

'You can't drive alone to Tan Tan.' His brow furrowed. 'What is your hotel?'

'Isn't the Hotel Salam the only hotel in Goulimine?' My reply was rather cheeky.

'I will be there at 8am and we will go together,' he confirmed.

'We have twenty rooms,' said the manager of the Hotel Salam plucking a key off the rack. 'But as important writer, I have allocated you Atlas

Suite. On right is bar—last before Sahara. Left is restaurant with Moroccan menu—*tajine* of camel meat, camel-meat couscous and camel-meat kebabs. Goulimine people like camel meat best. Dessert is camel custard.'

'You mean caramel custard,' I corrected him.

I'd filled the car at Au Rendezvous des Hommes Bleus garage well before Sheikh Ma el-Ainin arrived, black hair brylcreemed and looking dapper in a navy suit. Tall for a Moroccan, he had to fold up his legs up like a praying mantis to get in. He can't be coming for the ride, I thought. He must have business, or a secret amour in Tan Tan.

Leaving Goulimine, the road cut across a stony plain splashed with pools of sand. Every tree had been cut down for fuel and apart from wizened euphorbia, goats had vacuumed every piece of vegetation.

'*Les chevres,*' said Sheikh Ma el-Ainin reading my thoughts.

For a while we drove in silence and finding myself oddly disassociated with the barren landscape, I thought of other things. Who was behind the plane crash that had killed General Zia? Zia had authorised my visit to Gwadar and I was grateful to him. Should I stay an extra day in Tan Tan to wash my clothes?

Suddenly we encountered mayhem. Soldiers were chasing two figures fleeing across a shallow wadi and in the distance I heard the pop-pop-pop of gunfire.

'*Eeee! Polisario,*' shrieked the sheikh. '*Arrete! Arrete!*'

Jesus. What's happening? I thought and slowing down, I shouted out the window.

'*Quel est le problème?*'

'*Faites demi-tour. Vite!*'—turn around, quickly, shouted a red-faced officer running along beside us.

But it wasn't a case of parking and waiting out the fracas. Clearly terrified something fatal was upon us, the sheikh ordered me to return to Goulimine.

'*Vite. Plus vite,*' he kept shouting, and drawing up at Au Rendezvous des Hommes Bleu garage, he jumped out—a pleasant young man, but lacking the bottle of his great-grandfather.

The manager of the Salam was surprised to see me back, but there was no time to explain. Tossing down a coffee in the last bar before the Sahara,

I hit the road again for Tan Tan. As I approached the wadi, I found my hands were sweating on the wheel, but everyone had vanished as though a genie had scooped them into a bottle, and I wondered whether they were really Polisario, or just plain smugglers?

Upon reaching Tan Tan I was gobsmacked. Caught in a time warp, the settlement resembled a film set for a desert western, starring the legendary Blue Men of the Sahara. Everything, mosque, houses, shops—even the petits-taxis—was painted mustard and *bleu de Tan Tan*. Parking on the sandy Place Tan Tan, I set off to explore. Luckily the town was small since it was beneath the hauteur of Blue Men—independent and resourceful, but equally vain and aloof—to offer their service as a guide. On passing me, they averted their gaze and wound their black *lithams* around their tan faces.

Ignored, I wandered through a rustic souq selling tents, sandals and skewers for cooking kebabs over a camp-fire. An inquiry about the 'best hotel' in a pharmacie led me to the Hotel Royal but on looking in, I found it awash with army personnel, and a dozen smaller establishments clearly catered to long haul truckies. Each one was worse than the one before it. None was suitable to include in the guide, and conspicuous in my jeans and hat—at least I too was blue—I decided to press on to Tarfaya.

Mid-afternoon found me driving south on a strip of tarmac commandeered by flying fish trucks. In places the plateau looked as though it had been snipped off with a pair of dressmaking scissors and unable to get down to sea level, fishermen were perched in suicidal spots along the cliff-tops. The sight of someone fishing always made me happy and I pulled over behind a fellow wearing a brown beanie and several jumpers against the wind.

'*Labas,*' I called out to him. '*Puis-je prendre votre photo?*' And twisting around, he obligingly held up a huge *dorade* (sea bream) from his basket.

Merde. I was going to kill him. '*C'est la pêche la plus dangereuse du monde,*'—it's the most dangerous fishing in the world, I shouted.

'I've five *gosse* (kids) to feed,' he yelled back.

'What happens if you hook a monster.' I extended my hands.

'*Coupez. Ou de prendre un plongeon dans l'Atlantique.*'—cut it off. Or take a dive into the Atlantic. And baiting up, he cast into the void.

Along a spectacular coastline between here and Tarfaya, dunes rolling in from the Sahara reached the beach where the rusting hulks of ships lay just offshore. I debated whether to walk across for a photo, but remembering the ambassador's warning—'Land mines are all over the Western Sahara'—thought better of it.

I had read *Wind, Sand and Stars* by Antoine de Saint-Exupéry in my final year at Royal North Shore and was especially interested in Tarfaya. His account of flying over the Sahara during a *chergui* when '… the desert itself seemed to levitate as hundreds of tonnes of sand were sucked into the sky …' had fascinated me. Cape Juby was a welcome landmark for pilots operating the early twentieth century Aeropostale Service between Toulouse and Dakar—but anxious for a wash and a meal, I drove past the lonely headland without stopping.

Madrid had relinquished the Cape Juby region, including Tarfaya in 1958, and what I found were the peeling remnants of Spanish occupation— a church, barracks, and beach-front villas—all half buried under wind driven dunes. And the town was tinier than I had expected. A few shops were clustered around a mosque and with rising panic, I realised there was no accommodation.

'*Quelle est la distance Laâyoune?*' I called out to a grizzled old man sweeping sand from a doorway.

'*Acerca de una hora,*'—about one hour, he replied in Spanish. And hitching up his scrotum, he walked over to the car.

'*Luchado con las fuerzas nacionales durante la guerra civil,*'—I fought with nationalist forces during the civil war, he said in a gravelly voice.

Driving after dark was breaking my golden rule, but the road was good and there was no traffic since by now everyone had completed his journey. At Tah the headlamps picked out a monument commemorating the Green March organised by King Hassan II in 1975 when 350,000 citizens marched to this point to assert Moroccan rights to the Western Sahara. Nearing Laâyoune, a jerboa hopped across the road like a mini-kangaroo, then ahead I spotted a line of lights.

After Tan Tan's hotels, the Parador was paradise—clean, modern, restaurant and pool. Everything I could wish for after the stressful drive. I fell upon my couscous and could not understand a waitress saying that staff considered Laâyoune a punishment post.

Next morning I saw she was right. Capital of the Western Sahara, Laâyoune did not fit the usual description of a holiday resort. Interest was socioeconomic—schools, a hospital and a football stadium, all part of massive spending by Rabat to confirm the region was indisputably part of Morocco. The new town was exactly that. Its twin centres were linked by a long boulevard and a *mechouar* (parade ground) was flanked by monuments, resembling space-capsules topped with coronets. They can be floodlit, should the king arrive at night, I was informed by a wall-eyed man who co-opted himself as guide.

Together we visited the Artisan's Centre where Saharaui women were making crafts in anticipation of the arrival of thousands of tourists. Their dress, a flimsy, synthetic material patterned in yellow, reds, and greens resembled an Indian sari. Would I care for tea, asked their teacher, a smiley African-looking woman. The tea ritual was a necessity and while anxious to complete my sightseeing, to refuse would have been discourteous. But I didn't take sugar? The ceremony was thrown into confusion. Was I diabetic?

Laâyoune was ringed by white-domed houses, like stalkless mushrooms stuck in the sand. To the south lay a coastal inlet dusted with pink flamingos, before the plateau ended on an immense sea of rippling, russet-coloured dunes. How strange, I thought, to have been so attracted to the desert as a child only to discover the endless dunes confronting, even hostile. I had planned to drive as far as the phosphate mines at Bou Craa— root of the Saharaui dispute—but wind had blown sand banks on the road and to hit one would have spelt disaster. In truth, I'd wanted to continue to Dakhla, the last town before Mauritania, but this entailed a round-trip of almost 1,000 kilometres (621 miles), so instead I called a halt at a café standing in the middle of nowhere.

I've often thought I'd found the middle of nowhere on my travels, only to realise that I was actually on the edge of somewhere, but the Café Lemsid was definitely in the middle of nowhere.

CAMELS TAKE OVER AFTER ZAGORA, IN THE DEEP SOUTH, 1990

Painted caramel and raspberry red, it resembled a giant sweet that had dropped off a desert transport, and surrounding it lay the detritus of local civilisation: burst tyres, perished fan-belts, broken crab-traps and empty port-a-gas cylinders. A rug was stuffed in a hole in the wall to keep out wind-blown sand, and among items stacked behind its counter were boxes of Gunpowder tea, flour, candles, packets of soap-powder, balls of string and inevitably, tinned sardines. The owner said fresh fish arrived daily from Boujdour, so that even in this god-forsaken place I was able to sit down at a broken table for lunch. A lame, fish-eating chicken hopped about for scraps: it would never be killed and eaten, I decided—it was much too horrible. As I settled my bill, a grand-taxi pulled up and I half expected it to disgorge a host of characters from a Fellini film—dwarfs, transvestites, and dancing bears—but they were merely crushed passengers from Dakhla, relieved to stretch their legs on the long drive to Agadir from where, a few days later, I flew back to England.

***

Life in London was still the same. Had I really expected it to be different? Broad shoulder pads were in, Madonna was topping the charts and Buckingham Palace had confirmed that the Princess Royal and her husband were to separate. How was your trip, asked friends? But it was

THE CAFÉ LEMSID WAS DEFINITELY IN THE MIDDLE OF NOWHERE, 1989

only a courtesy. Busy with their own lives, they could not relate to my travel experiences.

Myra and Cathy were still flogging furniture in their shop on Lillie Road; someone had bought a studio on the Costa del Sol and travel writer colleagues had been walking in the fens and cruising the Caribbean with 1,600 passengers. Weren't you frightened of going to Yemen on your own? Can one get a drink in Doha? Even old friend Henry—met on a flight from Beirut in 1975—could only talk about his grandchildren.

'We'll be seventeen for Christmas dinner,' he informed me.

As others were preparing for the 1990 ski season in Europe, I flew to Marrakech to drive over the High Atlas to Ouarzazate, the gateway to what travel brochures called the 'kasbah country'.

Marrakech still embodied the hot heart of Morocco, but inevitably with the passing years, it too, had changed. Twenty charter flights a day now landed at the airport; foreigners were buying up old *riads* (houses) in the médina, children wanting bonbons trailed me everywhere I went, and in the Criée Berbère—the former slave auction site—fake watches and nylon jackets now competed with traditional handicrafts.

Touching a basket that I thought might be useful for bread, had prompted every basket-seller to jump to his feet, taking me back to the crafts market in Accra, the capital of Ghana. When word went out that

I was looking for an *akua'ba* doll (a fertility doll from Ashante), hundreds of wooden dolls had been rushed across. There were short dolls, tall dolls, dolls with earrings and others without, dolls rather the worse for wear, and others too new. I was shown dolls with breasts and dolls with flat chests and as scores of baskets were waved in my face, I had found a choice impossible. And while the Djemaa el-Fnaâ still had its entertainers, from a few orange-juice stands, it had become a huge food court with hundreds of stalls cooking on port-a-gas-grills. Each stall had a scout to rope tourists in—just like on the Riviera—and a bench to sit and eat *harira* soup, brochettes, boiled sheep head, squid, or sardines. As I was eating my calamare and chips, I noticed a woman in a patched djellabah begging from the tour groups. When I stood up to pay, she had darted across and stuffed my left-overs in her mouth.

Troubled by the woman, I experienced difficulty falling asleep and when sleep came, I had a dream that has pursued my travelling life. Of being somewhere in the Middle East only to find I've forgotten my camera. Or that I didn't bring film. A similar dream of insecurity that Aileen used to experience, of finding herself naked on the aircraft having forgotten to put on her uniform.

As usual my angst was a waste of emotional energy. While climbing to 2,260 metres (6,561 feet) the Tizi n'Tichka pass over the mountains was not insurmountable—even though I was driving another Renault 4. Ash and walnuts, and then oak and pines, soon replaced the date palms and eucalypts of Marrakech. The danger was a timber truck hurtling around a bend and I constantly sounded the horn—alerting boys holding out fossils and other diggings. Fifty minutes from Marrakech, I stopped for a Blue Man walking back from the Djemaa el-Fnaâ. Would I take tea in his home?

My heart was pounding as I left the P31 for a mountain track. Was I about to be raped on the Tizi n'Tichka? What a silly thought. Azrur lived with his wife and a child, in a two-room hut whose tiny rammed-earth garden contained a single rosebush with a single flower. As Azrur was changing his clothes, his wife picked the rose (it was the colour of a vintage burgundy) and handed it to me. I had brought three chocolates for my journey and I gave her the one left, but instead of popping it in her mouth, she carefully broke it into three: a piece for her husband, a piece for her child, and a piece for herself. It was a humbling experience for me.

Back on the P31, alpine vegetation was replaced by barren scree, then over the summit an adobe village heralded the kasbah country. It was warmer now and getting out to remove my jacket, I heard a cry from above. A woman was running down the hillside. Did I have an aspirin? Giving her the box, I inquired the way to Telouet. Next left, a lonely detour on a potholed road, a final bend and there it was—the imposing chateau-like headquarters of the Glaoui brothers, feudal warlords who'd ruled the Atlas, until the mid-twentieth century.

Scattering chickens, I drew up and parked outside a massive cedar door, expecting a *gardien* to appear at any moment. The door was open a crack so I slipped inside to find myself in a decaying belle-epoque décor with a sound of dripping water. The rooms, part stone, part rotting wood, were in poor repair. Tiles had dropped off the walls and strips of plaster had detached from the ceilings. An upper quarter with an oak-panelled floor surveyed the country through a wrought-iron grill: had this been the Glaoui's bedroom? I emerged from the building like a child who has plucked an orange from low hanging fruit in an orchard. I had read *Lords of the Atlas*[54] by Gavin Maxwell, but like the ruins of Mohen-jodaro, I never expected to have the kasbah to myself.

Descending to the bone-dry plains, I passed Aït Benhaddou, a massive *ksar* ranged along a river bank. As I stopped to take a picture, a boy had galloped up and said that for only three dirhams, I could ride across on his mule. No thanks, I told him and continued on to Ouarzarzate where a pack of sweaty cyclists was checking into my hotel—loud American voices indicating they were going to Zagora, my own destination.

I had driven down the Draa Valley to Zagora on another occasion and magic is the only description of the massive *ksour* lining the river. Formidable strongholds of towers and *agadirs* (granaries), they had once housed large extended families in hundreds of rooms, whose tiny windows reminded me of houses in the Yemen. Whether to avoid the cyclists, or just on whim, a little way from Ouarzazate, I turned off the tarmac on a road signposted Foum Zguid.

I had long ago learnt to navigate using the sun, but I grew uneasy as I drove on without sign of civilisation. Should I turn back? Suddenly I glimpsed a figure walking along ahead and catching up, I swung open the passenger door. A tiny, old man wearing a turban and cobalt blue robes got in beside me, his only possessions were a cane and a leather satchel. Leaning across, I belted him in and we were off, but the car crackled with apprehension. He was seated beside a woman driver—a foreign woman.

Sensing his discomfort, a little way on I stopped and getting out, I picked a bunch of pink rock roses growing by the roadside.

'Zagora!' I handed them to him and pointed to the way ahead.

A faint smile flitted across his face.

'*Waka,*'—OK, he replied.

For the next hour we drove on a wretched track through a rocky landscape without sign of life, but just as I envisaged us ending up in Algeria, we entered a lush oasis of shady palms and patchwork quilts of wheat. The old man signalled for me to stop, and after washing in an irrigation canal, he removed a tiny mat from his satchel and knelt on it to pray. Then on we went—bump, bump—until joining the tarmac again at Agdz, a modest town on the banks of the Draa.

Taking my small blue passenger with me, I went into a café and ordered two mint teas.

'I passed this man on the road,' I told the waiter. 'Can you tell me where is he going?'

There was a brief exchange before the youth responded in hesitant French.

'He is a *marabout* (holy man) from Taroudant on a pilgrimage to the *zaouia* in Tamegroute.' He snapped his tea towel at a fly.

'*Il est si heureux,*' called another customer. 'He'd been walking for six days when you came along.'

'Tell him I need to find a hotel in Zagora. Then I will take him to Tamegroute,' I said.

It was late afternoon when I pulled up at the *zaouia*, a dusky pink building with a green tile roof, associated with the Naciria brotherhood, a powerful Sufi clan in the seventeenth century. We both got out and the

WITH THE *MARABOUT* IN THE DRAA VALLEY, PHOTOGRAPHED BY A DATE-SELLER

old *marabout* came around and gently kissed my hand, before he walked slowly towards the gate where he stopped, turned, and made a little half-wave. Then he was gone, and I drove back alone.

Beyond a rusting sign *Tombouctou 52 jours* (by camel), there was little to see in Zagora except for the Amazrou Palmeraie that was rumoured to contains the ruins of an Almoravid fort. To find it required a guide and from several loitering outside my hotel, up stepped Hamid, a rat-faced man wearing a blue *gandura* (cotton garment without hood) and an untidily wrapped black turban. He'd learnt reasonable English from acting as a tourist guide, but his first words were to tell me he did wonderful massages.

'I can even put things back,' he poked his abdomen.

Assuming he meant a hernia, I drove off. We never found the fort, but the oasis was cool and picturesque. A woman riding sidesaddle on a donkey and others filling water-jars from a spring, reminded me of scenes on the bible cards handed out at Sunday school at Saint Augustine's.

'My parents were Bedouin who lived in a tent,' Hamid suddenly announced. 'I can only write my name. Perhaps you need someone more intelligent with you.'

Yes, I thought, but instead I said—'sometimes in life, kindness is better than intelligence.'

As we walked among the date palms, a boy had approached us with a baby sparrow crushed in his hand. Giving him a dirham, I popped the bird in my camera bag only to have another child appear with a second bird, that I exchanged for a biro.

'I will release them in my hotel garden,' I explained to Hamid.

'We eat sparrows for breakfast,' he replied.

Next morning I awoke to the sounds of donkeys braying in Zagora's Sunday souq and to avoid being pestered by other guides, I took Hamid with me.

My interest in the market was the cure-alls sold by *guerisseurs* (healers) but now Hamid struggled with translations. There were cocoons to be soaked and swallowed for runny tummy; gum-mastic to chew for a quickly heart, cowrie shells ground with lemon-juice to dab on acné—he touched a blemish on his cheek, ginger to make a woman work harder in bed, and chameleons—he indicated several bulb-eyed creatures clinging to sticks—for use as fly-catchers.

'Or they are dried and burnt against the Evil Eye,' and although it was hot, he gave a little shudder.

The market was held on an open patch of land, but just like in a covered souq, everything had its place. There were date sellers surrounded by bees and henna traders with sacks of leaves. There was a spot for spices, a space for slabs of glistening rock salt, and a corner for killims woven by women whose skills at the loom, according to Hamid, added to their dowry value.

And although I'd paid him generously the previous evening, as I was leaving Zagora he produced a bottle of *Eau de Rose*. 'It cost 125 dirhams,' he said.' 'But as you are my friend, my brother—*soyez bienvenue au Maroc*—it is yours for 100 dirhams.' And he stuck it under the dashboard.

Morocco for the Independent Traveller was published in 1990 and holding it in my hands—the biggest thrill for a writer—I wondered how many people would actually follow my advice, or even if they did, how could they know the background to writing such a guide? Or to researching a book on Pakistan, or to my adventures with the queen and other mortals?

***

In 2011, I decided to return to Tan Tan, the town that had once intrigued me. I would fly to Agadir, rent a car and make a sentimental loop of the Western Sahara. Renault had ceased production of the Renault 4, so I set off, happy to be on the road again, driving a shiny, black automatic Toyota Corolla. My attire was simple: navy cotton trousers run up for $5 by a tailor during a visit to Cochin, worn with a white, knee-length *shalwar* and my blue hat, by now so faded I doubted that Her Majesty would recognise it.

Taroudant, at the head of the Sousse—a long, fertile valley extending inland from the coast—was my first stop, and by habit I pulled over for a Moroccan and his son waiting by the highway. They hopped in, grateful for the ride, but I was equally pleased—I'd always wondered about the goats in the argan trees, a spiny species endemic to the Sousse.

'Sometimes you see up to fifteen in the branches,' said Mohammed, who taught English in a local lycée.

'Goats love argan nuts, but they cannot digest the kernels that they pass in their *merde*. The shepherd following a herd collects the droppings for women to crush the seeds.' He rattled off the uses. 'Argan oil good for massage, after-shave, herpes and hair.'

'Hair!' I took a hand off the wheel. Curly hair had been the bane of my life. At school I was called Curly-Top to which I responded Rat's-Tails, but I longed for silky hair to toss over my shoulder like the model in *l'Oreal* advertisements. I would buy some oil in Taroudant and hope for a miracle.

An historic market centre for Berber farmers, Taroudant had a laid-back rural air. The pace of life was slow, people shopped in traditional souqs—one Arab, one Berber—and its médina was bathed in a scent of orange blossom from surrounding orchards.

In the seventeenth century, the town had briefly been capital of the Saadi sultans from the Draa Valley who built its lofty ramparts, the colour of lightly cooked toast. On my last afternoon, I made a circuit of the walls by calèche, just like the old days in Marrakech. I wanted to stay, but with

only a week away, I had to press on to Tata—on the Sahara side of the
Anti-Atlas.

Needing petrol, I pulled into a garage on the outskirts of Taroudant.
Ahead was an SUV with a Blue Man driver and two French women tourists
wearing safari outfits and black Tuareg turbans.

'Bonjour—where are you going?' I greeted them.

'Tata,' they replied 'Et vous?'

'Tata.' I said.

'Mais vous êtes tout seul?'—but are you alone? asked one.

I screwed on the petrol cap. 'Oui.'

'C'est fantastique,' her friend applauded.

It hadn't felt fantastic. Although I had driven some 3,000 kilometres
(1,864 miles) for the Collins guide, I worried about Route 109 that resembled
a wriggly worm on the map.

'La route est bonne, mais tortueuse,' confirmed their driver.

Leaving the Sousse, the road cut through a final argan grove before
winding upwards through some of the most spectacular scenery in Morocco.
I'd never seen such beauty in utter wilderness. At one especially scenic spot
where a ridge in the Anti-Atlas resembled folds of rippled caramel, I passed
the French taking photographs. A little way on, although I'd left Taroudant
with a full tank and an empty bladder, I needed to go to the loo. There were
any number of rocky hiding places, but I feared humiliation lest the French
catch up and about to burst, I screeched to a halt at a solitary roadside
shop-house.

'Bonjour, puis-je utiliser votre WC?' I addressed a group of men
seated outside.

A youth among them got up and beckoned me to follow him to a shed
on the hill. When there was a violent banging on the door, I decided that
everyone crossing the Anti-Atlas must stop here, but it was Berber mother
bringing a pail of water. Bless her.

Coming down from the mountains, the Western Sahara presented as
a couple of camels grazing on acacias and a Bedouin tent shimmering in the
haze. Some 10,200 years ago, the region was a vast savannah, supporting an
abundance of game hunted by Neolithic man. The diverse geology—cliffs,

caves, and horizontal rock slabs—had made an ideal palette for carving crude representations of domestic stock and wildlife, even rhinoceros and giraffe, but all was now a sandy wilderness.

Tucked at the base of the Anti-Atlas, Tata exuded the raffish air of a frontier town. Its long, arcaded streets were lined with blush-pink shops, the market square had a parking lot—for donkeys—and there were Blue Men, even Blue Women, wearing billowing black chadors over their indigo robes. This was the old Morocco and I liked it at once. My bed was in a centuries-old kasbah, straight out of the Glaoui era. Restored as a guesthouse, it had steep steps and secret corridors—some opening into inner courtyards, others entering rooms so low, that you had to crawl in. How a bath had been hauled up was a mystery, but I soaked in it up to my chin.

'Each tree requires 200 litres of water a day,' said Patrick Simon, the proprietor of Dar Infiane, as we looked down on the great Tata oasis filled with thousands of date palms.

'You can buy a clock in the souq, but irrigation is still regulated by a centuries-old system of floating a bowl with a tiny hole in a bucket of water. When it fills and sinks, time is up and it's the next man's turn.'

He swept a suntanned arm over the panorama. 'The whole of Tata province is steeped in tradition and pre-historic art.'

Although on holiday, I felt my nose twitching. 'I'd like to get some pictures of petroglyphs,' I said.

'You'll pass engravings en route to Goulimine,' he replied. 'Turn left, 7 kilometres (4.3 miles) before Akka, and find someone to show you.'

Turning off the tarmac as instructed, I reached a cluster of houses the colour of Dairy Milk chocolate. The only sign of life was a small shop, and going in, I sketched some pictures of 'primitive animals' in my spiral notebook.

The trader nodded, but he couldn't leave his store and as I stood there, wondering what to do, a skinny young man came skipping up and on drawing near, I saw he was dribbling on his djellabah. Shown my drawings, he gave a hysterical laugh. Clearly I couldn't find engravings with the village idiot—the shopkeeper would come, but we had to be quick.

AGE-OLD WAY OF MEASURING WATER USE IN THE DATE OASES OF TATA, 2011

We set off along a brutal track before stones scraping the low-slung chassis forced me to stop. The shopkeeper jumped out and scaling a ridge, he weaved about before giving a shout in Tachelhit, the Berber language of the Western Sahara, and catching up I made out creatures pecked in the flat, brown, rocks. I recognised a gazelle, and an eagle, but concerned about missing a customer, the shopkeeper wanted to get back when we found the young man laughing uproariously. From what I understood, he'd sold a packet of cigarettes, but he hadn't taken the money.

Giving the shopkeeper fifty dirhams, I was headed back to the tarmac, when an obese black woman, swathed in royal blue robes and wearing a lump of amber on a long silver pendant, flagged me down. She looked as though dressed for a ball, but evidently she was going shopping.

'Akka?' I called out the window.

'Akka.' She nodded vigorously.

'Akka,' my passenger declared fifteen minutes later of a dusty settlement with one long street that reminded me of Temora.

'Akka?' I repeated, just to be sure.

'Akka!' she yelled.

Indeed we had arrived, and she wanted to get out.

Akka had a mechanic where I bought petrol from a boy who poured it into the tank from a jerry-can held on his shoulder. His mate gave me an orange as I paid the bill and set off driving to Goulimine with rocks— rocks—rocks on one side, and desert on the other. The Australian woman, Paula Constant, had walked across the Western Sahara and while I admired this feat, my desert walks had started and ended in Dishdaba. Checking the speedo I saw I was flying, but there was no traffic and although the region was possibly covered in petroglyphs, I wasn't stopping.

Goulimine was my first shock of the changes in store. Boasting six internet cafés, it had tripled in size and the hotel bistro menu listed dishes in six languages. The Saturday camel market apparently attracted hundreds of tourists from Agadir, but on Tuesday I was a solitary visitor.

As for Tan Tan, the evocative desert outpost of twenty years ago had morphed into a dull administrative centre of mechanics and café-terrasses. Apart from a camel arch at the entrance to town, there was nothing in the sense of *shenswürdigkeiten*—'things a sightseer should see'—is how author Robert Dessaix translates the word in his travel memoir *Arabesques*. Gone was the mustard and blue—every building was a dirty white—and hugely disappointed, I drove straight through only to be stopped at the exit by a gendarme with a brush moustache, just like Captain Renault played by Claude Rains, in the 1942 film *Casablanca*.

'*700 dirham, madame, infringement de traffique.*' He said it crisply.

'*Votre permis de conduire, s'il vous plaît.*' He rested a hand on my window.

'I did not see any stop sign.' I turned off the motor.

'*Vous devez payer madame,*' he pointed to a sign in Arabic.

'700 dirham is excessive,' I said, refusing to speak in French. 'I'm all alone and I've given rides to many Moroccans.' I mopped away tears in hope of clemency.

'*Il ne faut pas prends les gens avec vous! Vous pouvez être violé, volé madame. Même les femmes peuvent être agressifs. Vous devez payee.*'— you mustn't take passengers. You could be robbed or raped, madame. Even women can be aggressive. You must pay up, he scolded.

Fucker. I said under my breath and with no alternative, I withdrew seven brown one hundred dirham notes from my wallet with the present king, his father, and grandfather on one side, and the Green March on the reverse.

'*Que c'est triste que tout doit changer,*' I thought on the drive back to Agadir.

But it wasn't only Tan Tan. The explosive growth of tourism and infrastructure during the last decades had rendered unrecognisable so many places I'd once enjoyed. I stopped for a camel to cross the road. It was the last one I saw. Stunted trees appeared and desert melons. Soon I'd left the Sahara behind, but while disappointed, I'd found things new. There will always be pristine places, I reflected. It's a matter of setting out to find them.

The clamour of Agadir Airport came as a shock. Unshaven porters pushing baggage trolleys besieged me and at check-in I joined a queue of pink-skinned tourists clutching leather pouffes and copper trays: one man—the party clown—was wearing a djellabah. In the departure hall, long-haired windsurfers from Essaouira sat in untidy groups on the floor and people with Fit and Funky on their tracksuits were jogging on the spot. Selecting a seat in a corner, I opened the book I hadn't had time to read and forty minutes later my Easyjet flight took off for Gatwick.

Closing my eyes, I wondered what I would remember best, if fated never to return to Morocco.

First would be the friendly people, and second would be the exotic handicrafts, but I finally settled on colours: the red ramparts enclosing the médinas in a hot embrace; the pyramids of saffron and paprika in the souqs; the fudge-coloured *ksour* along the Draa; the shiny green tiles on the shrines and, last but not least, the fifty shades of blue.

In her book *Dreaming of East,*[55] the Canadian author Barbara Hodgson says that Lady Isobel Burton, who had accompanied Sir Richard on travels

A WEEKLY SOUQ IN THE DEEP SOUTH OF MOROCCO, 1990

to the Levant, believed that a woman smitten by the east, would not fit back into her former life. I can identify with this since after years on the road, I am now at home in an eastern society and an alien in my own.

Some people are fortunate enough to find their niche, others never settle down, and while friends speak of living life each day as it comes, only travel brings a life lived in the moment.

Chapter 8

Correspondence with Mum

Letter from PERSEPOLIS   *26 October 1971*

Dear Mum

*I've had the most interesting day visiting the ancient Persian city
of Persepolis. I love Iran, such an exotic country with courteous
people and a delicious cuisine. In fact this letter is all about food!
Am travelling with Vida Fatemi, an expert guide as she is a history
graduate from Shiraz University. Of course Persepolis is in ruins, but
vivid bas-reliefs indicate the pageantry of past events. Vida pointed out
the famous Immortals (personal bodyguards of the Achaemenian kings)
whose numbers never fell below 10,000 men. Other carvings showed
the Egyptians leading a bull, the Assyrians cups, hides and a Bactrian
camel, all gifts from the Persian dominions (unsure what these were,
will have to check).*

*Persepolis was conceived as a regal place for the king to receive his
subjects at Nowruz (that's Persian New Year). And just 10 days ago,
the Shah crowned himself in a splendid ceremony recreating the 2501st
anniversary of the founding of the Persian Empire by Cyrus the Great
(perhaps you have read about it in the SMH). Vida and I wandered
through the banquet tent (200 feet long x 80 feet wide) and sat down on*

the blue and gold velvet chairs, so recently warmed by the bottoms of kings and queens, crown princes and sheikhs.

The Shah spent millions on the occasion. Everything was flown in from Europe-Italian drapes, Limoges china with the Pahlavi coat-of-arms and Baccarat crystal glasses for the 5000 bottles of wine. Although Persian cuisine ranks with the world's best, 159 chefs, bakers and waiters were brought from Paris to do the catering. I found a crushed menu under a chair. It listed quail eggs stuffed with golden caviar, crayfish mousse, roast lamb baked with truffles, and baked peacocks stuffed with foie gras. Swoon! Apparently Iranians are furious at the cost of the banquet calling it 'imperial arrogance' and Khomeini (in-exile in Paris) said it was a 'Devil's Festival'. Vida told me in response, the Shah had asked what was the Imperial Court supposed to serve its honoured guests—bread and radishes?

At the Darius Inter-Continental Hotel, built for the event, I met the Iranian chef who had to cater for the 750 people accompanying the dignitaries. His name is a mouthful—Samad Kishehsayadanzadeh and his biggest shock was receiving three hour's notice that the 84 chefs from Maxim's would come for lunch. Said he had no choice but to prepare something simple, but exceptional. Good advice I think. They had Consomme Royal to start, roast beef as main, and a choice of crème caramel, or pistachio nut custard. Samad made us a lovely lunch. I had fesanjan (a dish I'd dreamt of tasting)—roast duck with walnuts and pomegranates. Vida's was good too: grilled trout with pistachio nuts (they grow everywhere in this southern part of Iran).

The weather is superb, crisp but sunny. I shall post this letter in Shiraz. There is nothing in Persepolis. Just the ruins.

Love Chris

Letter from BAHRAIN   21 December1976

Dearest Mum

You'll be wondering where I am as indeed you might. I've had a wretched trip. Never want to come back to the Gulf again. Have had enough of the Arabs. I'm in Bahrain as I was refused entry to Doha— reason 'I had written bad things'. I was deported on the next flight. The Arabs think money buys all ... In Sharjah I was told I could have anything I wanted so I took it seriously, and ordered a $30 bottle of wine, and made a phone call to Aileen which cost $140. Only to discover I had to pay myself! Having received me last time, this time the sheikh was too busy. Instead he sent his driver round with a gift of a silver tea service...

The weather is grey and overcast, but I managed a swim in the Lower Gulf. My $70 a night hotel room in Abu Dhabi had no hot water. When I turned on a tap it ran mud. During celebrations for UAE National Day, they held a Falconry Conference attended by all the rulers including Sheikh Zayed. They put the birds in one of these $70 rooms, then moved them out as guests were complaining about noise and smell. I had a quick look inside—the walls were splattered with blood from servants throwing them raw meat. I was shown an albino falcon caught in Pakistan, for which the Arab had paid $150,000. Crazzzzy.

People seem to think my book will sell so I must get back and finish it— deadline is 31 January. Am fed up with the thing. Couldn't have chosen a more difficult region to write about. One night in Sharjah I had to sleep among cockroaches on my driver's kitchen floor as the only hotel was full of oilmen. Fujairah (the smallest state on the Arabian Sea) has no hotel at all. There I slept in the desert beneath a Range Rover with a pistol under my pillow. Maybe I'll add to this later—it's not a very cheery letter at Christmas but as always, I will raise a glass. Bahrain is not short of alcohol!

Lots of love Chris

Letter from *KHARTOUM*   *20 September 1980*

Dear Mum

When I think of you sitting by the lake I wish I was there too. Will call from London so you will know I'm safely out of this place, but thought to write a few lines for someone to talk to in this awful city of Khartoum. What a vile place. An odour of urine, faeces, and dust accentuated in the twin town of Omdurman—across the Nile—by the scent of incense and badly cured skins.

By some miracle I have done the work (as you know I came out here to produce the Sudan Airways flight magazine). When I say it is miraculous, it truly is. I had to get one copy of the contract printed but can you believe that no one had any ink in the entire city.

Khartoum—no street lights, not even in the main street—women give birth by candlelight, no sewage system, little water, roads with cavernous holes, long queues for petrol and very little bread. As I write, there are people sitting outside the restaurant window who are really hungry. I collect rolls off the breakfast table and put them in my camerabag to give them.

And it's so hot: 40 Celsius. To keep up morale I decided to get my hair done. First I tried a cheap beauty salon. It stank of perms and sweat and I think the shampoo woman actually hated me. Water covered the floor and the sink was filled with rollers and teacups. I couldn't face it again so I thought damn the cost, I'll go to the Hilton.

Walking back along the Nile with my new hairdo, I saw this brown cloud gathering over Omdurman. It was a violent dust storm called a 'haboob' blowing off the Sahara. Trees were dancing all around and holding onto my expensive blow-dry I had to run like hell as the sky turned black and rain came pelting down. I reached the Araak Hotel where I'm staying, and raced up to my room as I'd left a window open for air (no air conditioning). Everything, including my typewriter, was covered in red sand. I called housekeeping who sent up a seven feet tall Dinka woman with a dustpan and broom. It took the two of us more than two hours to clean the room!

Anyway as you can see conditions have been/are very trying. Further compounded by the laziness of the Sudanese though they are very likeable. Did I tell you I had afternoon tea with the Mahdi's grandson before leaving London? He was very tall and dignified and served a fresh orange cake. You must have read about the Mahdi and the siege of Khartoum. The palace where General Gordon was killed on the steps is still here on the banks of the Nile.

Lots of love from the Sudan

PS: government announced a ban on alcohol and the manager of the Hilton had to empty 5,000 bottles of vintage wine into the Nile! There must be drunk perch from Khartoum to Wadi Halfa (that's the border with Egypt).

Letter from DUBAI   *25 July 1981*

Dear Mum

Happy to get your card and hope you are feeling better. I wrote you a long letter with beautiful stamps from Baghdad, but discovered the airport did not have a post box. Had to give it to my minder. I wonder if you'll get it? Wonder if they opened it? Am nearing the end of a fearfully hard trip—it's thanks to the comforts of the Hilton here that I am still well, though very tired. Dubai is cooler than Iraq, but it is very humid. Even the elastic in my bikini melted in 30 mins by the pool. Temperature went up to 49.4 followed by a driving sandstorm..

Yesterday received a call from the royal palace in Amman inviting me to visit in late August. We (publishers and self) have invited Queen Nour to write a foreword to my book on Jordan so this is likely what it's about. Am pleased since a hairdresser there is the only person who cuts my hair well.

My driver here is a serious old Indian Muslim who told me he married a 12 year old girl in Bombay. Anyone would drive better than Adeb, my driver in Jordan, who spoke no English and picked his nose with one hand while steering with the other. Yesterday I flew by helicopter to a gas-field 30 miles out in the Gulf. I was in a special harness, sitting with my feet on the runner board. It was so windy my legs nearly blew off but I was not frightened.

My reading on this trip is a book about an Englishman's experiences in the Foreign Legion. I had a friend who is a captain in the Legion—met him on the 'Pierre Loti' when I sailed down to Mombasa. His company was stationed in Madagascar. A nice man. Wore a black patch over an eye lost in the Battle of Suez.

Another journalist killed in Lebanon. I met him here at a conference. Syria is no doubt behind it. They also murdered the publisher of 8 Days for whom I do a lot of freelance photography. They soaked his arm in acid, then shot him through the head. We were supposed to meet up in Riyadh as he wanted me to go to Beirut with him. Lucky I didn't. At times I do wonder what I'm doing, recalling those days cleaning pans at RNSH. To beat the heat, sometimes I've been up at dawn climbing oil storage tanks and minarets.

Must go down and eat. There is plenty of Australian meat here—very cheap—only $3 a kilo according to Hajji (driver) who told me he got diarrohea from eating camel meat curry in Abu Dhabi. Last night I had lobster, but it's too hot to eat much. Give everyone my love. Will call when I'm back in London.

Chris xxxxxxxxxx

Letter from KARACHI AIRPORT   *26 November 1981*

Dearest Mum

*Writing this from the Hotel Midway-House near Karachi Airport.
My flight to Baluchistan has been cancelled due to snow. Did not
expect it to be so cold. Spent today getting hair done and doing a
little shopping. I found the most beautiful fish in the market. Not your
common goldfish, but shimmering silver-and-black striped fish like tiny
mackerel. Others are transparent. The man said they are glass fish.
Utterly mad, but I bought them, so am now travelling with a school
of fish. I carry them in a biscuit jar in my hand luggage. I wonder if
they'll make it back to London?*

*I feel very cut off as I'm the only person staying in this transit hotel.
I remember Aileen telling me there was always competition between
the two airline crews who stayed at Speed Bird House (as it was then
called). One year BOAC's Karachi manager erected a tent in the
garden for both to share Christmas, but the Qantas mob set fire to the
tree, burning down the tent and everything in it.*

*I've enjoyed splendid seafood while in Karachi. And it's very cheap.
Six blue-swimmer crabs only $2, lobster just $4. How is the fishing at
the Lake? Please give my greetings to everyone. I have bought some
small Xmas gifts to send home—an embroidered shawl, sandalwood
'worry beads' and a leather wallet. I hope Misty is well and the virus
is no longer affecting dogs in the area. Will end here. PIA accidently
sent my suitcase to Lahore and I must check to see if it has been found.
Otherwise I shall arrive in Quetta with just my toothbrush and a tank
of fish.*

Love Chris

*ps. Hope your back does not ache too much while you are painting.
What a great interest for you.*

Letter from BANGLADESH   *12 June 1987*

Dear Mum

Got your letter—my how your garden has grown. Hope this will reach you in time to wish you a 'Happy Mother's Day' when I shall be thinking of you.

The heat in Thailand was awful but Dhaka is relatively cool because the rains have started. These occur as powerful thunderstorms creating chaos. Flights are grounded, drains overflow etc. One night I was stranded in Sylhet—the tea-growing region of Bangladesh. A giant spider crawled into my bathroom causing great panic as you know I'm terrified of spiders. A boy from reception stuffed a blanket in the hole, but I couldn't sleep. It was the size of a dinner plate.

Ramadan has begun. It is very strict here—I could not find anything to eat all day. They sounded an air raid siren at 2.30am for people to wake and prepare a meal before dawn prayers. Then nothing until sunset when food stalls do a roaring trade. In any event, the food is FRIGHTFUL. They only seem to grow rice and pumpkins. Forget about meat, and any chicken is all skin and bone as they are not fed— people eat their 'meal'.

Bangladeshis are pleasant—very curious, usually non-aggressive. But photography is very hard as everyone races to be in the picture. Yesterday the crowd around me was so dense that a policeman let into them with his baton. Today my rickshaw was stoned. The driver was cut on the leg, but the hood was up so I was protected. In the melee my camera fell out, but a boy retrieved it and miraculously it was undamaged. No one is helping me. Officials are useless. Only way is to go it alone.

Bangladesh is so poor. The ill just die from lack of care. I wandered unheeded through a big hospital near here and did not see any nurses. Just the sick and dying looked after by relatives. In fact Dhaka is a rather pleasant city with large parks. It is also relatively clean although I stepped in a huge pile of human excrement while taking pictures...

Rain has interrupted my work this afternoon so have taken to bed. All the bumpy rickshaw rides have caused back pain. The hotel staff are kind but I am very lonely. I have booked a trip on an old paddle steamer for a 24 hour voyage into West Bengal. Will take food with me. Am reading Dominique LaPierre's book 'City of Joy'—see if you can get it from the library. He paints a very accurate picture of what life is like in Calcutta—which is about 40 miles west of here. Well my dear, space ended, give my love to the family and a big hug for you.

Chris xxx

Letter from SINAI   24 March 1990

My dear Mum

This will likely take months, but thought to write as you won't ever have had a letter from Sinai. It was occupied by Israel from 1967-82 and returned to Egypt under the Sadat 'peace initiative'. I have taken more than 1500 photos, but many will be poor due to bad weather. Haze in Aswan and pollution in Cairo. I have spent a fortune returning to important sites such as the pyramids and the Aswan Dam in an attempt to get good light. I will be here four days, mainly to visit St Catherine's monastery founded, 1400 years ago. I do not intend to climb up Mount Moses where God is supposed to have given Moses the tablet with the Ten Commandments. But everyone does.

Aswan was lovely but overrun with tourists. The Aga Khan is buried on a sandhill overlooking the Nile. The Begum—now very old—spends winter here in a white villa surrounded by pink hollyhocks. Each day she visits the mausoleum to place a rose on his tomb. I saw her sailing on the Nile with a dyed red poodle and a boatman in Persil-white robes. Yesterday I walked through the botanical gardens on Elephantine Island. They were planted by Lord Kitchener while he was awaiting orders to relieve the Mahdist siege of Khartoum.

I acquired two tiny Nubian ducklings in Aswan that were being mistreated by a man in the market. Cost a dollar. They used to swim around the bidet in my hotel—the Old Cataract—Room 507 (where King Farouk used to stay). They missed their mother terribly, so at night I would cuddle them as I sat watching the TV news with a G&T. They liked to get up into my curls. The room boy came in once with some tonic and when I got up to sign the bill, I had to take them out of my hair. I think he thought I was mad. I fed them on mashed cucumber and they slept in the bottom drawer of the mahogany wardrobe, but they were making rather a mess. As ducks do. Even tiny ones. When I left, I gave them to the room maid who promised she wouldn't eat them.

All now—will call from London.

Love Chris

Letter from ZAMBIA   3 June 1994

My dear Mum

My last day in Zambia after a fantastic trip. It is a beautiful country, rich in wildlife, and the Zambians are great people—good looking, friendly and with a good sense of humour. In 10 days we have travelled by road, river and plane visiting about 20 safari camps. The main feature is the River Zambesi which teems with hippo and crocodiles. Canoe safaris are very popular but they are very dangerous—hippos biting off legs etc.

I fished in one spot in a remote game park watching for crocodiles which snatch you off the bank, and the possibility of a lion grabbing you from behind. I caught five tiger fish but did not stay long as I was too scared. In fact I was frightened 90 percent of the time. We had no untoward experiences, but it was always potentially dangerous. One driver split up two male lions walking through the bush at dusk—they passed us sitting in an open jeep—only four feet away. Even our tour leader said it was foolhardy.

We stayed in a tented camp by the Kafue river in the floodplains of the Lochinvar National Park. Hippos roaring all night long kept the other writers awake, but ha-ha, I took a sleeping tablet. Next morning, an elephant uprooted a tree near where we were eating breakfast. The manager said a lion had walked through the kitchen the previous day.

I was thrilled to go white-water rafting on the Zambesi. It is one of the world's wildest rafting areas—several rapids are grade 5. The others would not come so I went with an American tourist and three African guides. I was determined not to fall out, but it was a wild ride as the river was a mass of whirlpools following the rains. Actually, I only learned of the hazards afterwards and think I was very lucky, as rafts frequently capsize. We went through great walls of water—at rapid 18 we nearly flipped and I thought, this is it!. We finished at rapid 23 beyond which a guide said lived a large crocodile. He told me on another trip, a crocodile had bitten a raft and deflated it. But canoeing is the more dangerous. One party of tourists camping by the river in small tents lost a girl to lions when she went outside to relieve herself.

What I loved about Zambia was that there were hardly any tourists— unlike Kenya which is overrun with people sitting in buses staring at the animals. We have identified 200 species of birds and about 30 animals including a leopard which killed a warthog right beside our vehicle. I fly home in three hours with a seven foot tall giraffe bought from a roadside crafts stall. I hope I have taken good photos—my small exhibition at the Royal Geographic Society went well—I wish it didn't cost so much to have pictures enlarged and framed. I've had my hair done while waiting to leave Lusaka, so now I must pack. Hope all well in Australia.

Will call you from London

Love Chris

Postcard from GALILEE   20 March 1984

Dear Mum

This is written by the shores of Lake Galilee. The picture of a fish mosaic is in a church built on the spot where Jesus is said to have performed the miracle of the loaves and fishes. Wish I felt as deeply about it as the tourists evidently do. Am travelling with a bus load of Baptists from Oklahoma, organised by my friend Raji Khoury, a Christian Arab travel agent in East Jerusalem. They are nice simple folk—I feel such a heathen. Don't think I can stand the Middle East much longer—the loneliness is too great. After this trip, I think I will give up being a travel writer. It is not a normal life.

Lots of love Christine

ps. Will call from London.

Postcard from UZBEKISTAN   16 November 1993

Dear Mum

Writing this airborne en route to Samarkand. The visit has been an ordeal—awful food, no food, and boring tourists. The Uzbeks are v. poor, but pleasant—ours is the first ever holiday group. It's the only way to visit the country at present. The markets sell not much more than rugs, kebabs and pomegranates. The old town of Khiva was freezing (-9c) but it looked like fairyland with icicles hanging off the snow-covered buildings. I have never worked in such dangerous conditions. Occasionally crawled on hands and knees to take a photo. One man slipped and broke his arm. You may not receive this card for months—ha, ha.

C x

ps. Samarkand has some splendid mosques and religious colleges. We saw the mausoleum of Tamerlane.

Postcard from BANJUL   *25 January 1994*

Dear Mum

I am sorry to hear of your accident with the old leg! Keep it elevated and try not to fret about the garden for a while. The bushfires sound terrible. I heard about them here in Gambia. I've had a dreadful, dreadful trip—no light or water where I'm staying in Banjul. The country is so poor and people are very aggressive and demanding. A man wanted money when I took a picture of a tree. 'It's my tree' he yelled.' Won't go on about it on a postcard, but I was robbed on the beach when I turned my back from taking photos. Two men took everything. Not to worry as I was unhurt although they stuck a knife in my ribs (it was blunt). Managed a day fishing, but sea was so rough I had to be dropped off. But I still caught the most fish! Looking forward to getting back—the mice will be into everything in my kitchen. Will write proper letter after I unwind.

Love Chris

Postcard from ALGIERS   *17 October 1999*

Dear Mum

Was invited here for a tourism conference, but the French translation system didn't work so I could not understand anything. Went downtown with heart-in-mouth as Algiers is not entirely the safest city in the world. Visited the great basilica of Our Lady of Africa—it has a black virgin over the altar. Someone tapped me on the shoulder in the market and said it was dangerous, so I went back to the hotel. It has a wonderful view of the bay and a fantastic hairdresser. A shame no one to celebrate my 59th but that's the lot of a travel writer. Oh yes, Algiers has a gem of an art gallery with paintings by Utrillo, Matisse and Renoir. Despite the tension, I really like the city. No wonder the French fought so hard to hang on to it.

Love Chris

ps. The bureau de poste is like a palace. I've posted this card there.

Letter from MUM

Dearest Chris

This is only a note to thank you for the book with the lovely inscription in front—everyone is very impressed. I spent most of last week showing it to family and neighbours and all think you've done a wonderful job. And beautifully produced with all the pictures of the Arab countries you visited. I am glad you used that one of you having breakfast of dates and camel milk with the old sheikh in the desert in Dubai. It's the nicest one of you ever. I loved your usual humour here and there and I hope to just loaf and read it next week. I showed the newsagent Len Campbell who was very impressed—everyone got a big surprise and my darling, I'm so proud of you. Starting from scratch and all alone. I went to Alan Langwell's 91st birthday party yesterday and 'The Gulf States and Oman' went too and was greatly admired. Have you sent the sheikh a copy? The one who looked after you in Sharjah. Ita Buttrose should also be sent a copy. That Mrs Sanders who brought it back from London was very kind so I'll get her a lottery ticket as thanks.

I'm sending with this the money you wanted. It only leaves $55 in your account now as you lost $19 on withdrawing it.

We are having glorious weather, but it remains very changeable. I'm not looking forward to summer. The mozzies were so dreadful last year and the high humidity is so trying. When I tried writing a letter, my arm constantly stuck to the aerogramme with perspiration. The garden is looking spring-like and the jasmine is just magnificent. It is crawling all over the pergola. That stick of frangipani I picked up on the foreshore has sprung and is growing into a beautiful tree. I wonder where it came from? I can't wait for it to burst into flower. My roses don't do very well though. I don't think they like the salty air. Must go up the town now. Being Monday the larder's a bit low.

Lots of love sweetie

Mum x

ps. Mr Moffat caught five fine mullet off the jetty yesterday.

Letter from MUM

Dear Chris

We are having the worst heatwave I've ever known. I've ceased to use hankies. Mop up with a washer and have a towel under my arm to stop it sticking. I received your own dear letter today, written with your hand stiff with the cold and by the time I'd read it, it looked as though it had been out in the rain. I've just given Jet a swim in the lake but had to hose him down afterwards—there seem to be sea lice in the weeds.

Your blue dress for the trip with the Queen sounds regal. What about a handbag and shoes? And don't you need gloves? On TV I've been watching Royal Heritage, a magnificent film. Last Sunday it showed the Queen entertaining on the 'Britannia', she looked gorgeous in pale blue with a glittering diamond tiara and evening handbag dangling from her arm. She rose and said a toast to the President of Finland, or King ...(I'm not sure) then he rose, and made a toast to the Queen and her realm. I was staggered by the beauty of everything. The photographer must have been right beside the table. All the fuss about Lord Snowdon's pictures. He had an exhibition out here – not nearly as good as your work. Next step, the Queen's photographer, try and get some photos of the palace gardens and the family.

I forgot to mention that the Aramco Magazine came in the post with your own photo among the rest of the contributors and the beautiful pictures with your article on Marrakech. I'm so proud of you darling, you're better than the best. Pity you can't arrange an exhibition of your work. Julia has been offered space to exhibit her watercolours in a shop in town, but she must find a second person for it to be worthwhile.

It's now 38c and Jackie (cat) is very restless and panting. I'm sorry the duck you cooked for Christmas was so skinny. Our turkey was 7lbs and we had lots of meat. The cherry sauce you made must have been nice with it. I've made it in the past, but lazy me, this year I bought a jar of cranberry sauce which I didn't eat anyway. There's our ferry, the 'Wangi Queen', going down the lake with all the flags flying. And two teenagers just went into the lake fully clothed to cool off. It must be hard for the birds to find a meal during those terrible gales and snow covering the ground in England.

Well sweetie, I will go up and post this now, then try and cool off a bit.

Mum xx

Letter from MUM   30 September 1980

Dear Chris

I still think it very unwise to go to Pakistan. A mediator has just left on a peace mission to Iraq—see what results come of it. The whole thing may turn into all-out war. They say at present they won't be involved, but oil is our vital necessity.

I am reading a very refreshing book 'On Home Ground' by Gwen Moffat about mountain climbing in Scotland. She and husband were both mountain guides but there wasn't much of a living in it so she turned to writing. 'Space Below my Feet' got a terrific write-up: must try and get it—her love of the great outdoors and animals appeals to me. I'm following a TV documentary on Nepal—lovely scenery. I think you went there and said the people don't have W.C.s so they go outside which is rather unhygienic. By the way, Gwen Moffat has also given talks on the BBC 'Women's Hour'. Something you should do—never say, or write anything that hurts the family though.

I picked a big bunch of pansies from the garden. I have a patch to hide the veggies—lettuce, beans and spinach abound. The lemon tree is feeling its age with the dry conditions. I see on your last visit, you drank all the cumquat liqueur I made from the small tree at the back door.

I had my golf friend Kay for afternoon tea on the verandah yesterday. I baked some scones and we watched the sailing races. Your London flat must look nice with the new blue paint. I'm still unsure if I'll have my kitchen done—costs are awful and last time I had to clean up the mess with ammonia. That Jiff you used on the sink took all the shine off: it's only for use on porcelain—baths, basins and the like.

Well darling, I had better say 'happy birthday': it only seems the other day you were a little bombshell—you've turned out well I'm proud to say and made an interesting life for yourself. I will write to you—Julia gave me an address in Rawalpindi—said she'd call. I won't. It's too frustrating through foreign exchanges. I have your birthday present. Something you can always have. I may send you a picture of it later on. Love to you my dear—we're all getting old aren't we—I weigh 8 ½ stone.

Love Mum and Mickie xxx

ps. Mickie has the heaviest coat I've seen on any cocker spaniel. The woman who usually clips him is abroad so I'll have to take a bit off his legs or he'll die of heat exhaustion.

Letter from MUM   **19 February 1983**

Dear Chris

Thank you for your card and letter. I think I've thanked you before. Also for the lovely scarf. I had a very nice birthday. Was called for on Sunday and had a lovely baked dinner and champagne and was home again early afternoon. Country friends sent me a bunch of proteas: they have a lovely old home at Dyers Crossing, off the Pacific Highway.

You sounded fed up with your trip. Tell me why do you go to the same places all the time? You always seem to be going to Egypt and you must have been to Morocco on half a dozen occasions: if you keep on travelling so much, you will end up without any friends.

It's a gorgeous day here, a light north-easterly wind and sailing boats everywhere. They're also having a ferry race—four ferries are out on the lake now. It will probably finish at Belmont. I've had friends in for afternoon tea and drinks. Planted some poppies and I've been scratching elsewhere in the garden. Pulled out the last tomatoes. They have been cropping since December. Lettuce is done now.

Here is a little addition written later I thought you'd be interested in—news from the Herald and also on TV. A large shark attacked a boat and bit the front off. The men managed to escape in a dinghy and say they are determined to kill the shark. I wish them luck. Six young whales came ashore in a weak condition at Crescent Head and the public went to their rescue. They were towed back out to sea—one died—but they all came ashore again and there were more deaths. They were finally taken by a lorry of some sort to Brisbane and put into a special pool. One more has died but the others are still alive. Last I heard. Must wind up now.

Lots of love my dear one

Mum xxoxx

ps. Auntie Mollie and I were down on the jetty getting oysters and one had a mother blue-ringed octopus in it with her eggs. We put it in a jar and took it to the Reptile Park to see if they wanted it for antivenene. They are highly venomous as you know.

Letter from MUM   2 May 1985

Dear Chris

Your letter of 15/3 which I have sent on to Julia: she will be most interested as was I. It put me right there and I could picture it all. Your new London friends sound interesting. You are indeed lucky— today's newcomers become very lonely in most places after moving from somewhere familiar. Many don't even know who lives next door. I suppose the neighbours have watched you sweating over the restorations and no doubt admired your hard work.

These days workmen want easy jobs, just like cleaners who'd sooner arrange flowers than get up on a chair and dust a lampshade. I must say my cleaner is extremely kind and ready to do anything, but rules only allow her to clean the floors. It's an agency that is subsidised by the state govt. I have a new gardener. He is most willing and I pay him less than Mr Owen who has retired.

You have not told me about your curtains. Or haven't you got that far yet? Do you still have my little paintings. And did you get them framed? I may take up a brush again but there's never time. I'm reading a book I heard discussed on the radio 'Diet for Life'—a cookbook for arthritis. I could not follow the diet, but have learned a lot about what and what not to eat. All the vitamins we need are contained in what we eat. Tablets pass into the liver and kidneys and are lost. You should read it.

You seemed very interested in the shark story. Well here's another one, a woman's encounter with a saltwater crocodile in the Northern Territory. She was canoeing and saw what looked like a log but as she rowed, the log followed her. She got to the river bank and endeavoured to climb up the muddy bank and as she reached up for the limb of a paper-bark tree, the croc leapt and grabbed her back into the water. It had her by the thigh and rolled around and around trying to drown her. Then it let go and grabbed her other leg, rolling over and over again but she managed to escape and crawl up the bank where she tore up her singlet to make a tourniquet to quell the bleeding. She finally managed to reach a ranger's hut and after many trips by landrover and boat, she got to Darwin Hospital. She was flown down to Royal North Shore where she spoke about the experience on TV. She will need many skin grafts poor thing and may not be so keen on the great outdoors after this.

Love Mum xx

ps. A Timorese fisherman had his leg taken by a shark off Broome.

Letter from MUM   *16 June 1993*

My dear Chris

Lovely to hear from you, but too bad you have the 'flu again. I think you need a good tonic. You never pick up like you used to. Perhaps London weather doesn't agree with you as you always say you hate it. Do you keep warm in winter clothes? This is what I have on: cotton singlet, wool singlet, long sleeve spencer, wool slacks, wool jumper and wool jacket, wool socks and fur-lined boots. I'm in the lounge with the heater on and it's nice and cosy.

Glad the trip went well and you were also able to enjoy some sailing and diving. I received the magazine with the article on the Comores. I had never heard of these islands. Fancy Richard Burton's last wife also invited. Does she write? It's not like you to go on a press trip but good to have the company for once. Julia and I discussed the dangers of working alone in some of the wild places you go to. We agreed that one day Chris will just disappear and that will simply be that.

The garden in your home in France sounds lovely. I like the sound of blue wisteria climbing up the wall but why not put in a few veggies? My beans are 6 feet high and I'm eating the silver beet; have to water each day, we've had some rain but the soil soon dries out. The days are drawing in—it's almost dark at 5.30pm. I'm having my eyes tested tomorrow, they get very sore so perhaps I need new lens. I'm feeling well apart from the arthritis. I take Panadol tablets when necessary.

I went to the RSL club the other morning and played bingo, a most boring game. On the way out I put three 10 cent pieces in a pokie and out fell thirteen more which was much more fun.

Lots of love dear and God bless

Mum xx

Oh! I have a blue tongue lizard who I feed pieces of chicken each evening. He is getting used to me. I have to keep the screen door shut as I saw him glide out of the kitchen the other day.

Endnotes

1   Ethel Mannin, *Land of the Crested Lion: A Journey Through Modern Burma,* Jarrolds, London, 1955.

2   *Mermaid Singing:* Australian writer Charmian Clift's story of her sojourn on the Greek island of Kalymnos in the 1950s, Bobbs-Merrill, USA, 1956.

3   A small, burrowing freshwater crustacean that numbers some 150 species in Australia.

4   In November 2000, Haile Selassie's remains were accorded a Christian burial in the Holy Trinity Cathedral in Addis Ababa.

5   Wilfred Thesiger, *The Danakil Diary-Journeys through Abyssinia, 1930-34,* HarperCollins, London 1996.

6   Wilfred Thesiger, *Arabian Sands, Chapter One Abyssinia and the Sudan,* Longman, London, 1959.

7   Laurens van der Post: as quoted in *Ethiopia-Cultures of the World* by Steven Gish, Benchmark Books (NY) 1996.

8   One of ten children sired by Ras Makonnen, Haile Selassie was born in the village of Ejersa Goro, just outside Harar, on 23 July 1892.

9   Richard Goodman, 'Arthur Rimbaud, Coffee Trader' *Saudi Aramco World vol.52. no.5, Sep/Oct 2001.*

10 Released in 1989.

11 Brigadier General Teferi Bente was chairman of the Dergue. He was shot during a meeting of the hierarchy on 3 February 1977.

12 Sainsburys is a major British supermarket chain.

13 Elizabeth de Stroumillo (1926-2010) was the *Daily Telegraph's* full-time travel editor during the 1970s. She was known for her encouragement of young writers whom she considered had talent.

14 British Overseas Airways Corporation merged with British European Airways in 1974 to become British Airways.

15 A former diplomat, Michael Shea, became press secretary to Her Majesty Queen Elizabeth from 1978 to 1987. Died 17 October 2009.

16 1 Kings 10:11-13 refers to her famous journey to Jerusalem.

17 www.windweaver.com/sheba/Sheba3.htm.

18 An Arabic sweetmeat made from ghee and sugar. Variations of halwa, also known as halva, are made with carrots and almonds in South Asia.

19 Richard Ryther Steer Bowker, physician, surgeon and politician. Born 1815 Yorkshire, England. Awarded diplomas in botany and *materia medica,* Paris 1836. MD University of St Andrews, 1839. First visited Australia with the emigrant ship, *Shepherd* and then migrated to Melbourne in the *Georgiana,* 1841.

20 Caliph Abu Jafar Abdullah al-Ma'mun ruled 813-833.

21 Abu Yusuf Yaqūb ibn Isāq al-Kindi 801-*c.*873.

22 Muhammad ibn Mūsā al-Khwārizmī 780-*c.*850.

23 M. M. Ahsan, *Social Life Under the Abbasids,* Longman, UK, 1979.

24 Christine Osborne, *Middle East Cooking,* Prion, UK, 1984.

25 Also known as Tell al-Muqayyar, an important Sumerian city-state *c.* 2025-1738 BCE.

26 Sir Leonard Woolley (1880-1960), best known for his excavations at Ur in Iraq.

27 *Abhaya mudra* symbolises peace and protection. It is made with the right hand raised to shoulder height, the arm crooked, and the palm facing outward.

28 *Masgouf* is the traditional Iraqi way of cooking carp. It is split, spiced with pepper, salt and tamarind and staked out on sticks to grill around an open fire.

29 During the British occupation of Egypt in the 1800s, Egyptian workers wore the letters W.O.G.S. signifying they were Working on Government Service.

30 Prophet Muhammad *c.*570 – 632.

31 Famous gentleman's barber and perfumer operating in London Mayfair since 1875.

32 Eric Newby, *A Short Walk In The Hindu Kush,* Secker & Warburg, London, 1958

33 Unleavened flat bread eaten throughout South Asia.

34 *Eid ul-Adha* is the feast following the fast of Ramadan in Pakistan.

35 Poetic form, likely originating in sixth century Asia, whose theme is love, specifically an illicit and unattainable love.

36 *Hijra,* transvestite entertainer.

37 Or *maulana,* a religious man.

38 Shah Abdul Latif (1689-1752), *The Voice of Silence.*

39 Word for bandit used in Pakistan, from the Hindustani *dakaiti*

40 Begum Viqar-un-Nisa Noon, was Austrian by birth, English by upbringing and a Pakistani by choice. In 1945 she married Sir Feroz Khan Noon, then Indian High Commissioner in England. She converted to Islam and was chairman of the Pakistan Tourism Development Corporation during the 1970 and 1980s.

41 182 kilograms. *The Guinness Book of Records* of 1981 listed Mohammad Alam Channa as 232.4 cm (7 feet 7 inches) and for a short time he was credited as being the world's tallest man. This would contradict the author who measured him in the shrine. Suffering numerous ailments, he died aged forty-two in New York in1998.

42 7,315 metres.

43 *An Insight and Guide to Pakistan* was published in 1983.

44 A Berber word for the countryside or hinterland.

45 *Maghreb*—Morocco, Algeria,Tunisia and Libya.

46 Jeanette Hoorn, *Moroccan Idyll,* The Miegunyah Press, Melbourne, 2012.

47 Also known as agarwood, is a resinous hardwood obtained from the bark of the genus Aquilaria in south-east Asia. Highly scented, it is used in essential oils and incense.

48 ONCFM: Office National des Chemins de Fer du Maroc.

49 Ibn Juzayy: *A Gift to Those Who Contemplate the Wonders of Cities and the Marvels of Travelling.* A medieval book recounting the journeys of Ibn Battūtah.

50 Jean Joseph Benjamin Constant, *Drying Clothes,* 1875, Aberdeen Art Gallery and Museum, Scotland.

51 *Window at Tangier,* 1912, Pushkin Museum of Fine Arts in Moscow.

52 Literally a scrubber, or masseuse in the hammam.

53 A genre of classical music brought back by Moorish refugees from Andalusia.

54 Gavin Maxwell, *Lords of the Atlas:The Rise and Fall of the House of Glaoua,* Longman, UK, 1966.

55 Barbara Hodgson, *Dreaming of East: Western Women and the Exotic Allure of the Orient,* Hardie Grant, Australia, 2005

Acknowledgements

My father J.K.Osborne heads those people who helped me during my travelling life. Dad typed my first handwritten article and submitted it to the *Sydney Morning Herald*. He was lost off a boat near Coffs Harbour in 1966. Mum, who likely needed a cup of tea after reading some of my letters, was a constant support and a great correspondent. Kay Annoni who stopped when I was hitchhiking in Spain in 1965 has remained a loyal friend along with Irma Rodriguez from Club Méditerranée days on Moorea in 1968. On a professional level I would like to thank Chaille McKenzie, former editor of *Signature* magazine who commissioned articles on South East Asia which received the 1970 PATA award for travel writing. I owe huge thanks to the PTDC for hosting my visits to Pakistan in the 1980s. More recently I owe thanks to Markus Schneider of the Oberoi Sahl Hasheesh in Egypt, and in Morocco to Sharyne Naamane of Complete Tours in Agadir, to Sibyl de Beaufort of the Riad Dar-el-Hana in Taroudant, to Emma Joyston-Bechal of the Riad Zamzam in Marrakech and to Ahmed Azami of the Dar Anebar in Fez. Thanks also to Gatwick Express for providing tickets to the airport—the only relaxed part of many journeys. Sydney author Trish Clark is thanked for her generous advice as well as Diana Hill and Allison M. Dickson for their encouragement.

I am indebted to Hilary Bradt MBE for her comments on Ethiopia, to Tim Mackintosh-Smith for checking the chapter on Yemen and to Robert Fisk for reading the chapter on Iraq. Jeremy Hoare who designed the original website is warmly thanked. Thanks to my niece Rosemary Sutherland of Paperhorse Designs for creating the present website. My sister Julia made many helpful suggestions to the text of TWMH and Margaret Hogan has done a great job with its design. Finally there are two important people, no longer with us, whom I wish to mention: Sister Irene Campton who steered me through the difficult years at Royal North Shore and my aunt, Joyce Hindley who made childhood holidays such fun at Lake Macquarie. My old friend Aileen Aitken died in 2012.

Books by the Author

The Gulf States and Oman, Croom Helm, UK, 1977

An Insight and Guide to Jordan, Longman, UK, 1980

An Insight and Guide to Pakistan, Longman, UK, 1981

People at Work in the Middle East, Batsford, UK, 1984

Cooking the Middle Eastern Way, Prion, UK, 1985-94-97

Middle Eastern Food and Drink, Wayland, UK, 1988

South East Asian Food and Drink, Wayland, UK, 1988

Australian and New Zealand Food and Drink, Wayland, UK, 1989

Essential Thailand, AA Publishing, UK, 1990

Essential Bali/Jakarta, AA Publishing, UK, 1990

Essential Seychelles, AA Publishing, UK, 1990

Essential Malaysia, AA Publishing, UK, 1992

Independent Travellers Guide to Morocco, Collins, UK, 1990

Morocco, Moorland, UK, 1994

Insight Guide UAE and Oman, (Co-author), APA, UK, 1998-02